ENGLISH DOMESTIC
Or,
HOMILETIC TRAGEDY
1575 to 1642

———

Number 159 of the
Columbia University Studies in English
And Comparative Literature

ENGLISH DOMESTIC
Or,
HOMILETIC TRAGEDY
1575 to 1642

Being an Account of the
Development of the Tragedy
of the Common Man
Showing its Great Dependence on
Religious Morality, Illustrated with
Striking Examples of the
Interposition of
PROVIDENCE
For the Amendment of Men's Manners

By HENRY HITCH ADAMS

Published by
COLUMBIA UNIVERSITY PRESS
on Morningside Heights in New York
in the Year of Our Lord 1943

To

My Mother and Father

PREFACE

FOR MANY YEARS, domestic tragedy has needed an interpretation which would establish the place of the genre in dramatic history and which would relate the plays to the intellectual movements of their own times. The form has long been recognized, but because it frequently falls outside the ordinary classification of plays in a given period and because individual domestic tragedies are often inferior as dramas, the discussions of the type have been more or less perfunctory. Sometimes historians of the theatre have related it to the realism which existed in drama in the last decade of the sixteenth century or to the sentimentalism of the eighteenth century. Neither of these interpretations adequately describes the genre at either period of its development. Shortly after work was begun on the present volume, it was discovered that a complete history of domestic tragedy is too large a subject for a single book. The original plan was to seek out these tragedies wherever they might be found and to attempt to link them in some developmental pattern leading through the English eighteenth-century domestic tragedies, the German *bürgerliche Trauerspiele,* and the tragedies of Friedrich Hebbel and eventually tracing the chain to Ibsen, the real father of the modern social-problem play. The treatment of the Elizabethan domestic tragedy was planned as an introductory chapter. However, the section on Elizabethan drama grew into the size of a book, and it was decided to postpone the remaining portion of the study for a later investigation. The year of the closing of the theatres in England, 1642, was selected as an arbitrary stopping place, although before that time domestic tragedies had died a natural death.

The ascription of two of the Elizabethan domestic tragedies to Shakespeare has made them the center of critical controversy, but little work has been done on these plays as a group. However, a person who sought information on this group of plays has had to turn to Hans Wolfgang Singer's *Das bürgerliche Trauerspiel in England,* published in 1891, or to chapters in handbooks on the drama of the period. Singer's work is devoted largely to listing the plays, summarizing the plots, and describing their historical settings. He recognizes that the plays are a departure from the critical canons, but makes little effort to relate them to the thought of the time. An unpublished dissertation by Edward Ayres Taylor on the Elizabethan domestic tragedy is devoted mainly to the historical background of the murders which form the subjects of many of the plays. The alterations from the sources are explained in neither intellectual nor dramatic terms.

The emphasis in the present book is different. It was found that among the critics no clear definition had been agreed upon as completely acceptable. Before a study could be started, it was necessary to define the genre and to decide what plays belonged to it. For this reason, existing lists of domestic tragedies were of little use, and a completely new compilation has been made. The aim has been to include every play of the period which in some way partakes of the attributes of the genre. The most obvious characteristic, and the only one not occasionally violated, was the humble station of the hero of the tragedy. He is always someone below the ranks of the nobility. This criterion has been the main basis of selection of each play, and every tragedy here considered has as its protagonist a shopkeeper, farmer, gentleman, tradesman, or other person of corresponding social position. As is shown in Chapter One, the inclusion of such a hero was directly contrary to the humanistic ideas of tragedy, for in classical tragedy there was no place for the citizen hero. In the English morality plays, this person becomes established as a suitable character for serious drama.

Domestic tragedy, throughout its history, has attempted to teach. As the plays of Ibsen showed the defects in the social system, Elizabethan domestic tragedies inculcated lessons of morality and religious faith in the citizens who came to the theatres by offering them examples drawn from the lives and customs of their own kind of people. The choice of the hero, the moralizing, and the religious teaching are the only consistent attributes of all these plays.

The aim of this study has been twofold. First, to interpret these plays as they might have appeared to the audiences who saw them in the public theatres. To this end, an attempt has been made to supply the reader with the religious and moral background which the average playgoer of that time would possess. This is necessary if a clear understanding of the meanings of the plays is to be attained. Chapters Two and Three are intended to supply this background. The second method of approach to these plays has been more obviously aesthetic and is an attempt to evaluate them in relation to other plays of the period and as a part of the history of drama.

A few explanations should be offered at this point. The word "tragedy" is always used in this book to mean a play, poem, or narrative ending in death for the protagonist and, unless specifically defined, never refers to the art form capable of giving the highest aesthetic satisfaction to the reader. Similarly, the word "hero," unless otherwise stated, always is used as a synonym for "protagonist" and does not necessarily mean that the "hero" has any heroic qualities.

The phrase "orthodox tragedy" is employed to refer to tragedy of the Elizabethan times which is not domestic, that is, any tragedy of whatever type whose protagonist belongs to royal estate.

The dates for the plays considered are, in general, taken from Harbage's *Annals of English Drama* and from Chambers's *The Elizabethan Stage*. Only occasionally has a play been assigned to a year other than that given by one or both of these two writers.

I have supplied a short title and modern spelling for all works in the text of this book, but in the first footnote mention of each work and in the Bibliography I adhere to the old form. Where I have worked from a modern edition, I have made no effort to conform to my usual practice of reproducing old spellings and old title pages.

I have made quotations from the plays in editions which were convenient to my hand and which, therefore, should be readily accessible to the reader. I have followed the normal division of plays into acts and scenes. Where no such divisions have been made by an editor, I have not attempted to supply them. Instead, I have referred to the page number of the volume I have been using. This is, however, not the drawback it might at first appear. Since, in all these cases, the edition used is the only one readily available, the reader can easily locate the references.

Thanks are due to the following publishers for their kind permission to incorporate copyrighted material: the University of California Press for Willard Farnham, *The Medieval Heritage of Elizabethan Tragedy;* the Clarenden Press for F. S. Boas, *An Introduction to*

Tudor Drama, and C. F. Tucker Brooke, *The Shakespeare Apocrypha;* the Columbia University Press for J. E. Spingarn, *A History of Literary Criticism in the Renaissance;* Houghton Mifflin Company for C. F. Tucker Brooke, *The Tudor Drama,* J. Q. Adams, *A Life of William Shakespeare,* and Felix Schelling, *Elizabethan Drama;* the Macmillan Company for A. W. Ward, *A History of English Dramatic Literature to the Death of Queen Anne,* and S. H. Butcher's translation of Aristotle's *Poetics;* the Macmillan Company and the Cambridge University Press for L. B. Campbell, *Shakespeare's Tragic Heroes, Slaves of Passion,* and G. R. Owst, *Literature and Pulpit in Medieval England;* Charles Scribner's Sons for *Encyclopaedia of Religion and Ethics,* edited by James Hastings; Sidgwick and Jackson, Ltd., for Wilhelm Creizenach, *The English Drama in the Age of Shakespeare,* and Harold Jenkins, *The Life and Works of Henry Chettle;* the Vanderbilt University Press for R. W. Battenhouse, *Marlowe's "Tamburlaine," a Study in Renaissance Moral Philosophy.* Thanks should also be given to the Huntington Library for allowing me to reprint the last stanza of *A Moſt Notable and Worthy Example of an Vngratious Sonne.*

To the many friends who have aided me in writing this book, I owe more than I can set forth here. I am grateful to Miss Jean Macalister and Miss Dorothy H. Litchfield of the Columbia University Library for their help in locating and obtaining copies of the works which form the basis of Chapter Three. To Professor Joseph Wood Krutch, my debt is heavy. Professor Oscar James Campbell has read and reread the manuscript, and his scholarly direction has materially lightened the load. At every stage in the development of this book, he has been a counselor and guide, offering assistance above and beyond the call of duty. My greatest debt is, however, to my parents. Without their aid, this book, in all probability, could not have been written.

HENRY HITCH ADAMS

Ann Arbor, Michigan
December, 1942

CONTENTS

I. Critical Backgrounds   1

II. Popular Theology   6

III. Nondramatic Literature   26

IV. Morality Plays   54

V. Plays from Legend and History   75

VI. Sixteenth-Century Murder Plays   100

VII. Seventeenth-Century Murder Plays   126

VIII. Thomas Heywood's *A Woman Killed with Kindness*   144

IX. The Decline of Domestic Tragedies   160

X. Conclusion   184

Appendix A. Lost Domestic Tragedies   193

Appendix B. Heywood and Brome's *The Late Lancashire Witches*   204

Bibliography   207

Index   221

Chapter One

CRITICAL BACKGROUNDS

*Let us sit upon the ground
And tell sad stories of the death of kings.*

IN THESE WORDS Shakespeare's Richard II laments his pathetic situation and attempts to find comfort in the tragic fate of other kings. To Richard, to his forebears, and to most of his successors, tragic protagonists were necessarily men noble of character and high of social and political position. To the present generation, on the other hand, the tragic hero need no longer be a person of exalted estate. Many modern tragedies depict catastrophes overtaking men like ourselves, men whose problems are common ones, men whose deaths do not cause thrones to totter or convulsions to run through the universe.

This change in conception of the tragic hero has given rise to a new dramatic form, now usually called domestic tragedy. The term is vague, for the word "domestic" has two meanings. It may designate any phase of family life. In this sense of the word even *Hamlet* may be properly called a domestic tragedy. The word "domestic" also means familiar, local; and the term "domestic tragedy" is most frequently applied to those tragedies which present common people as heroes. The lowly social station of the tragic protagonist is the one invariable characteristic of the genre. Other features are the natural result of this *sine qua non*. For example, the playwrights set the action of their plays in the family merely because their plots inevitably concerned the everyday problems of the "common" hero. Even critics who have employed the expression "domestic tragedy" correctly usually have applied it primarily to sentimental plays of the eighteenth century such as George Lillo's *The London Merchant*. But Elizabethan domestic tragedies are not primarily sentimental. The common man as hero, then, is the essential feature of domestic tragedy as the term will be employed here. It is a tragedy of the common people, ordinarily set in the domestic scene, dealing with personal and family relationships rather than with large affairs of state, presented in a realistic fashion, and ending in a tragic or otherwise serious manner.

The earliest known domestic tragedies appeared in the sixteenth century, almost two thousand years after the great Greek dramatists had written their masterpieces. Domestic tragedy is one of the youngest children of the tragic Muse. It has suffered since its birth all the woes of a younger son, snubbed by respectable critics, but it has survived scorn and abuse to become, under the guidance of Ibsen and O'Neill, perhaps the greatest achievement of the modern theatre.

The reason for its early disfavor lies in the fact that dramatists through the ages followed the example of classical tragedy in presenting only kings and princes as heroes. Renaissance humanists, looking back with reverence on centuries of established usage, would have been aghast at any violation of the accepted rules so radical as that of which domestic tragedy was to be guilty.

Classical tragedy justly occupies one of the highest pinnacles in the literary range. It was the first dramatic type to reach complete artistic development. In its origins it was a form of religious observance, and its characters were often gods. When it came to deal with men, it sought to discover a suitable successor to the post vacated by Zeus and his fellow Olympians. Only men of the highest social and political eminence deserved that honor. Thus, the Greek tragedies tell stories either of the gods or of heroes. That Aristotle, noting in *The Poetics* the nobility of all the heroes of tragedy, elevated the convention to a law need occasion no surprise. Having excluded as tragic protagonist the completely virtuous and the completely evil man, he continues:

There remains, then, the character between these two extremes—that of a man who is not eminently good or just, yet whose misfortune is brought about not by vice or depravity, but by some error or frailty. *He must be one who is highly renowned and prosperous,*—a personage like Oedipus, Thyestes, or other illustrious men of such families.[1]

Many recent commentators on *The Poetics* have been so concerned with the interpretations of the word ἁμαρτία, translated above as "some error or frailty," that the sentence following it has received relatively little comment. However, early interpretations and emendations of

---

[1] S. H. Butcher, *The Poetics of Aristotle*, 4th ed., pp. 45–47. The italics in the quotation are mine.

this particular passage had enormous influence on medieval and Renaissance critical theory and on classical drama as written in Italy and France during the sixteenth and seventeenth centuries. Many of the medieval and Renaissance writers knew nothing of the requirements of a stage play. After Plautus and Terence, Roman drama passed gradually from the stage, ousted by the more primitive appeal of the Circus. The mimes did little to carry on any tradition of theatrical tragedy. Most scholars agree that the tragedies of Seneca were written for recitation, not performance. Thus it came about that the limitation of the words "comedy" and "tragedy" to drama faded from the minds of men. Any kind of writing that showed a progression from good fortune to bad became a tragedy; any that showed a progression from bad to good fortune, a comedy. But even the Dark Ages never forgot the classical imperative that the characters of tragedy had to be drawn from the ranks of the high and mighty; only comedy might deal with the common and lowly man.

Medieval writers drove the wedge ever deeper between tragedy and comedy. The social eminence of the characters and the style of the plot continued to be the bases for distinction between the two forms. It was only as the *De casibus virorum illustrium* type of tragedy acquired the idea of retributive justice [2] that its purpose approached that which was later to animate domestic tragedy. In the fundamental conceptions of character and tragic dignity, the formal tragedy of the Middle Ages affords no possible basis for domestic tragedy. Spingarn has prepared a useful list to show the distinctions between tragedy and comedy at the end of the fifteenth century.

i. The characters in tragedy are kings, princes, or great leaders; those in comedy, humble persons and private citizens.

ii. Tragedy deals with great and terrible actions; comedy with familiar and domestic actions.

iii. Tragedy begins happily and ends terribly; comedy begins rather turbulently and ends joyfully.

iv. The style and diction of tragedy are elevated and sublime; while those of comedy are humble and colloquial.

v. The subjects of tragedy are generally historical; those of comedy are always invented by the poet.

---

[2] Willard Farnham, *The Medieval Heritage of Elizabethan Tragedy, passim.*

vi. Comedy deals largely with love and seduction; tragedy with exile and bloodshed.[3]

It will be noted that domestic tragedy runs counter to three of these six rules. The protagonist occupies a humble station, the action and style of writing are both familiar and domestic. Almost the only rule obeyed by writers of Elizabethan domestic tragedy was the fifth, as stories notorious in local annals were usually selected. Even the classical authors, held up to admiration, had occasionally provided a happy ending, as in the case of *The Eumenides* of Aeschylus. Elizabethan domestic tragedy included both the exiles and bloodshed attributed by medieval writers to tragedy and also the loves and seductions connected with comedy.

In view of the unanimity of the critics, it is indeed remarkable that tragedy was ever able to descend from its Olympian heights to the lowly vale of common man. Wherever the origins of domestic tragedy may be, they are not to be found in countries where the writers were ruled by critical opinion, for there it had an insurmountable obstacle to overcome.

In Tudor England, where domestic tragedy got its start, the relationship between playwright and dramatic theorist was not as close as on the Continent. The critics of England re-echoed all the classical rules. William Webbe in *A Discourse of English Poetry*, describing the rise of the historical form of tragedy, said:

There grewe at last to be a greater diuersitye betweene Tragedy wryters and Comedy wryters, the one expressing onely sorrowfull and lamentable Hystories, bringing in the persons of Gods and Goddesses, Kynges and Queenes, and great states, whose partes were cheefely to expresse most miserable calamities and dreadful chaunces, which increased worse and worse, tyll they came to the most wofull plight that might be deuised.[4]

This repeats the attitude of Chaucer's translation of Boethius and that in his *The Monk's Tale*. Webbe refers, of course, to drama, not to narrative.

Sir Philip Sidney, most eminent of Elizabethan critics, in his *The Defense of Poesy*, to support his main thesis, argues the moral effect of

[3] J. E. Spingarn, *A History of Literary Criticism in the Renaissance*, 2d ed., pp. 66–67.

[4] William Webbe, *A Discourse of English Poetrie*, in G. Gregory Smith, *Elizabethan Critical Essays*, I, 248–49.

drama. Thus he is forced to say that the virtue of tragedy lies in the lesson it teaches to kings, since they are its only subjects.

So that the right use of *Comoedie* will, I thinke, by no bodie be blamed; and much lesse of the high and excellent *Tragedie*, that openeth the greatest woundes, and sheweth forth the *Ulcers* that are covered with *Tissue*, that maketh Kings feare to be Tyrants, and Tyrants manifest their tyrannicall humours, that with sturring the affects of *Admiration* and *Commiseration*, teacheth the uncertaintie of this world, and uppon how weak foundations guilden roofs are builded: that maketh us know: *Qui sceptra saevus duro imperio regit, Timet timentes, metus in authorem redit.*[5]

Sidney had little respect for the tragedies of his own time, asserting that *Gorboduc* was the only one which did not violate the Senecan rules, and hence the only one worthy of serious consideration and respect. Whatever may be said of his position, his analysis was accurate, for the Elizabethan dramatists obviously were not slavish imitators of the ancients. On the contrary, the English classicists seem to have exerted surprisingly little influence upon the composition of stage plays. Perhaps this was because Elizabethan plays were intended for popular audiences. Most of the English dramatists had none of the literary pretensions of continental writers. English critics had small connection with the popular theatre, and their dicta did not have the same stifling influence on dramatic growth. To be sure, Tudor dramatists adopted some Senecan conventions, but they added many of their own in the development of romantic drama. Their practice was almost as great a departure from the rules of the strict classicists as was domestic tragedy itself. Stage plays had got off to a head start and were far in advance of the conservative influences which were so effectively blocking dramatic experimentation in other parts of Europe. The implacable rules fixed by classical opinion had to be violated boldly before any new development in tragedy could put in its first tentative appearance.

It is natural that these theatrical conditions should have proved favorable to the growth of so unorthodox a sort of play as domestic tragedy. Although isolated examples of such dramas survive from France and Italy, they are not significant because in both countries the drama had become formalized under court patronage. In England, court circles failed to gain exclusive control of the theatres, and domestic tragedy came to its first great flowering.

[5] *The Defence of Poesie*, in *The Complete Works of Sir Philip Sidney*, ed. Albert Feuillerat, III, 23.

Chapter Two

POPULAR THEOLOGY

REEK TRAGEDY treated primarily the problem of evil. Aeschylus attempted in his plays to expound his own theological and philosophical system. Aeschylus, Sophocles, and, to a lesser extent, Euripides presented gods and important personages to illustrate large problems of man, god, and destiny.

The new tragedy of the common people, with which this book is concerned, also dealt with the problem of evil. Questions of right and wrong in everyday life loomed large to the shopkeepers, artisans, and other respectable citizens who made up a great part of the audience in Shakespeare's time.[1] These people had an infinite capacity to stomach large doses of moral instruction. In tragedies written about men like themselves, they expected a discussion of the problems of life and death. As earnest Christians, they viewed death as a passage to the next world, either to rewards for virtue or to punishments for sin. They had absorbed from their preachers ideas about the methods of attaining salvation and avoiding damnation, ideas which became the intellectual texture of the domestic tragedies of the time. These dramas appealed to the same type of audience and to the same interests and prejudices as did the morality plays. Therefore, it need occasion no surprise that the authors of the first English domestic tragedies contrived to combine sound moral and theological persuasion with their melodramatic plots. Their tales of murder, rebellion, seductions, and infidelity served the same purpose as the exempla of the sermons preached every Sunday in every parish church.

The ordinary Elizabethan domestic tragedy presented a tale of infidelity and murder. A wife falls in love with another man and plots with him to murder her husband. The crime is delayed by various circumstances, but eventually the deed is done. The wife and her lover are quickly revealed in some natural or supernatural way to the agents

---

[1] Alfred Harbage, *Shakespeare's Audience, passim.*

of justice, are sentenced to death, and pay the penalty for their crimes. Before their deaths, however, the murderers turn to thoughts of repentance, plead for God's mercy, and exert every effort to prepare for heaven.

The typical domestic tragedy followed a pattern, the sequence being: sin, discovery, repentance, punishment, and expectation of divine mercy. For an understanding of these plays, it is necessary to know the contemporary religious ideas, the exact meanings and applications of the terms "sin," "repentance," "mercy," "Providence," and the like. A knowledge of the popular theology of Elizabethan England is as important for an appreciation of these plays as is a familiarity with the modern capitalistic system for an insight into the drama of the last fifty years.

The writings of eminent clergymen of the period on abstruse doctrinal and metaphysical problems are far less important in showing the popular views of theology than are the sermons delivered on Sundays in local parish churches. In these sermons, clergymen reiterated basic ideas which became part of the beliefs of even the most perfunctory churchgoers. It is easy to discover these ideas because of the existence of a book of the authorized sermons which were required by law to be read in the pulpits of Her Majesty's churches. This book was developed in an effort to curb the religious unrest among the people.

On the accession of Elizabeth to the throne in 1558, both secular and ecclesiastical authorities desired to establish the Protestant religion on a firm basis in England, to have done with the doctrinal upheavals which for over a generation had caused acute distress to both clergy and laity. In the interests of unity and stability, the Articles of Religion, sometimes known as the Thirty-nine Articles, were adopted by convocation in 1563. Also thirty-three sermons, written about the middle of the sixteenth century, were ordered to be read regularly in the churches of the country. The first twelve appeared in print in 1547, another twenty in 1563, and one more in 1572. The preface to an edition of these sermons in 1562 makes its purpose abundantly clear: "to avoid the manifold enormities which heretofore by false doctrine have crept into the Church of God," and since some ministers "have not the gift of preaching sufficiently to instruct the people . . . the Queen's most excellent Majesty . . . hath . . . caused a Book of Homilies, which heretofore was set forth by her most loving Brother . . . Edward the Sixth, to be printed anew." [2] The preface enjoins the following:

All which Homilies her Majesty commandeth and straitly chargeth all Parsons, Vicars, Curates, and all other having spiritual cure, every Sunday and Holy-day in the year, at the ministering of the Holy Communion, or if there be no Communion ministered that day, yet after the Gospel and Creed, in such order and place as is appointed in the Book of Common Prayers, to read and declare to their parishoners, plainly and distinctly, one of the said Homilies, in such order as they stand in the book; except there be a Sermon, according as it is enjoined in the book of her Highness' Injunctions: and then for that cause only, and for none other, the reading of the said Homily to be deferred unto the next Sunday or Holy-day following.

And when the foresaid Book of Homilies is read over, her Majesty's pleasure is, that the same be repeated and read again, in such like sort as was before prescribed. [3]

The Eightieth Canon of 1603 required that a copy of the homilies be placed in every parish church. [4] These facts show that the doctrine contained in the sermons not only had the sanction of the officials, but that every churchgoer would be thoroughly, perhaps painfully, familiar with them. Thus the evidence here presented, together with that from other available texts, affords a basis for understanding the ideas of the man in the street on such subjects as salvation, repentance, charity, Providence, and similar theological conceptions.

The book of homilies is too lengthy and repetitious to make a complete discussion of its sermons advisable. Many of the topics treated, while fundamental to a complete faith, found no reflection in the later drama, and the present book will call attention only to those ideas which by reiteration must have impressed themselves on the people—ideas which came to be the bases for many works of contemporary literature.

Two fundamental articles of faith are constantly reiterated: first, that God is instantly aware of all sin; second, that no man except Christ ever lived without sin. The first of these appears too frequently to need illustration. The following expression of the second concept is characteristic:

---

[2] *Certain Sermons, or Homilies, Appointed to Be Read in Churches, in the Time of the Late Queen Elizabeth of Famous Memory*, 1852 ed., p. xi.

[3] *Ibid.*, p. xii.   [4] *Ibid.*, p. v.

So doth blessed St. John the evangelist, in the name of himself, and of all other holy men (be they never so just) make this open confession: *If we say we have no sin, we deceive ourselves, and the truth is not in us: if we acknowledge our sins, God is faithful and just to forgive us our sins, and to cleanse us from all unrighteousness. If we say we have not sinned, we make him a liar, and his word is not in us* (1 John i. 8–10).[5]

Although every man on earth sins in the sight of God, the theologians made distinctions in the types of sin. For example, they emphasized the traditional distinction between mortal and venial sin. Miss Campbell writes:

Thomas Aquinas defined the difference between venial and mortal sin:
"Therefore when the soul is so disordered by sin as to turn away from its last end, viz. God, to Whom it is united by charity, there is mortal sin; but when it is disordered without turning away from God, there is venial sin." . . . mortal sin is imputed to reason only, not to sensuality.

. . . .

This distinction it is absolutely necessary to make if we are to see the difference between the villain and tragic hero in Shakespeare. The tragic hero sins under the influence of passion, his reason failing to check his passion. His passion may lead him to madness, but as long as his passion is in conflict with reason, he has not committed mortal sin. When, however, passion has taken possession of his will, has perverted his will, when in perfect accord with passion his reason directs evil through the will, then we have a villain, one who is dyed in sin, and one whose sin is mortal.[6]

This distinction is implicit in the action of the domestic tragedies, although few cases of mortal sin are dramatized in them.

Another division, really implied in that of St. Thomas Aquinas, is established in the sermon "An Information for Them Which Take Offence at Certain Places of the Holy Scripture." The anonymous author divides mankind into three classes, ungodly men, sinners, and scorners.

By these three sorts of people, *ungodly* men, *sinners*, and *scorners*, all impiety is signified, and fully expressed. By the *ungodly*, he understandeth those which have no regard of Almighty God, being void of all faith, whose hearts and minds are so set upon the world, that they study only how to accomplish their worldly practices, their carnal imaginations, their

---

[5] *Ibid.*, p. 12.
[6] Lily B. Campbell, *Shakespeare's Tragic Heroes, Slaves of Passion*, pp. 99–101.

filthy lust and desire, without any fear of God. The second sort he calleth
sinners; not such as do fall through ignorance, or of frailness; for then
who should be found free? What man ever lived upon earth (Christ only
excepted), but he hath sinned? . . . Though the godly do fall, yet they
walk not purposely in sin, they stand not still to continue and tarry in sin,
they sit not down like careless men, without all fear of God's just punishment for sin; but defying sin, through God's great grace and infinite
mercy, they rise again, and fight against sin. . . . The third sort he calleth *scorners,* that is, a sort of men whose hearts are so stuffed with malice,
that they are not contented to dwell in sin, and to lead their lives in all
kind of wickedness; but also they do contemn and scorn in other all godliness, true religion, all honesty and virtue.

Of the two first sorts of men, I will not say but they may take repentance and be converted unto God. Of the third sort, I think I may without
danger of God's judgment pronounce, that never any yet converted unto
God by repentance, but continued still in their abominable wickedness,
heaping up to themselves damnation, against the day of God's inevitable
judgment.[7]

In the domestic tragedies many of the first two kinds of evildoers appear, but few of the scorners. This distinction will explain the denial
of repentance to certain characters in the later plays.

Man, left to his own devices, so the homilies taught, runs headlong
to sin, along the primrose path to the everlasting bonfire. He can escape
hell only through God's mercy. Christ made His sacrifice that mankind might be redeemed, and God desires to save those who, not having
lost their way entirely, are willing to turn again to His mercy with
complete and lasting faith. For only through God's mercy can man
return to grace. It is not man's will but God's great love for mankind
that renders repentance efficacious.

Thus we have heard how evil we be of ourselves: how of ourselves and by
ourselves, we have no goodness, help, nor salvation; but contrariwise, sin,
damnation, and death everlasting: which if we deeply weigh and consider,
we shall the better understand the great mercy of God, and how our
salvation cometh only by Christ.[8]

The complicated problem of the salvation of man and of the operation of God's mercy provoked much of the religious controversy of the
day. On questions concerning the efficacy of repentance, of good works,

[7] *Certain Sermons,* pp. 348–49.   [8] *Ibid.,* p. 15.

of penance, and of virtuous living there was a wide diversity of opinion. In spite of this confusion, the view reflected in the dramas of the time, as well as the general impression to be gathered from the authorized sermons, was that earnest repentance would bring with it forgiveness of sins and admission into heaven. Belief in God without the desire to seek forgiveness for sin was considered as a dead faith, "which bringeth forth no good works, but is idle, barren, and unfruitful." [9] The lively faith necessary for salvation ordinarily required good works, but they could be dispensed with in the case of a man converted just before his death. Even on the steps of the scaffold, the ungodly man might repent the error of his ways and pray for divine forgiveness and thus hope to escape damnation.

And this is not only the common belief of the articles of our faith, but it is also a true trust and confidence of the mercy of God through our Lord Jesus Christ, and a stedfast hope of all good things, to be received at God's hand: and that although we, through infirmity, or temptation of our ghostly enemy, do fall from him by sin, yet if we return again unto him by true repentance, that he will forgive and forget our offences for his Son's sake, our Saviour Jesus Christ, and will make us inheritors with him of his everlasting kingdom; and that in the mean time, until that kingdom come, he will be our protector and defender in all perils and dangers, whatsoever do chance: and that though sometime he doth send us sharp adversity, yet that evermore he will be a loving Father unto us, correcting us for our sin, but not withdrawing his mercy finally from us, if we trust in him, and commit ourselves wholly unto him, hang only upon him, and call upon him, ready to obey and serve him. This is the true, lively, and unfeigned Christian faith, and is not in the mouth and outward profession only, but it liveth, and stirreth inwardly in the heart. And this faith is not without hope and trust in God, nor without the love of God of our neighbours, nor without the fear of God, nor without the desire to hear God's word, and to follow the same in eschewing evil, and doing gladly all good works. [10]

The idea that good works were necessary adjuncts to Christian faith had its practical drawbacks. Developed to a logical conclusion it could result in drawing up a kind of cosmic balance sheet in which the profit derived from good works could balance the losses incurred through sin. The authors of domestic tragedies carried this idea to almost the same absurd conclusion as did Sir Despard Murgatroyd in Gilbert and

[9] *Ibid.*, p. 31.   [10] *Ibid.*, p. 32.

Sullivan's *Ruddigore*. This bad baronet, faced with the necessity of committing a daily crime, would get it over the first thing in the morning and then do good for the rest of the day. Good works, St. Chrysostom showed, might help a man; but divorced from faith, they could never insure the sinner's attainment of heaven.

"A man must needs be nourished by good works, but first he must have faith. He that doth good deeds, yet without faith, he hath no life. I can shew a man that by faith without works lived, and came to heaven: but without faith never man had life. The thief, that was hanged when Christ suffered, did believe only, and the most merciful God justified him. And because no man shall say again, that he lacked time to do good works, for else he would have done them; truth it is, and I will not contend therein; but this I will surely affirm, that faith only saved him. If he had lived and not regarded faith and the works thereof, he should have lost his salvation again. But this is the effect that I say, that faith by itself saved him, but works by themselves never justified any man." Here ye have heard the mind of St. Chrysostom, whereby you may perceive, that neither faith is without works, (having opportunity thereto) nor works can avail to everlasting life, without faith.[11]

The example of the penitent thief was of great use to later playwrights who repeatedly exhibited last-minute repentances of sinners on the steps of the scaffold.

Repentance was considered necessary for all men. Clergymen, however, disagreed in their estimates of its efficacy as well as in their conception of the exact steps by which to approach the act itself. Ordinarily preachers allowed the widest possible latitude to divine mercy. Even the sermons of the most severe preachers might suggest to the ear untrained in fine theological distinctions that sincere repentance would save anyone. John Bradford, whose works received an unsolicited testimonial in *A Warning for Fair Women*,[12] stated in *A Sermon of Repentance*, 1553, that salvation might come to all who would repent. Bradford defined repentance or penance, equivalent words in his definition, as "a sorrowing or forthinking of our sins past, an earnest purpose to amend or turning to God, with a trust of pardon."

This definition may be divided into three parts: that penance or repentance should contain, First, a sorrowing for our sins: Secondly, a trust of pardon, which otherwise may be called a persuasion of God's mercy by the

---

[11] *Ibid.*, pp. 45–46.   [12] See below, Chapter VI.

merits of Christ for the forgiveness of our sins: and Thirdly, a purpose to amend, or conversion to a new life.[13]

Even the vilest of men might hope for salvation, according to Bradford, if they would forsake their evil ways and live their lives according to God's commandments. He therefore felt justified in using the harshest words to turn men to the paths of righteousness.

Search therefore your hearts all: all swearers, blasphemers, liars, flatterers, idle talkers, jesters, bribers, covetous, drunkards, gluttons, whoremongers, thieves, murderers, slanderers, idle livers, negligent in their vocation, &c. All such and all other as lament not their sins, as hope not in God's mercy for pardon, as purpose not heartily to amend, to leave their swearing, drunkenness, whoredom, covetousness, idleness, &c.; all such, I say shall not nor cannot enter into God's kingdom, but hell-fire is prepared for them, weeping, and gnashing of teeth. Whereunto, alas! I fear me, very many will needs go, in that very many will be as they have been, let us even to the wearing of our tongue to the stumps preach and pray never so much to the contrary, and that even in the bowels of Jesus Christ: as now I beseech you all, all, all, and every mother's child, to repent and lament your sin, to trust in God's mercy, and to amend your lives.[14]

To show how far a man might have fallen from the grace of God and yet be saved by repentance, Bradford, near the end of his sermon, devotes several pages to Biblical examples of persons who were or might have been forgiven. He includes Adam, Eve, Cain, Noah, Moses, David, Mary Magdalene, and the penitent thief, all of whom had or could have returned to God after careers of disobedience, murder, drunkenness, adultery, or betrayal. Following a digression on the necessity of leading a better life, he concludes:

But I will make an end, for I am too tedious.

Dearly beloved, repent your sins: that is, be sorry for that which is past; believe in God's mercy for pardon, how deeply soever you have sinned; and both purpose and earnestly pursue a new life, bringing forth worthy and true fruits of repentance. As you have given over your members from sin to sin to serve the devil; your tongues to swear, to lie, to flatter, to scold, to jest, to scoff, to vain jangling, to boasting, &c.; your hands to picking, groping, idleness, fighting, &c.; your feet to skipping, going to evil, to dancing, &c.; your ears to hear fables, lies, vanities, and evil things,

---

[13] *A Sermon of Repentaunce*, in *The Writings of John Bradford, M.A.*, ed. Aubrey Townsend, I, 45.

[14] *Ibid.*, pp. 52–53.

&c.; so now give over your members to godliness, your tongues to speak, your ears to hear, your eyes to see, your mouths to taste, your hands to work, your feet to go about such things as may make to God's glory, sobriety of life, and love to your brethren; and that daily more and more diligently: for in a stay to stand you cannot; either better or worse you are to-day than you were yesterday. But better I trust you be, and will be, if you mark well my theme, that is, "Repent you."

The which thing that you would do, as before I have humbly besought you, even so now yet once more I do again beseech you, and that for the tender mercies of God in Christ Jesus our Lord: "Repent you:" "repent you; for the kingdom of heaven" (that is, a kingdom full of all riches, pleasures, mirth, beauty, sweetness, and eternal felicity) "is at hand." The eye hath not seen the like, the ear hath not heard the like, the heart of man cannot conceive the treasures and pleasures of this kingdom, which now "is at hand" to such as repent; that is, to such as are sorry for their sins, believe God's mercy through Christ, and earnestly purpose to lead a new life.[15]

During the reign of Elizabeth, high officials in the Church of England held, in general, Calvinistic views on election. The Lambeth Articles issued in 1595 revealed the severest possible attitudes. In spite of these views of the high officials, the Sixteenth Article of the Articles of Religion set forth a more liberal dogma.

Not every deadly sin willingly committed after Baptism is sin against the Holy Ghost, and unpardonable. Wherefore the grant of repentance is not to be denied to such as fall into sin after Baptism. After we have received the Holy Ghost, we may depart from grace given, and fall into sin, and by the grace of God we may rise again, and amend our lives. And therefore they are to be condemned, which say, they can no more sin as long as they live here, or deny the place of forgiveness to such as truly repent.[16]

The doctrine that a man could depart from grace by his evil deeds and could return by repentance was one which would be more easily comprehensible to the man in the street than that proclaimed in the Articles of Lambeth. As the foregoing analysis of the sermon by Bradford shows, the hearer would leave the church with the feeling that unless he made earnest repentance, he was doomed to hell-fire; but if he did repent, he would, in all probability, be saved by the mercy of God. Therefore he could by his own choice assure his salvation.

This impression he would receive even more strongly from the

[15] *Ibid.*, pp. 80–81.   [16] *Certain Sermons*, p. 514.

authorized sermon, "An Homily of Repentance, and of True Reconciliation unto God," included among those Queen Elizabeth had appointed to be read in churches. In this collection, the doctrine that a
man must have faith before he could gain admission to the ranks of
the blessed was an answer to the extreme assertions of foreordination:

By this then you may well perceive, that the only mean and instrument
of salvation, required on our parts, is faith; that is to say, a sure trust and
confidence in the mercies of God; whereby we persuade ourselves, that
God both hath, and will forgive our sins, that he hath accepted us again
into his favour, that he hath released us from the bonds of damnation, and
received us again into the number of his elect people, not for our merits
or deserts, but only and solely for the merits of Christ's death and passion,
who became man for our sakes, and humbled himself to sustain the re-
proach of the cross, that we thereby might be saved, and made inheritors
of the kingdom of heaven.[17]

This doctrine made the question of repentance simple, for a return to
faith and contrition for sins would allow the penitent to take his place
among the chosen of God.

The "Homily of Repentance" shows the operation of this plan. The
sole requirement was that a man should once have had faith; even
baptism was held to be sufficient evidence of the fact. Indeed, the collection contains some examples of last-minute repentances which had
saved men who in their lives had neither had faith nor accomplished
good works. Thus even an ungodly man might receive the benefits of
repentance. The sermon begins with an account of the danger of falling
away from God, of the pains and sufferings meted out to all unrepentant sinners. In justice, all deserve and would suffer damnation,
were it not for the mercy of Jesus Christ, "who being true and natural
God, equal and of one substance with the Father, did at the time appointed take upon him our frail nature, in the blessed virgin's womb,
and that of her undefiled substance, that so he might be a Mediator
between God and us, and pacify his wrath." [18] The existence of a Mediator gave mankind hope for the forgiveness promised to penitents.

Now, unto all them that will return unfeignedly unto the Lord their
God, the favour and mercy of God unto forgiveness of sins is liberally
offered. Whereby it followeth necessarily, that although we do, after we

---

[17] *Ibid.*, p. 399. [18] *Ibid.*, p. 494.

be once come to God, and grafted in his Son Jesus Christ, fall into great sins, *for there is no righteous man upon the earth that sinneth not; and if we say we have no sin, we deceive ourselves, and the truth is not in us* (Eccles. vii. 20; 1 John i. 8), yet if we rise again by repentance, and, with a full purpose of amendment of life, do flee unto the mercy of God, taking sure hold thereupon, through faith in his Son Jesus Christ, there is an assured and infallible hope of pardon and remission of the same, and that we shall be received again into the favour of our heavenly Father. . . . and yet afterwards he [David] fell horribly, committing most detestable adultery and damnable murder; and yet as soon as he cried *Peccavi, I have sinned unto the Lord,* his sins being forgiven, he was received into favour again (2 Sam. xi. 4, 15, 17; xii. 13).[19]

Having once repented, a man could sin again and still obtain salvation by a fresh confession and a second act of repentance. However, so long as a man clung to the material advantages his misdeeds had won for him, penitence brought no remission of sin. King Claudius in *Hamlet* desires to have his conscience cleared, but his murder of his brother has won for him the crown of Denmark and Queen Gertrude. Since he refuses to give up either the throne or the queen, he cannot obtain forgiveness. In the domestic tragedies, the repentant sinners have surrendered the gains obtained from their sins, for most of them are about to give up life itself.

Perhaps the best summary of the whole matter of repentance as it was understood by the average Elizabethan appears at the end of this sermon, the "Homily of Repentance."

Repentance (as it is said before) is a true returning unto God, whereby men, forsaking utterly their idolatry and wickedness, do with a lively faith embrace, love, and worship the true living God only, and give themselves to all manner of good works, which by God's word they know to be acceptable unto him. Now there be four parts of repentance, which, being set together, may be likened to an easy and short ladder, whereby we may climb from the bottomless pit of perdition, that we cast ourselves into by our daily offences and grievous sins, up into the castle or tower of eternal and endless salvation.

The first is the contrition of the heart. For we must be earnestly sorry for our sins, and unfeignedly lament and bewail that we have by them so grievously offended our most bounteous and merciful God, who so tenderly loved us, that he gave his only begotten Son, to die a most bitter

---

[19] *Ibid.,* p. 499.

death, and to shed his dear heart-blood for our redemption and deliverance. And verily this inward sorrow and grief, being conceived in the heart for the heinousness of sin, if it be earnest and unfeigned, is as a sacrifice to God; as the holy prophet David doth testify, saying, *A sacrifice to God is a troubled spirit; a contrite and broken heart, O Lord, thou wilt not despise* (Psal. li. 17).

. . . .

The second is, an unfeigned confession and acknowledging of our sins unto God, whom by them we have so grievously offended, that, if he should deal with us according to his justice, we do deserve a thousand hells, if there could be so many. Yet if we will with a sorrowful and contrite heart make an unfeigned confession of them unto God, he will freely and frankly forgive them, and so put all our wickedness out of remembrance before the sight of his majesty, that they shall no more be thought upon (Ezek. xviii. 27).

. . . .

The third part of repentance is faith, whereby we do apprehend and take hold upon the promises of God, touching the free pardon and forgiveness of our sins: which promises are sealed up unto us, with the death and blood-shedding of his Son Jesus Christ. For what should avail and profit us to be sorry for our sins, to lament and bewail that we have offended our most bounteous and merciful Father, or to confess and acknowledge our offences and trespasses, though it be done never so earnestly, unless we do stedfastly believe, and be fully persuaded, that God, for his Son Jesus Christ's sake, will forgive us all our sins, and put them out of remembrance, and from his sight?

. . . .

The fourth is, an amendment of life, or a new life, in bringing forth fruits worthy of repentance. For they that do truly repent must be clean altered and changed, they must become new creatures, they must be no more the same that they were before.[20]

In the dramatic presentation of repentances of murderers and other sinners in domestic tragedies, the essential steps as outlined above are carefully followed. Contrition of the heart can be exhibited dramatically only by action and by the dialogue used for confession. Confession was not necessarily before a priest. Public acknowledgment of all sins was thought sufficient. This fact accounts for the presence in literature of an extraordinary number of "scaffold speeches," repentant

[20] *Ibid.*, pp. 502–8.

monologues in which the criminal, before his death, summarizes his evil life, confesses his sins, forgives his enemies, repents from the heart, "*ab imo cordis,*" [21] as one of them says, and throws himself on divine mercy. Thus writers dramatized the first three steps of repentance; obviously the condemned person was prevented by death from performing good works, but works were proofs of repentance and not part of repentance itself.

Repentance, a manner of settling the account between God and man, could not save a man from the earthly consequences of his sin. Indeed, mundane punishment was often welcomed as a penance. If a man suffered his penalty on earth, he was less likely to have to endure it in the next world. This comforting idea appears frequently in the plays.

One of the notions most useful to pamphleteers, writers of homiletic treatises, and playwrights was that Divine Providence intervened in the lives of men to assure the operations of divine justice. Divine Providence is a specific power of God which employs signs, portents, coincidences, seeming accidents, plagues, natural or unnatural phenomena, or minor miracles to dispense rewards and punishments according to His laws, either through His direct action or through His agents. The phrase "Divine Providence" was common enough in nondramatic literature, but was seldom employed by the playwrights. For this reason, providential operations have commonly gone unrecognized in investigations of the drama of the period. Critics of the individual domestic tragedies have dismissed providential interventions as "poetic justice." But there is a distinction between Thomas Rymer's poetic justice and the theological conception of Divine Providence. A dramatist who dispenses poetic justice distributes rewards and punishments artificially in response to his own moral standard, which may or may not coincide with Christian morality. A dramatist uses interventions of Divine Providence to show direct operations of what he understands as the will of God. When he dispenses poetic justice, a playwright acts as a god in a microcosm of his own creation. When he employs operations of Divine Providence, a playwright gives his interpretation of the will of God. In both the dramatic and nondramatic literature of the time, Divine Providence is employed to punish vice, to prevent crime against an innocent person, and to reveal criminals to the agencies of human justice. In one tale, for example, murderers cut the tongue from a

[21] Robert Yarington, *Two Lamentable Tragedies,* in A. H. Bullen, *A Collection of Old English Plays,* IV, 91.

young girl to prevent her from disclosing the fact that they have killed her parents. She miraculously recovers her speech, however, and denounces the criminals to the magistrates.[22] Biblical incidents, interpreted as acts of Divine Providence, were used as examples of what might befall unwary sinners. Other writers gathered rumors of miraculous occurrences and interpreted them as examples of God's vengeance for sin. Numerous pamphlets followed each visitation of the plague and stressed the wrath of God, His impatience with man's continued sin, and His Providence which was punishing the whole nation by means of the disease. Succeeding chapters will illustrate the use of providential intervention as a dramatic device in literature. A more immediate concern must be to discover in the homiletic writings of the time the views concerning the nature and operation of this power.

The idea of Divine Providence can be found in any religion in which the conception of divinity is theistic.

As used in religion, Providence is understood in a theistic sense to denote the care of God for His creatures, His general supervision over them, and the ordering of the whole course of things for their good. . . . In a very wide sense some such idea would seem to be indispensable to religion, although—as in Buddhism and some forms of pantheism—the word "providence" cannot be legitimately used as of a relation between "God" and "the world." In popular parlance it has too often included superstitions and unworthy ideas of deity, which responsible teachers would not countenance.

In the more restricted area of Christian theology Divine Providence is theoretically distinguished, on the one hand, from God's preservation of all His creatures, including man; and on the other, from His moral judgment. The latter is said to concern the character and education of man as moral creatures, their welfare and destiny, while Providence is concerned with the affairs and events of life and the way in which a Divine purpose is accomplished in and through them. The two are, however, almost inseparable, even in thought. The Christian doctrine is one of faith, resting upon the attributes and character of God generally, but especially as made known in Christ. Providence implies a God of unbounded wisdom, power, and goodness, who unceasingly directs human affairs, great and small, for the accomplishment of the highest spiritual ends.[23]

---

[22] See below, Chapter III.
[23] *Encyclopaedia of Religion and Ethics,* ed. James Hastings, X, 415.

The Elizabethans failed utterly to make the distinction pointed out in the second paragraph. By Providence they meant both moral judgment and the preservation from danger. Occasionally the same incident might reveal both, as in the case of the man whose horse fell and injured him while he was riding to kill his innocent son.[24] John Bradford, in the sermon already quoted, gives many ancient examples of Divine Providence and then turns to modern cases in the following picturesque passage:

But what go I about to avouch ancient examples, where daily experience doth teach? The sweat the other year [1551], the storms the winter following, will us to weigh them in the same balances. The hanging and killing of men themselves, which are, alas! too rife in all places require us to register them in the same rolls. And the least in children, infants, and such like, which yet cannot utter sin by word or deed, we see God's anger against sin in punishing them by sickness, death, misshape, or otherwise, so plainly that we cannot but groan and grunt again, in that we a little more have gushed out this gear gorgeously in word and deed.[25]

The means that God might employ in the operation of His Providence varied widely. He might inspire men or even animals to act in ways contrary to their natures, as in the case of the whale who approached the shore to save Jonah. He might send portents or cause other supernatural phenomena to help His people or punish His enemies. Any coincidence was considered an example of the workings of Providence. The punishment of any crime might be regarded as evidence of the action of the Lord. Stephen Charnock, in a discourse written about 1675, expressed ideas that also had wide currency at the end of the sixteenth century. Of this last method of Providence he said:

What more righteous than to make those vile affections and that unrighteousness their punishment which they make their pleasure, and to leave them to pursue their own sinful inclinations, and make them (as the psalmist speaks) Ps. v. 10. "fall by their own counsels?" A drunkard's beastliness is his punishment as well as his sin. Thus God delivers up some to their own lusts, as a punishment both to themselves and others, as he hardened Pharaoh's heart for the destruction both of himself and his people.[26]

---

[24] See below, Chapter III.   [25] Bradford, *op. cit.*, I, 61.

[26] *Discourses on Divine Providence,* in *The Complete Works of Stephen Charnock,* ed. Rev. James M'Cosh, I, 28.

An evil man might be used as the instrument of divine punishment to wreak God's vengeance on sinners, but even though he acted as the agent of God, he was still responsible to God and man for the consequences of his crime. He pursued his ends for selfish motives, and although his purposes happened to coincide with those of Providence, his case had to be judged on its own merits. Professor Battenhouse has pointed out that Elizabethans believed that tyrants were frequently permitted to reign over a people to punish them for their ungodly ways, but that the tyrant had to make his accounting with God for his crimes.

The concept of the Scourge of God has, therefore, two complementary aspects: it serves to explain historical calamities by showing that they are chastisements of sin permitted by God; and it assures tyrants that God is not helpless before their power but that He will, when He has used them, destroy them utterly.[27]

Battenhouse makes the further statement: "It is not too much to say that the doctrine of Providence was the chief apologetic interest of Reformation times." [28] As Professor Farnham has shown, during the sixteenth century the idea of fortune gradually retreated in the minds of writers, to be replaced by that of God's retributive justice.[29]

The assumption that God was immanent and active ruled out all question of chance. Everything that happened was in accordance with His knowledge and a result of His Providence. By recognizing the manifestations of this Providence, a man could pass accurate judgment on the merits of his companions, on the condition of the world, and on his own state of grace. The essential paradox was that a man who acted as an instrument of Divine Providence in an attempt to redress a wrong or to overthrow a prince committed a sin by his action.

If external forces failed, there was yet a way in which Providence could act. A criminal, God had provided, would punish himself by the remorse, by the growing fear, by any of the fundamental passions which might cause his natural humors to go adust,[30] and so cause him to suffer from abnormal melancholy. If this extremity failed to bring

---

[27] Roy W. Battenhouse, *Marlowe's "Tamburlaine," a Study in Renaissance Moral Philosophy*, p. 113.

[28] *Ibid.*, p. 86.

[29] Willard Farnham, *The Medieval Heritage of Elizabethan Tragedy, passim.*

[30] Farnham, *op. cit.*, p. 335; Campbell, *op. cit.*, Chapter VII.

the punishment, there remained the direct and drastic action of God as expressed through some great disaster or plague. Professor Battenhouse has shown conclusively that this kind of intervention by Providence is the explanation of the sudden illness of Tamburlaine on the eve of one of his triumphs.[31] It is clearly this force that strikes down Mr. Worldly Man at the height of his riches and earthly power, at the conclusion of the morality, *Enough Is as Good as a Feast*.[32]

Ordinarily, instead of direct intervention or the use of evil men as instruments of His Providence, God employed established authorities. The king was the anointed of God, and magistrates were his agents. To them it was given to judge and punish or to liberate, according to the merits of the case, and the commoner who was dissatisfied with their judgments had no human redress. He could, as the sermons told him, only wait patiently for the interposition of Providence. "But we must refer all judgment to God, to kings and rulers, and judges under them, which be God's officers to execute justice, and by plain words of Scripture, have their authority and use of the sword granted from God . . ."[33] If a man thought the decisions of a magistrate unjust, he could not rebel or make any attempt to overthrow that official, "but we must in such case patiently suffer all wrongs and injuries, referring the judgment of our cause only to God."[34] According to the idea of Providence, it was impossible for God to allow an unjust decision to go long unpunished.

Two quotations, one from the seventeenth century and one from the twentieth, may well sum up and clarify the idea of Providence as it was understood by the men and women who made up Shakespeare's audiences. Stephen Charnock wrote:

> God glorifies his righteousness and justice. There is a measure of wickedness God stays for, which will be an object of his justice without exception. . . . When men come to such a height, as to slight and resolve to break the laws of God, then is the time for the honour of his righteousness in his own institutions, to vex them in his sore displeasure: Ps. ii, 3, 5, "Then shall he speak to them in his wrath, and vex them," &c. When? When they resolve to "cast away his bands and cords from them," ver. 2 [3]. He is forced to rise then, when men make void his law, and tread down the honour of it; when they would not have God to have a standing

---

[31] Battenhouse, *op. cit.*, pp. 243–58.   [32] See below, Chapter IV.
[33] *Certain Sermons*, p. 102.   [34] *Ibid.*, p. 107.

law in the world, or a people to profess him: Ps. cxix. 126, "It is time for the Lord to work, for they have made void thy law." When the grapes of wickedness are thus fully ripe, then is God's time for the honour of his justice to cast them into the wine-press of his wrath, Rev. xiv. 19, 20. This is God's set time, when he may glorify, without any exception, his justice in punishing his enemies' sins, his wisdom in defeating his enemies' plots, his power in destroying his enemies' strength, and his mercy in relieving his people's wants.

. . . .

To conclude this: God's providential judgments are to be remembered; though they are for the punishment of the age that feel them, they are also for the instruction of the age which succeeds them.[35]

Miss Campbell restates the Elizabethan conception of Providence as a means of moral teaching through artistic media.

Even as tragedy came, then, to prove that justice must prevail, that God did punish evil, it came to stress more and more the teaching of Renaissance philosophy, that the man sins who would undertake to execute privately the justice of God. The great popularity of the so-called revenge tragedies attests the interest which the Renaissance took in this theme. God will Himself execute justice through calamity visited upon the sinner, or through justice executed by the magistrates as His agents, or through the troubled heart and uneasy conscience which are the penalty of sin.

. . . .

Thus are tragedies the *exempla* by which men are taught the lessons of moral philosophy. . . .[36]

Certain sins represented often in the plays were the subjects of entire sermons. In these discourses, the language employed and the attitudes revealed closely resemble those presented in the public theatres by "atheistical" playwrights. "A Sermon against Whoredom and Uncleanness" in the authorized collection discusses at length a theme highly popular with the dramatists and the writers of moral tracts. In this homily appear the familiar ideas of Providence, repentance, and divine mercy. The sermon begins with scriptural admonitions against fornication and continues with descriptions of the evil of this sin.

Hitherto have we heard how grievous a sin fornication and whoredom is, and how greatly God doth abhor it throughout the whole Scripture. How

---

[35] Charnock, *op. cit.*, I, 103–4, 115.   [36] Campbell, *op. cit.*, pp. 23–24.

can it any otherwise be than a sin of most abomination, seeing it may not once be named among the Christians, much less it may in any point be committed. And surely, if we would weigh the greatness of this sin, and consider it in the right kind, we should find the sin of whoredom to be the most filthy lake, foul puddle, and stinking sink, whereunto all kinds of sins and evils flow, where also they have their resting place and abiding.[37]

The author then shows how adultery leads to other sins, idleness, theft, envy, wrath, and even murder, and how it may discomfort the fornicator by the presence of bastards, and other direct evidences of the power of Providence. This congregation of sins leads to the inevitable damnation awaiting unrepentant sinners. The preacher fulminated against the filthiness of the sin and offered illustrations which show the action of Divine Providence in punishing adulterers. He chose his first example from the Bible to show God employing His Providence to punish Sodom and Gomorrah and the world of Noah. Then the preacher described the punishments meted out to fornicators in other countries by the agents of God's Providence, the princes and the magistrates. The ideas here presented are fundamental to an understanding of such plays as *A Woman Killed with Kindness* and *The English Traveller*.

One other question, that of swearing, needs consideration before this review of popular theology is concluded, for in the domestic tragedies, oaths were frequently used as dramatic devices. The Elizabethans distinguished several kinds of oaths. It was lawful to swear before a judge and in making solemn promises, to swear allegiance and obedience to laws, to promise fidelity in matrimony, and similar cases; but to swear an oath lightly, for insufficient purpose, was a sin, for this was taking "the name of God in vain." When one swore a lawful oath, it was a religious act, and to break it was to incur God's displeasure and to subject oneself to the danger of the intervention of Providence. That is why the ghost of her former lover haunts the heroine of *The Vow Breaker; or, The Fair Maid of Clifton*. She has sworn with him an oath of trothplight, and has married another man.[38]

While lawful oaths were to be kept at all costs, it was held that unlawful oaths, those by which the swearer vowed to commit a sin or to do an ungodly act, constituted a double offense against God and ought not to be fulfilled.

[37] *Certain Sermons*, p. 118.   [38] See below, Chapter IX.

Therefore, whosoever maketh any promise, binding himself thereunto by an oath, let him forsee that the thing which he promiseth be good and honest, and not against the commandment of God, and that it be in his own power to perform it justly. And such good promises must all men keep evermore assuredly. But if a man at any time shall, either of ignorance or of malice, promise and swear to do any thing which is either against the law of Almighty God, or not in his power to perform, let him take it for an unlawful and ungodly oath.[39]

The sin of perjury was thought particularly likely to provoke the intervention of the Providence of God. In addition, perjurers forever divorced themselves from the mercy of Christ, from the forgiveness of sins promised to all penitent sinners. All kinds of oaths, both lawful and unlawful, as well as the consequences of breaking the one and keeping the other, appear frequently in the plays to be discussed.

The tenets of popular theology here presented form the intellectual and moral substance of the Elizabethan domestic tragedies. Echoes of the language of the sermons and tracts were heard on the stages as the domestic tragedies were acted. The surprising strength of the influence of theology on these plays will be made clear in the pages that follow.

[39] *Certain Sermons*, p. 70.

Chapter Three

NONDRAMATIC LITERATURE

THE NONDRAMATIC LITERATURE of the sixteenth and seventeenth centuries contains many tales similar to those dramatized in domestic tragedy. These stories helped to establish the customary attitudes of the people toward the events and deeds which provided dramatists with plots for tragedies of domestic incident. The narratives also serve to illustrate crudely the operations attributed to Divine Providence, operations generally employed far more subtly by the playwrights. In the nondramatic works, the supernatural agency usually bears the name "Divine Providence," "God's just judgment," "God's Providence," or some similar descriptive term, but in the plays the same power is seldom labeled. Thus, a study of the popular nondramatic literature will aid in the recognition and identification of the real homiletic interests of the dramatists as expressed in the domestic tragedies.

The ethical and theological bases of the early domestic tragedies were constructed from materials drawn largely from sermons. It is natural, therefore, that the authors of this new dramatic genre should model their plots on stories which had descended from those used by preachers to supplement their sermons and to aid their congregations in grasping moral lessons. The earliest of these tales were called "exempla." An "exemplum" was "a short narrative used to illustrate or confirm a general statement." [1] They were almost infinite in number. The exempla were international property both in origin and use, and preachers altered them to suit their immediate purposes. Two of the best-known collections, the *Gesta Romanorum* and *The Exempla of Jacques de Vitry*, illustrate the distinctive features of the type. Although the second was not of English authorship, and both were written in Latin, later collections appeared in the vernacular. In content, these tales differed widely from one another, for exempla were drawn

[1] J. A. Mosher, *The Exemplum in the Early Religious and Didactic Literature of England*, p. 1.

from the lives of mythological kings, from saints' lives, from adventures of crusaders, from animal tales, and from Biblical stories. Only a very few showed the catastrophic results of sin committed by the common people. In the *Gesta Romanorum* several stories of this kind appear. Among these is an interesting instance of the intervention of Providence to prevent the death of an innocent person. A woman whose husband is on a crusade plans to kill him so that she may marry her lover. Her plan is to have her paramour stab an effigy of her husband. This deed, the author assumes, will be fatal to the crusader. Warned in time by a wise master, the knight is able to reverse the spell, so that the third blow dealt by the would-be murderer rebounds and kills the man who wields the weapon. The wife then buries him under her bed. On his return, the knight exposes her sin, and she is condemned to be burned.[2]

At first glance Providence does not seem to intervene in this tale, but with the sermons of the last chapter freshly in mind, one easily recognizes the wise master to be an agent of God. Although the exemplum has a second or allegorical significance, its literal meaning is of the kind repeatedly given to the homilies. A domestic situation in which a wife conspires with her lover to murder her husband and a supernatural manifestation of the power of Providence in a realistic tale are both frequent elements in dramatic and nondramatic works of literature throughout the period under consideration.

The *Exempla ex sermonibus vulgaribus* of Jacques de Vitry, a book widely read in England, contains several stories of persons of low social station who feel God's retributive justice. One tells of a nun who, hiding from a knight bent on her seduction, when he is about to give up the search, cried out "cucu," that he might find her. His will accomplished, he leaves her to disgrace and misery, the consequences of her folly.[3] Another relates with a strong appeal to pity the ruin of a young woman's reputation by the slander of a rejected suitor.[4] A third anecdote shows a young thief on the way to the gallows because his parents' lack of care has caused him to turn to a life of crime.[5]

A story from an English collection illustrates the direct operation

[2] *The Early English Versions of the "Gesta Romanorum,"* ed. Sidney J. H. Herritage, pp. 1–3.

[3] *The Exempla of Jacques de Vitry; or, Illustrative Stories from the Sermones Vulgares of Jacques de Vitry,* ed. Thomas F. Crane, Tale LVIII, pp. 22–23.

[4] *Ibid.,* Tale CCLXXXI, p. 117.   [5] *Ibid.,* Tale CCLXXXVII, p. 121.

of Divine Providence. A woman who had hated another for seven years was forbidden to take Communion at Easter until she had forgiven her enemy. This she pretended to do and took Communion with disastrous results:

Than, whan servis was do and all the pepull had eton, the neythbores com with this pore woman unto this worthy womans hous with presentes, to chere hure, and thanked god hiʒly that thei were accorded. But than this wretched woman seid, "Wene than that I forʒave this woman hure trespasse with myn herte as I dud with my mouthe? Naye! Than I preye god that I never take up this rush at my fote." Than she stowped down to take it upp, and the dewell strangled hure even there. Wherefore ʒe that make any lovedayes, loke that thei be made withowte anny feynynge, and latt the herte and the tonge accorde in hem.[6]

Many other exempla could be cited, but they would merely amplify the characteristics already illustrated.

At the preacher's disposal there had accumulated a mass of stories of marvels wrought by relics, by the sacred Host itself, or by some other means of divine intervention in the affairs of men; stories, likewise, of life and death, of mystery and adventure, many of which would have a vivid human interest for the ages of Chaucer and Lydgate. Examples in this category are far too numerous and accessible already to require any fresh illustration at this stage. We may note of them, in passing, that, unlike some classes of anecdotes we have considered, they were obviously intended to be taken very seriously. No one need doubt the truth of modern marvels of divine retribution, argues Bromyard, in view of the marvellous happenings recorded in the Old and New Testaments. The inspired word of Scripture was adequate warrant.[7]

The widespread influence of these exempla has been discussed thoroughly by Dr. Owst and others. The material, available in large quantities for anyone who cared to use it, was continually employed by writers and preachers for didactic purposes. Thus it would be likely to occur to a literary artist that here was not only a great mass of accessible material, but also a method of treatment already worked out for him. To construct his stories and poems, he had only to expand, amplify, and adapt the plots of these exempla.

[6] MS. Roy. 18. B. xxiii, fol. 71, quoted in G. R. Owst, *Literature and Pulpit in Medieval England*, p. 156.

[7] Owst, *op. cit.*, pp. 168–69.

II

At least three of the tragedies in *The Mirror for Magistrates* are stories of the sort dramatized in the domestic tragedies. As the title suggests, this work was designed to teach moral lessons to persons in high places. But some of the examples, particularly those dealing with rebels, speak even more directly to the common man. Indeed, William Baldwin calls the work "A Briefe Memorial of / sundrie Vnfortunate Englishe men." [8] In the earlier suppressed edition, the title page read: "A memorial / of fuche Princes, as fince / the tyme of King Richard / the feconde, haue been / vnfortunate in the / Realme of / England." [9] This change from "Princes" to "Englishe men" supports the idea that the tales were not to be limited to men of noblest station. Planning his work as a series of examples of God's retributive justice rather than as instances of the arbitrary turning of fortune's wheel (Boccaccio's scheme in his *De casibus virorum illustrium*, as well as Lydgate's in his *The Fall of Princes*), Baldwin intended to make his lessons apply to all men, "vnto this presente time, chiefly of suche as Fortune had dalyed with here in this ylande: whiche might be as a myrrour for al men as well noble as others, to shewe the slyppery deceytes of the wauering lady, and the due rewarde of all kinde of vices." [10] In the various editions appear three tragedies of common men. Two of them deal with rebellion. The third is the pitiful story of Jane Shore, a king's concubine. The 1559 edition contains the tale of Jack Cade, a famous rebel, whose story resembles that of Jack Straw, the hero of a play produced about 1591. The tragedy of "The Blacksmith" also narrates the events of a rebellion. Jane Shore, the mistress of Edward IV, became the heroine of Thomas Heywood's two-part chronicle history, *Edward IV*, and of the lost play, *Shore's Wife*, by Henry Chettle and John Day.

Jack Cade's story is the only one of the three included in the original edition of 1559. Cade, "base borne, of no abilitye, and lesse power," [11] is temporarily triumphant. The author makes Cade admit that he is not well born, although it would have suited the conventional purpose of "tragedy" better if he had the rebel insist on the descent from the house of Mortimer which the real Cade actually claimed.

[8] *The Mirror for Magistrates*, ed. Lily B. Campbell, p. 68.
[9] *Ibid.*, plate, between pp. 6 and 7.   [10] *Ibid.*, p. 68.   [11] *Ibid.*, p. 170.

> This shift I vsed the people to perswade
> To leave their Prince, on my side more to sticke,
> Wheras in deede my fathers name was Kade
> Whose noble stock was never wurth a sticke.
> But touching wit I was both rype and quicke,
> Had strength of lims, large stature, cumly face,
> Which made men wene my lynage were not base.[12]

Cade's career found its way into dramatic literature at least once, for Shakespeare uses his rebellion in *2 Henry VI* to reinforce the general theme of the play that though anarchy arises when the royal ruler is weak, it is a sin to revolt against any king. The sermon on rebellion, it will be remembered, taught that only God's Providence could properly dethrone an evil king. A subject who raised his hand against God's anointed committed a sin. This is taken for granted by Shakespeare in his chronicle-history plays and is the moral of Cade's tragedy in *The Mirror for Magistrates*. At the end of his story, Cade tells the reader:

> Full littell knowe we wretches what we do
> Whan we presume our princes to resist.
> We war with God, against his glory to,
> That placeth in his office whom he list,
> Therfore was never traytour yet but mist
> The marke he shot, and came to a shamefull ende
> Nor never shall til God be forst to bend.

> God hath ordayned the power, all princes be
> His Lieutenauntes, or debities in realmes,
> Against their foes still therfore fighteth he,
> And as his enmies drives them to extremes,
> Their wise deuises prove but doltish dreames.
> No subiect ought, for any kind of cause,
> To force the lord, but yeeld him to the lawes.[13]

"The Blacksmith," whose history first appeared in the edition of 1563, gives a specific warning to those who would rebel that the Providence of God will choose and implement His chosen agents.

> Who that resisteth his dread soveraygne lord,
> Doth dampne his soule by Gods owne very worde.
> A christen subiect should with honour due,

---

[12] *Ibid.*, p. 173, ll. 50–56.   [13] *Ibid.*, pp. 176–77, ll. 148–61.

> Obey his soveraygne though he were a Iue:
> Whereby assured when subiectes do rebell,
> Gods wrath is kindled and threatneth fyer and hell.
>
> . . . .
>
> Which is the chiefe cause no treason preuayles,
> For yll must he spede whom Gods wrath assayles:
> Let Traytors and Rebels looke to spede then,
> When Gods mighty power is subiect to men.
> Much might be sayd that goeth more nere the pyth,
> But this suffiseth for a rurall Smyth.[14]

To every man brought up in the theological tradition of the immanence of Providence, the subsequent failure of the rebels because of
dissension in their own ranks would be interpreted immediately as a
normal manifestation of God's interference in human affairs.

The fate of Jane Shore, whose tragedy was also included in the 1563
edition of *The Mirror*, strangely enough is an example of the turn of
fortune's wheel, and not, as might have been expected, of God's retributive justice. "But whether through sentimentality or through proneness
to see the world as merely mutable, Churchyard makes almost nothing
of the sin which might be credited to his heroine." [15] Indeed, he glosses
over her fault by emphasizing the good she has done in helping those
less fortunate than she. At her downfall, Jane could have forgiven
Richard III had he made her punishment a warning to others against
sin, but she cannot forgive him for acting arbitrarily and from personal
hostility.

> Yf that such zeale had moved this Tyrantes minde,
> To make my plague a warning for the rest,
> I had small cause such fault in him to finde,
> Such punishment is vsed for the best:
> But by yll wil and power I was opprest.
> He spoyled my goodes and left me bare and poore,
> And caused me to begge from dore to dore.[16]

Although the author of the tragedy missed the main theological possibilities of this piece, Heywood, in his play, *Edward IV*, realized them
all. Churchyard combined the sentimental, feminine appeal of the ex-

---

[14] *Ibid.*, p. 412, ll. 275–92.
[15] Willard Farnham, *The Medieval Heritage of Elizabethan Tragedy*, p. 293.
[16] *The Mirror for Magistrates*, ed. Campbell, p. 385, ll. 351–57.

king's mistress with the medieval homiletic belief in the fickleness of fortune. The moral is directed both to kings who might take mistresses and to commoners who might aspire to positions above their station. In spite of his orthodox moral purposes, Churchyard hesitated to include Jane's story with those of princes, for he makes her apologize as follows:

> And nowe a time for me I see preparde,
> I heare the lives and falles of many wyghtes:
> My tale therfore the better may be heard,
> For at the torche the litle candle lightes.
> Where Pageantes be, small thinges fil out the sightes.
> Wherefore geve eare, good Baldwyn do thy best,
> My tragedy to place among the rest.[17]

At the end of her story, the usual moral is appended.

> Thus long I lyved all weary of my life,
> Tyl death approcht and rid me from that woe:
> Example take by me both maide and wyfe,
> Beware, take heede, fall not to follie so,
> A myrrour make of my great overthrowe:
> Defye this world, and all his wanton wayes,
> Beware by me, that spent so yll her dayes.[18]

The Mirror for Magistrates, ostensibly offering examples of how vices of great princes and magistrates are punished,[19] included stories of lesser people who had in some way provoked the intervention of the Providence of God or became the victims of the turn of fortune's wheel. The political lessons were reinforced with Christian morality. The technique of employing moral material as it had been developed in works like *The Mirror for Magistrates* was adopted with little alteration by authors of domestic tragedies.

III

The literary descendants of *The Mirror for Magistrates* Professor Farnham has enumerated and described in his *The Medieval Heritage of Elizabethan Tragedy*.[20] At least one of these works is of first importance for the present investigation. In 1580, Anthony Munday,

---

[17] *Ibid.*, p. 375, ll. 50–56.

[19] *Ibid.*, p. 65.

[18] *Ibid.*, p. 386, ll. 386–92.

[20] Farnham, *op. cit.*, Chapter VIII.

who, the year before, had contributed to the providential literature his
The Mirrour of Mutabilitie, a collection of examples from the Scriptures, again illustrated his theme, this time with incidents taken from
domestic life in his *A View of Sundry Examples.* This work relates no
less than twenty murder stories of the sort popular with pamphleteers
and dramatists of the following generation.

The narratives are so interlarded with scriptural quotations and
references to Biblical story that none may escape the significance of the
work as a moral tract. In a dedicatory preface, the author apologizes
for the meanness of his material. He adds, however, that his present
work should not be despised, for, in "this little labour is contained as
much affection, and as liberally bestowed, as any hee whatsoever that
offreth a greater gift. The poore Widdowes mite pleased Christe better
then the riches that the other offred . . ." [21] Munday calls each of
his anecdotes an "example," thus indicating the purpose he intended
his volume to serve. In this work the tales are more local in origin
and more domestic in character than those in the early collections of
exempla. Munday tells his stories as gospel truth and expects everyone to believe them. The work contains four sections: first, accounts of
recent English murders; second, marvels and portents which occurred
abroad; third, more English murder stories; and fourth, "a short discourse of the late earthquake." His contemporaries were, of course,
more credulous than readers of the present generation, so that the intrusion of marvels did not lessen the moral effectiveness. Also it must
be remembered that the Providence of God was omnipotent, so that
to disbelieve in miracles was to show lack of faith.

Munday introduces his first example thus:

Beholde how the world is given to wickednesse; for one disdayneth that
his neyghbour should thrive by him; another coveteth his neyghbours
goodes unjustly; some one is bent to this vice, some to that. Some care
not so they lyve in their jollitie and pleasure, who goeth to wracke, whome
they murder, whome they spoyle; the proofe whereof is evident.[22]

The first narrative, the most interesting in this collection of Munday's, tells of one George Browne, who, with the aid of his victim's
wife, murdered George Sanders. The story of this murder was later

---

[21] Anthony Munday, *A Vievv of Sundry Examples,* in *John a Kent and John a
Cumber,* 1851 ed., pp. 73–74.
[22] *Ibid.,* p. 78.

(1599) to serve as the plot of the anonymous *A Warning for Fair Women*, although Munday's version was not the source of the drama. The murder appeared at least twice in the nondramatic prose of the time, once in Stow's *Chronicle* and once in an anonymous pamphlet of 1573 entitled "A BRIEF DISCOURSE / of the late murder of / Master George Saunders / a worshipfull Citizen of London: and / of the apprehension, arraignment, / and execution of the principal / accessories of / the Same." [23] The play seems to have been taken from this *Brief Discourse* together with some details based on Stow's narrative. The moral emphasis in Munday's account far exceeds that in any other of the versions; they stress much more strongly the melodramatic features of the events without omitting entirely the familiar moral comments. Munday's version is brief enough to be quoted in full. Its tone is representative of the entire collection, so that this tale told in its entirety will serve better than any summary to give an idea of the author's narrative methods. His digressions from the story made in order to introduce the essential pious comments are characteristic of his style.

Not long since, one George Browne, a man of stature goodly and excellent, if lyfe and deedes thereto had beene equivalent; but as the aunctient adage is, goodly is he that goodly dooth, and comely is he that behaveth him selfe comely, so may it be witnessed in this man, who more respected a vaine pride and prodigall pleasure, which remayned in his person, then commendation and good report that followeth a godlie and vertuous life.

But nowe a dayes everie courageous cutter, euerie Sim Swashbuckler, and everie desperate Dick, that can stand to his tackling lustely, and behave him selfe so quarrelously that he is ashamed of all good and honest company, he is a gallant fellowe, a goodly man of his handes, and one, I promise you, that as soone comes to Tyburne as ever a one of them all. This is a vaine-glorious vertue, (which some tearme it) but it can be called no vertue, because it dependeth not uppon any goodnesse.

A view to vaine vaunters.

A fellowe worthy of commendation.

[23] A. F. Hopkinson, ed., *Play Sources: the Original Stories on Which Were Founded the Tragedies of "Arden of Feversham," & "A Warning for Fair Women," to Which Is Added Thomas Kyd's Pamphlet, "The Murder of John Brewen,"* p. 49.

This George Browne, (before named) addicted to the voluptuous-nesse of this vaine world, to unlawfull lyking, to runne at his libertie in all kinde of lewde behaviour, murdred cruelly maister George Saunders, an honest, vertuous, and godly Cittizen, well knowne, of good name and fame; among his neigh-bours well thought of; abroade and every where well esteemed; of wealth well stored; of credit well allowed; of lyving Christianly disposed; and of those that knewe him well beloved.

A report of maister Saun-ders.

This man being met by this George Browne, (who by the consent of maister Saunders wife was appointed to kyll him) after he perceived what was his intent, and howe he sought to bathe his handes in his guyltles blood, fell to entreataunce, that pittie might take place in his bloody brest.

George Browne meeting him by S. Mary Cray.

But he, a wretch, more desirous of his death then wylling his welfare, more mindful of murther than savegard of his soule, so bent to blindnesse, that he ex-pected not the light, strooke the stroke that returned his shame, dyd the deede that drove him to destiny, and fulfilled the fact, that in the end he found folly.

His devilish intent and perverse practices.

O, minde most monstrous! O, heart most hard! O, intent so yrksome! whome neyther preferment might perswade, rytches move to regard, affection cause to respect, former freendship force to fancie, nor no vertue of the minde seeme to satisfie. Where was the bonds of loyaltie? where was the regard of honestie? where was the feare of the Almightie? where was the care of Christianitie? or where was the hope of eternall felicitie? and last, where was thy duty to God, thy Prince, and countrey? Alas! each of these seemed cleane vanquished in thee: they were smally regarded; yea, little or none accoumpt made of. It is yet evidently seene in that common crew that give them selves to boasting and bravery, to swearing, fighting, quarrelling and all such divelish practices. But what sayth Esai? *Shall the axe boast it self against him that heweth therwith, or shall the sawe make any bragging against him that ruleth it? That were even lyke as if the rod did exalt it self against him that beareth*

A hard heart that could doo so cruell a deede.

All feare of God cleane layde aside.

Esai, 10, 15.

it, or as though the staffe should magnify it self, (as who should say) it were no wood.[24]

This narrative, so religious in tone, bears curiously little resemblance to the usual treatment of a murder story. Nothing can be interpreted as the hand of Providence or can be made to fit into the theological pattern of sin and repentance. Most of his other examples are obvious cases of providential manifestations, but here, in one of his best stories, Munday is content with general comments on the power of evil. However, his central theme is God's wrath; and this tale shows how wickedness brings punishment through providential manifestations on the whole world.

A tale more representative of the volume is the *"Example of Anne Averies, that bought the Towe. 1575. Febru. 11."* Anne, having bought the tow, refused to pay for it, saying that she had done so and calling down God's vengeance upon herself if she spoke not the truth.

Gods judgement so just, seeing her unjust dealing, presently accorded thereunto, and before the face of all the standers by, she was immediately stroke to the earth, not able to rise without help, nor yet to blaspheme the name of God as she had done, but holding out her hand, wherein she held thirteene pence, which she should before have payed for the towe withall; and her mouth beeing put to such a vyle office, that from thence issued that which should have discended at the lower partes. So was she carried from thence, where she was fayne to lye in a stynking stable, and few dayes after yeelded her life.[25]

As *A View of Sundry Examples* continues, the author presents several brief statements that someone had cruelly murdered someone else, concluding this section with pious quotations in support of his general thesis. There is no record that any of these murders was ever dramatized. The undramatic character of the anecdotes may account for their failure to appeal to the playwrights. The motivation for the crime is seldom given, since the murderer normally appears as an unregenerate villain. If any explanation is offered, it is usually the simple one that the scoundrel is a man who has fallen into evil ways and has become addicted to gaming and other vicious occupations.

The second section of Munday's pamphlet presents examples of providential portents such as monstrous children who utter warnings at the moment of their birth. Most of the cases are recorded from

---

[24] Munday, *op. cit.*, pp. 78–80.   [25] *Ibid.*, p. 82.

foreign countries, and the number of details varies in direct proportion to the geographical distance from England. The author gives no description at all of a wonderful babe born in London, but presents striking details of a marvelous child born in "Dutchland." [26]

Munday soon abandons his wonder book to return to his murder stories. In one, the slayer is haled before the corpse of his victim, "and presently, in the sight of all the standers by, it presently bled both at the nose and at the mouth; wherupon hee was accused, and hee did presently confess it." [27] Such selections as these give ample evidence that Munday's pamphlet belongs to the literature illustrating the ways of Providence. His work is important because each of the stories deals with a middle- or low-class person whose fall is supposed to warn other middle- or low-class persons against a similar fate. If the author missed seeing in the story of George Sanders the dramatic possibilities of the device of Divine Providence, the playwright who employed the material in *A Warning for Fair Women* was not so obtuse.[28]

In 1587, George Turberville wrote a book called *Tragical Tales and Other Poems*, a collection of ten narrative tragedies in verse. Three of them have middle-class protagonists, and in one, a ghost as a providential agent reveals an unsuspected murder.[29] Turberville's remarks on the propriety of selecting tragic heroes from the lower classes indicate that the problem disturbed him. With an uneasy conscience he broke the time-honored rules for the writing of tragedy. He defended his boldness as follows:

> Which sith is so, I may with better face
> A pardon craue of you that Ladies be,
> For bringing here a homely wench in place,
> And ranking her with dames of gallant glee:
> Who sith did rage in fancie as the rest,
> Why should she not be plast among the best?
>
> Put case her byrth was base, her image lowe,
> Her parents poore, her liuelod bare and thin,
> Sith Cupid did his golden shaft bestowe
> Vpon her brest, when liking entred in,
> Let her receiue the guerdon that is dewe
> To faithfull loue, and march with Cupids crewe.
> . . . .

---

[26] *Ibid.*, p. 89.   [27] *Ibid.*, p. 92.   [28] See below, Chapter VI.
[29] George Turberville, *Tragicall Tales and Other Poems*, 1837 reprint, p. 183.

> The mind is all that makes or marres the thing:
> A Carter loues as whotly as a King.[30]

In spite of this apology, most of the tragedies deal with the customary high-born figures. When he descended from the heights of the court, he mitigated his departure from critical canons by laying the scenes of his tales in distant lands, to capture the respect paid to unfamiliar things and to avoid the contempt felt for the familiar. The theological note is not as strong in Turberville's tragedies as in most similar works of the period. Still, in his defense of the right of common man to be the protagonist of tragedy, Turberville lent his influence to the innovators.

IV

Many of the most instructive cases of the operation of Divine Providence crop up in generally forgotten quarto pamphlets written by hack writers to capitalize on the sensations of the moment. These little books repeat the warnings of the sermons and moralities and use the techniques which they established. The authors of the quartos probably had no more moral purpose than the present-day writers of confession stories whose works usually illustrate the operations of poetic justice. However, the accepted practice in these works accustomed the audience to religious terms and theological modes of thought in sensational literature.

A young man who stabbed himself rather than suffer the loss of his ears for perjury is the subject of the anonymous pamphlet, *A Fearful Example Shewed upon a Perjured Person*. This attempt at self-destruction is called "the iuft iudgement of God vpon this party, the better to make his odious offéce feene manifeft & to be apparent to many other . . ." [31] The recovery of the youth from his self-inflicted wound does not, in the eyes of the author, vitiate the lesson.

The writer of the brief narrative of the murder of *Page of Plymouth* [1592] [32] states the facts succinctly and with little reliance on the religious devices so prominent elsewhere. The outline of the story may be found in Appendix A. Here the purpose is to afford another illus-

---

[30] *Ibid.*, p. 259.

[31] *A Fearefull Example, Shewed vpon a Periured Perfon*, p. 4.

[32] *A True Discourse of a Cruel and Inhumaine Murder, Committed vpon M. Padge of Plymouth*, in *The Shakespeare Society Papers*, II, 79–85. See also Appendix A.

tration of the literature of Providence. Even though the murder is discovered in a straightforward way, and the murderers are accused without the presence of any supernatural manifestations, the author says:

Thus did the Lord unfold this wretched deed, whereby immediately the said mistris Padge was attached upon the murther, and examined before Sir Francis Drake, Knight, with the Maior and other majestrates of Plimouth; who denied not the same, but said she had rather dye with Strangwidge then to live with Padge.[33]

Also, and this is a device used in *Arden of Feversham,* the power of Providence, for a considerable period, saves the victim from injury and death. In this story, the death of Page is not explained, while in the case of Arden, it clearly occurs as punishment for his own sins. Perhaps in the present instance it may be laid to destiny. Although, according to the tenets of the time, Providence left nothing to chance, writers were not so precise in the ordering of the microcosms of their works as they believed God to be in his regulation of the outside world.

Several ballads on Page of Plymouth are extant. Indeed, most of the famous murders of the time stimulated the composition of popular broadside ballads. These single-sheet tales in doggerel usually gave a moral twist to the notorious events of the moment. One such ballad, on the death of Ulallia (Page's wife), tells of her repentance as she says:

> Farewell, falfe world, and friends that fickle be;
> All wiues farewell; example take by mee:
> Let not the Deuill to murder you infpire,
> Seeke to efcape fuch foul and filthie mire.

> And now, O Chrift! to thee I yeeld my breath,
> Strengthen my faith in bitter pangues of death;
> Forgiue my faults and folly of my times,
> And with thy bloud wafh thou away my crimes.[34]

Another, more extensive and more packed with details, makes her say, "Methinkes the heauens crie uengeance for my fact [*sic*]." [35] And she ends her career with the usual repentance, as does her lover, George Strangwidge, who was captured with her.[36]

[33] *Ibid.,* p. 84.

[34] John Payne Collier, *Broadside Black Letter Ballads, Printed in the Sixteenth and Seventeenth Centuries,* p. 72.

[35] *Ibid.,* p. 65.   [36] *Ibid.,* p. 69.

A highly amusing ballad recounting a grotesque operation of Divine Providence is preserved in a unique copy in the Huntington Library.[37] It begins as does the usual prodigal-son story and ends with a feast at which the boy opens a pie. Then out jump, not four-and-twenty blackbirds, but poisonous toads. The concluding stanza makes it clear to any reader who may have missed the significance that God had sent the loathsome creatures to punish the son for his sin against his father:

> All vertuous Children learne by this,
>   obedient hartes to fhow:
> And honour ftill your Parents deare,
>   for God commaundeth fo.
> And think how God did turne his meate
>   to poyfond Toades indeed:
> Which did his Fathers face denie,
>   becaufe he ftood in need.

Another ballad,[38] grimmer in its punishment, shows the penalty for cursing to be sudden death. Waking from a stupor into which he has been cast, the sinner begins to curse.

> He had no fooner fpoke thefe words
>   which I haue fhewed to you,
> But that a pace his heart blood did
>   foorth of his body flowe;
> For why out of his fingers endes
>   his blood did ftreame full faft,
> So did it foorth at his toes endes,
>   which made them all agafte.
>
> And yet the Lord proceeded foorth
>   this trayterous wight to fcourge.
> The blood gufht out, yea at his wrifts
>   much like the foaming furge;
> So did it alfo at his nofe
>   runne foorth aboundantlie,
> With other filthie excrements
>   which man doth loathe to fee.

---

[37] *A Moft Notable and Worthy Example of an Vngratious Sonne.*
[38] *A Fearfefull and Terrible Example of Gods Iufte Iudgement Executed vpon a Lewde Fellow,* in J. P. Collier, *op. cit.,* pp. 42–47.

> Thus died he, committing
> his foule to Furies fell,
> Which doe poffeffe th' infernall gulfe
> and laberinth of hell.
> Than was his body ftraight interde,
> although in truth forlorne,
> For whom it had been better farre
> if he had not beene borne.[39]

The ballads in general show only the operation of the devices already illustrated in other works in this chapter. A few repeat the stories of some of the domestic tragedies, and these are discussed in connection with the plays to which they are related. A consideration of the others would be unrewarding for the present purpose.

Arden of Feversham, usually thought to be the first of the extant domestic tragedies, appeared in 1592. In the same year, Thomas Kyd, held by many critics to have been the author of *Arden,* told a similar story in a pamphlet entitled *The Murder of John Brewen.*[40] The work begins with the customary theological outburst against the sin of murder. Kyd then proceeds with this story: Though Anne Welles loves John Parker, she marries John Brewen. In order to wed her lover, she poisons her husband. Parker then refuses to marry her. Angrily she exclaims that she had murdered her husband for Parker's sake. This statement, through the operation of Providence, is overheard. They are apprehended, condemned, and die unrepentant. The pamphlet concludes:

The Lord giue all men grace by their example to shunne the hatefull sinne of murder, for be it kept neuer so close, and done neuer so secret, yet at lengthe the Lorde will bring it out; for bloud is an vncessant crier in the eares of the Lord, and he will not leaue so vilde a thinge vnpunished.[41]

Kyd's literary ability raises this work above the level of its class. Except for its comparative excellence, there is little to differentiate this account of a murder from any other of those contemporaneous with it.

A more extensive and elaborate work, *The Theatre of God's Judg-*

---

[39] *Ibid.*, pp. 45–46.
[40] *The Trueth of the Moft Wicked and Secret Murthering of Iohn Brewen,* in *The Works of Thomas Kyd,* ed. Frederick S. Boas, pp. 285–93.
[41] *Ibid.*, p. 293.

ments (1597), by Thomas Beard, as the title plainly indicates,[42] attempted to reveal God's use of providential interventions to punish sinners. In his preface, Beard describes the extent of the power of God over human affairs. "And unto him belongeth the direction and principall conduct of humane matters, in such sort that nothing in the world cometh to passe by chance or aduenture, but onely and alwaies by the prescription of his will . . ." [43] This work has obtained some prominence because of its fictitious account of the death of Marlowe. The playwright's fate is presented as an example of punishment for the crime of atheism. Marlowe's story is only one of many drawn from the Scriptures, from history, and from local incident to illustrate God's punishment of sin. Numerous editions (1612, 1631, 1648, and 1672), each adding new and up-to-date examples of its own, testify to the popularity of *The Theatre of God's Judgments*.

In 1618, Edmund Rudierd composed a small book entitled *The Thunderbolt of God's Wrath . . . or, An Abridgment of the Theatre of God's Fearful Judgments*.[44] Rudierd shared Beard's desire to impress his readers with the powers of the Almighty and in order to reach a larger audience condensed Beard's work. The author commends his work, perhaps a little boastfully, as follows:

. . . it will ftead you more, to bring you to a hatred and lothing of finne, than any booke, that euer you read, of the like fubiect: yea or any other except the booke of all bookes, which is without comparifon, euen the holy bible; my reafon for this is, that it is fo full of terror againft both the doer, and fufferer of finne, that it will make any Chriftian heart to feare, and tremble: for feare, you may find many wonderfull and vnwonted iudgments, not only againft wicked finners, but alfo againft fuch as haue bin fauourers of finne: yea, and here you may fee how fearfully the enemies of religion, and religious people, haue bin by Gods heauie hand plagued.[45]

---

[42] *The Theatre of God's Judgements; or, A Collection of Histories out of Sacred, Ecclesiasticall, and Prophane Authors, concerning the Admirable Judgements of God upon the Transgressours of His Commandements.*

[43] Roy W. Battenhouse, *Marlowe's "Tamburlaine," a Study in Renaissance Moral Philosophy*, p. 92, quoted from Beard.

[44] *The Thunderbolt of Gods Wrath against Hard-hearted and Stiffe-necked Sinners; or, An Abridgement of the Theater of Gods Fearefull Iudgements Executed vpon Notorious Sinners.* Of Rudierd, nothing is known. He says in his "epistle dedicatory" that he "wrote a fhort treatife againft idle and vaine ftage-plais, lafciuious and vnchaft (mixt) dauncings," but if he did, this work has vanished.

[45] *Ibid.*, the Epiftle Dedicatorie.

Rudierd and Beard continue the tradition of interpreting the scriptural miracles as illustrations of the intervention of Providence. Their examples drawn from contemporary life, like the death of Marlowe, are no less striking proof of God's immanence in the affairs of mankind. Witness the following:

In *London*, there was fometime three maides going to fchoole, of which, one was called *Dennis Benifield* of twelue yeares of age: thefe were reafoning what God fhould bee, a good olde man faith one, nay an old doting foole faith *Dennis:* but the next day coming home from market, was ftricken by the Lord on the one fide, which was very blacke and fo died . . .[46]

It was unnecessary for a writer to present so striking an occurrence to establish the fact that Providence had intervened. Even a normal operation of justice would be so understood, as the following bit shows:

A certaine other young man, poifoned his owne father for his wealth, but the iuft God inftead of the goods, brought a fhamefull death vpon him: for being drawne through the ftreetes he was burnt with an hot yron, and tormented nine houres in a wheele to dea[t]h.[47]

The most interesting section of Rudierd's book is, however, his account of the death of Marlowe, worth repeating here since it is not the one usually given by moralists of his time and is certainly nothing like the actual facts.

We read of one *Marlin*, a *Cambridge* Scholler, who was a Poet and a filthy Play-maker, this wretch accounted that meeke feruant of God *Mofes* to be but a Coniurer, and our fweet Sauior but a feducer, and a deceiuer of the people. But hearken yee braine-ficke and prophane Poets, and Players, that bewitch idle eares with foolifh vanities: what fell vpon this prophane wretch, hauing a quarrell againft one whom he met in a ftreete in London, and would haue ftabd him: But the partie perceiuing his villany peruented him with catching his hand, and turning his owne dagger into his braines, and fo blafpheming and curfing, hee yeelded vp his ftincking breath: marke this yee Players, that liue by making fooles laugh at finne and wickedneffe . . .[48]

The desire of Beard and Rudierd to show case after case of God's anger and retribution was perhaps not shared by narrators of the notorious murders of the day. Nevertheless, they employed the same

[46] *Ibid.*, p. 35. [47] *Ibid.*, p. 54. [48] *Ibid.*, p. 29.

terms, presented similar lurid details, and emphasized orthodox Christian morality. The yellow journalism of the time used the language of the theological tract.

The anonymous pamphlet, *Two Most Unnatural and Bloody Murders*, appeared in 1605. The two plays, *A Yorkshire Tragedy* and *The Miseries of Enforced Marriage*, dramatized the first of these homicides. The story runs as follows: Caverley, an orphan, has become trothplight to one girl, but is forced to marry another. Wasteful living exhausts his property. His brother, who has foolishly given surety for a debt of the prodigal, is sent to prison. Remorse for this brother's fate starts Caverley on his career of crime. He kills two of his children and stabs his wife. As he gallops off to make away with his other child who was at nurse twelve miles away, he is pursued by the authorities of the law. "But God that ordreth the life of a wren, hath then a care of his reaſonable creatures."

And his hart had made ſharp the knife to cut his own infants throte, (O God how iuſt thou art) his horſe that flew with him frõ his former tragedies, as appointed by God to tie him from any more guilt, and to preſerue the infants life, in a plaine ground, where there was ſcarce a pibble [sic] to reſiſt his haſt, the horſe fell down and M. *Cauerley* under him; the horſe got vp, & breaking from the hold his Maiſter had to ſtay him, ranne violently toward the Towne, leauing maiſter *Cauerley* not able to ſtirre from thence, where he was ſoone ouertaken by the purſuit: and indéede cea3de on by thoſe, did both lament his fall and pitty his folly.[49]

An unusual feature of the account is that after his capture, Caverley makes no formal repentance. Perhaps he had allowed his mind to be perverted by his evil courses and so had committed a mortal sin. The only hint of repentance comes at the end when he expresses regret that he has killed his children and adds, "I would I had thoſe beggars, either I to begge with them, or they to aſke heauens almes for me."[50] Although his failure to repent is carried over into *A Yorkshire Tragedy*, the conclusion of the play emphasizes a different sort of theological conception.

The agency of Providence is shown as prolonging the life of the victim in the second tale in this pamphlet.[51] It is indicated also that

[49] *Two Moſt Vnnaturall and Bloodie Murthers*, pp. 16–17.
[50] *Ibid.*, p. 18.   [51] *Ibid.*, p. 24.

the murder would have remained undiscovered had it not been for God's justice.

. . . and indeed, had not God dwelt in heauen, & looked downe vpon the crueltie of the fact, who neuer ſuffers murther to be vnreuenged, it was ſlily conueyed and ſo cloſely acted, that without a diuine inſpiration it had neuer béene reuealed, nor diſcouered.[52]

All went well with Peter after he had murdered his master, until he was foolish enough to go to church, where he heard a sermon on murder. Since there was a general belief that a sermon had the power to return a man to God, Peter's reaction is not unexpected:

. . . & *Peter* ſitting among the reſt, though all wept, yet there appeared no ſuch ſigne of guilt in any as in him, for he ſate like one had laine ſix daies in a graue, no cõſtruction could be made from his words but fren3ie, nor from his actions but diſtraction. The Preacher perceiuing his alteration, would néeds lie with him that night; but ere the morning he forced his own tongue by the terror which he pronounced, was in Gods iudgement, to reueale the treaſon his hand did, which no heart did ſuſpect.[53]

After this revelation of the identity of the criminal, justice works quickly and Peter is soon executed, and with him Mistress Browne, who had been an accessory before the fact. However, before death, they repent in the usual manner and hope for divine forgiveness.[54]

The circumstances of another famous murder survive in two brief accounts, although no play remains dealing with the subject. The case concerned the murder of Anthony James, his wife, Elizabeth, and their son, Anthony, and the mutilation of their daughter, whose tongue was cut out to keep her from revealing the perpetrators of the crime. The two surviving accounts, *The Most Cruel and Bloody Murder* and *The Horrible Murder of a Young Boy*, differ in some particulars, but both are written from the same point of view, and in both the purpose is the double one of showing the lurid details of the murder and the operations of Divine Providence. The first of these two versions offers more detail in the earlier part. After cutting her tongue out, the murderers sell the girl to a beggar from whom she escapes, and she is miraculously kept alive for four years "as is certenly by diuine prouidence of heauen, that by her theſe villanies should come to light."[55]

[52] *Ibid.*, pp. 24–25.   [53] *Ibid.*, p. 27.   [54] *Ibid.*, p. 28.
[55] *The Most Crvell and Bloody Mvrther*, p. [12].

Or, as the other story puts it, "But he that preferued *Daniel* in the Lions den . . . did not onely preferue the life of this childe, but alfo did giue vnto her an extraordinarie ftrength and vigor, whereby fhe was able, and did make fuch a noyfe, that a man comming by that way (not by chaunce, but furlye by the prouidence and appointment of God) . . ." [56] was able to save her life by tending her wound. After a suitable time, the girl recovers speech so that she can reveal the crimes. In both versions, the crowing of a cock, "that bird that put *Peter* in minde of his great finne in denying our Sauiour and his Maifter," [57] precedes the miracle. In one version, the son of the murderess repents, spending his last hours in prayers and the singing of Psalms.[58] The other tale ends with a brief sermon to the reader that could well have been used by a preacher at the conclusion of an exemplum.

A pamphlet which appeared in 1613 entitled *Three Bloody Murders* varies somewhat from the pattern customary in the accounts of miraculous discoveries of murders. The first story leaves the murderer unpunished, and the last shows the murderer as yet unrevealed. In the first of these accounts, the slayer of Cartwright flees beyond the seas, a fate thought to be temporary punishment. The corrupt magistrate, who fixed bail so low that the killer could make good his escape, is removed from office by the archbishop of Canterbury, who acts as the agent of God. There is a great deal of theological discussion in the course of the narrative, and this is only natural since the victim is a preacher. When the story is read in connection with other murder accounts of the time, it is scarcely possible to miss the moral significance even though the author avoids direct mention of Providence and repentance. The events are undoubtedly the basis for the lost play, *Cartwright*, mentioned in Henslowe's *Diary*.[59]

The second part of the pamphlet tells of one Elizabeth James who defrauds a young woman of her money. Then "this cruell woman, being empty of all grace, (as wee haue before fayd) no thought of death and iudgement, no loue to heauen, nor feare of hell in her bofome, moft mercilefly dragg'd this filly mayden by the hair of her head, into an inner Roome," [60] where she murdered her, cutting her

---

[56] *The Horrible Murther of a Young Boy*, p. 4.
[57] *The Most Cruel and Bloody Murder*, p. [17].   [58] *Ibid.*, p. [19].
[59] *See* Appendix A.   [60] *Three Bloodie Murders*, p. [15].

body up in small pieces and burying them in the garden. A dumb woman who had seen the crime was unable to make herself understood by the authorities.

But here ſée the certainty of the ſacred word of the Almighty; which ſayes, *that he that ſmites a man that he die, ſhall die for it. Exod.* 21 [xxi, 12.] Sée here (I ſay) the goodneſſe of this omnipotent God, that ſées ſinne, hates ſinne, and wil puniſh ſinne: When this dumb woman ſufficiently expreſſed her meaning, to make them vnderſtand her, a hungry dogge ſenting about for prey, in the garden of this bloody murdreſſe, ſented out the peices [sic] of that poore Maiden, that ſhe had there buried, and then neuer left ſcraping vp the earth, till he found the head of her, which (by the haire of it) he carried in his téeth, and there before the honeſt Keeper, Goodman *Iames,* the bloody harted woman his wife, and other of his Neighbors that were with him laid it down: vpon the ſight of this, they were all very much amaſed, the innocent perſons at the ſtrangeneſſe of it, and the murdreſſe with her feare.[61]

This double-barreled operation of Providence may possibly seem redundant, but it was by no means unusual at the time. To make their lessons perfectly clear, many of the plays employ four or five such providential interventions.

The last of the *Three Bloody Murders* is exceedingly brief, telling how a dog led a young man and a young girl to the body of a stranger. At the time of writing, the murderer was still unrevealed.

. . . and where they are God knowes, and will (no doubt) at his good wil and pleaſure reueale them. For, howſoeuer they doe yet ly hidden from the eyes of men, from the all-ſeeing eye of almighty God, they do not: but that's a thing we too ſeldom thinke on. For, as a reuerend Doctor ſayes concerning this: If we could alwaies haue in minde theſe three things, *viz.* that there is an eye about vs, that ſées all wée do, an eare that heares all we ſay, and a booke, in which all our words and déeds are written, we ſhould neuer ſin, (meaning capitally).[62]

As indicated in the above quotation, it mattered little if the murderer were not immediately revealed. The author could employ some conventional moral summary and so could publish his story while the events were fresh in the minds of the readers.

In 1614, a certain I. T. wrote a pamphlet which he called *A Horrible Cruel and Bloody Murder Committed at Putney.* Its construc-

[61] *Ibid.,* p. [17].   [62] *Ibid.,* p. [19].

tion is like that of a moral treatise, more attention being paid to remarks on the heinousness of the sin of murder than to the details of the crime. The faithless servants do not long enjoy the material rewards of their bloody deed. One of the perpetrators becomes conscience-stricken and takes the first step toward repentance by confessing to the authorities. His return to virtue is attributed to the agency of Divine Providence. By "the iuſt iudgement of God they enioyed not long" the rewards of the deed, "which God in his iuſtice will neuer [sic] ſuffer to bee hid or eſcape unpuniſhed." [63] There is, however, no formal theological repentance displayed on the part of any of the criminals.

V

The dramatic device of repentance was used repeatedly, however, in an exceedingly ambitious work by John Reynolds entitled *The Triumphs of God's Revenge*.[64] Its bibliographical history is too long to relate, but the first installment appeared in 1621. The six books were collected in a single volume in 1635, and by 1679, six editions had appeared. In his introductory material, Reynolds remarks that he has purposely set his histories in foreign lands, lest similar ones laid in England scandalize people or make him too many enemies. Also, he insists that his work is original and not, as detractors had charged, a translation.

The introduction to the first story illustrates the author's purpose.

It is a Hiſtory that hath many ſorrowful dependences, and which produceth variety of diſaſtrous and mournful accidents: wherein (by the juſt judgment of God) we ſhall ſee Ambition bitterly ſcourged, Revenge

---

[63] *A Horrible Creuel and Bloudy Murther*, p. [5].

[64] The title page of the 1679 edition, which was used in the present study, reads as follows: "THE TRIUMPHS OF GODS REVENGE Againſt the Crying and Execrable SIN OF MURTHER: Expreſſed in Thirty ſeueral Tragical Hiſtories. Written by *JOHN REYNOLDS*. *The Sixth Edition, Very Carefully Corrected*, to Which is Added, GODS REVENGE AGAINST The Abominable SIN of ADULTERY. Containing Ten Several Hiſtories, Neuer Printed before. Illuſtrated with New Sculptures." The title page of the 1635 edition reads, "The Triumphs of Gods Revenge, Against the crying, and Execrable Sinne of Murther: of His miraculous discoveries and severe punishments thereof. In thirty severall Tragicall Histories (digested in sixe Bookes) acted in divers Countries beyond the Seas, and never till now published, or imprinted in any language. Histories which contain great variety of memorable accidents, Amorous, Morall, and Divine, very necessary to restraine, and deterr us from this bloody Sinne, which, in these our dayes, makes so ample, and so lamentable a

ſharply rewarded, and Murther ſeverely puniſhed; by whoſe example, if all that profeſs Religion become leſs impious, and more truly religious, we ſhall then lead the whole courſe of our lives, in ſuch peaceful and happy tranquillity, as (arming ourſelves with reſolution to live and die in the favour of Heaven) we need net [*sic*] fear either what earth, or hell can do unto us.[65]

That is to say, all these histories are told with the idea of showing the operation of Providence. In many cases, Reynolds chooses middle-class protagonists, offering no apology for the selection. Instead, he is willing to employ anyone to illustrate his conception of the Providence of God as he sets it forth in the conclusion of the first history.

. . . theſe crimes of theirs, and the ſmoke of theſe their impious and diſ-pleaſing ſacrifices, have pierced the clouds, and aſcended the preſence of God, to ſue and draw down vengeance and confuſion on their heads; for although Murther be for a time concealed, yet the finger of God will in due time detect and diſcover it; for he will make inquiſition for bloud, and will ſeverely and ſharply revenge the death of his children.

But Gods Providence and Juſtice in the diſcovery thereof, is as differ-ent as miraculous; for ſometimes he protracts and defers it of purpoſe, either to mollifie or to harden our hearts, as ſeems beſt to his inſcrutable will and divine pleaſure; or as may chiefly ſerve and tend to his glory; yea, ſometimes he makes the Murtherer himſelf as well an Inſtrument to diſcover, as he hath been an actor to commit Murther; yea, and many times he puniſheth one ſin by and in another, and when the Murtherer ſits moſt ſecure, and thinks leaſt of it, then he heaps coals of fire on his head, and ſuddenly cuts him off with the revenging ſword of his fierce wrath and indignation.[66]

The third history is the first domestic tragedy in Reynolds's book. It concerns a gentleman's faithlessness to a farmer's daughter. Montaign seduces Josselina on a promise of marriage, but later declines to pro-ceed with the wedding. Wearying of her recriminations, he hires two lackeys to murder her. The jealousy of the wife of one of the lackeys becomes the instrument of Divine Providence. Montaign repents on the steps of the scaffold and hopes for divine forgiveness. Tedious passages of moralizing warn against murder and against unchastity.

---

progression." Quoted in Lily B. Campbell, *Shakespeare's Tragic Heroes, Slaves of Passion*, p. 13.

[65] Reynolds, *op. cit.*, 1679 ed., p. 2.   [66] *Ibid.*, p. 11.

The last story in the first book is one of a poor man and a poor woman. The man, Alibius, murders his wife so that he can marry a rich widow.

But as murther pierceth the Clouds, and crys for revenge from Heaven, fo we fhall fee this of *Alibius*, miraculoufly difcovered, and ere long feverely punifhed. . . . then, when all other means and inftruments wanted, to bring this his obfcure and bloody fact to light; Lo, by the Divine Providence of God, we fhall fee *Alibius* himfelf be the caufe, and the inftrument of his own difcovery.[67]

In this case, Alibius himself acts as the instrument of Providence, for, in his cups, he drops remarks which his daughter overhears, and this information enables her to denounce him to the authorities. Before his death he makes a full repentance in a "scaffold speech" which the author carefully outlines.

His fpeech at his end, was brief and fhort; only he freely confeft his Crime, and with infinit fighs and tears befought the world to pray for his foul; he lamented the vanity of his youth, and the diffolutenefs of his age; told them, that by his neglect of Prayer to God, and his too much confidence in the Devil, had brought him to this fhameful end; and therefore befought them again and again to beware by his example: and fo having folemnly freed his fecond Wife *Philatea* from being any way acquainted or acceffary with the Murther of his firft Wife *Merilla*, he recommending his foul into the hands of his Redeemer, dyed as penitently as he had lived diffolutely and prophanely.[68]

This speech, properly amplified and put in dramatic form, appeared on many stages in England between 1500 and 1642. Reynolds repeats it several times in the course of his book for the edification and instruction of the reader.

Supernatural interventions of Divine Providence either to reveal or to punish crime appear frequently in this work. In the seventh tale, a thunderbolt kills a murderess; [69] in the tenth and thirteenth, the device already employed in the case of Caverley, the fall of a horse, becomes the instrument of God's vengeance.[70] In the twenty-fifth, a mad bull, "no doubt but being fent from God," injures the murderer and causes him to repent.[71] The twenty-seventh history tells of an

[67] *Ibid.*, p. 50.
[70] *Ibid.*, pp. 129, 185.
[68] *Ibid.*, p. 54.
[71] *Ibid.*, p. 385.
[69] *Ibid.*, p. 85.

innkeeper and a priest who murder a goldsmith only to have his corpse dug up by a wolf, a most unusual manifestation of Divine Providence.[72]

An interesting history, the fifteenth, presents a case of most precise action on the part of Providence. Christina is the widow of a Burgemeister. Her son, Maurice, after the death of his father, has gone to Lausanne to school, but while there has contracted evil habits. To obtain money to continue his wild life, he kills his mother by throwing her down a well. Eventually the dream of one of the maids leads to the discovery of the body, the significance of the dream being obvious. Maurice is not suspected, however, and returns to his riotous living. Jailed for debts, he falls downstairs and breaks his right arm in two places so that it mortifies and has to be amputated. This was the arm with which he had killed his mother. In prison he goes mad and confesses his crimes, "for which he humbly craveth remiſſion, both from Heaven and Earth."

And although there be no doubt, but God will forgive his ſoul for this his foul murther, yet the Magiſtrates of *Morges*, who have gravity in their looks, religion in their hearts and ſpeeches, and juſtice in their actions, will not pardon his body; ſo in deteſtation of this his fearful crime, and inhuman paricide, they in the morning condemn him, that very afternoon to be hanged. At the prenouncing of which ſentence as he hath reaſon to approve the equity of their juſtice in condemning him to die, ſo he cannot abſtain from grieving at the ſtrictneſs of the time which they allot him for his preparation to death. *But as ſoon as we forſake the Devil, we make our peace with God.*

After a few more details, his "scaffold speech" is summarized.

He tells them he grieves at his very ſoul for the foulneſs of his fact, in giving his Mother her death, of whom he had received his life. He affirms, that drunkenneſs was not onely the root, but the cauſe of this his beggery and miſery, of his crime and puniſhment, and of his deboaſhed life, and deſerved death, from which with a world of ſighs and tears he ſeeks and endeavours to divert all thoſe who affect and practiſe that beaſtly vice. He declares, that his Mother was too virtuous ſo ſoon to go out of the world, and himſelf too vicious (and withall too cruel) any longer to live in it; that the ſins of his life had deſerved this his ſhameful death; and although he could not prevent the laſt, yet that he heartily and ſorrowfully repented

---

[72] *Ibid.*, p. [421], misnumbered 424.

the firſt. He prayed God to be merciful to his ſoul, and then beſought the world to pray unto God for that mercy; when ſpeaking a few words to himſelf, and ſealing them with many tears and far-fetched ſighs, he laſtly bids the world farewel; then inviting the Executioner to do his office, he is turned over.[73]

The egregiousness of this moralizing is characteristic of the thirty histories in the book. In each, the discovery of the crime and its perpetrators bears witness to the operation of God's retributive justice. In spite of his foreign settings, Reynolds clearly expected his book to win English converts to virtue by his exposure of the lamentable results of a career of vice. Although he included sensational details of a crime or of a duel, the reader carries from the book a far stronger impression of religious persuasion than of lurid action. The author continually interrupts his narrative to interpolate such remarks as, "But behold the mercy and juſtice of God!" [74] Several of the other stories in the book are domestic tragedies in the sense of the term as used in this study, but they add nothing to a knowledge of the use of Providence as a narrative device and so need not be summarized here.

VI

The 1679 edition of Reynolds's work contained ten further examples showing *The Triumphs of God's Revenge against Adultery*. This section has its own title page, and the pages are independently numbered. The style resembles that of *The Triumphs of God's Revenge against Murder*, but nowhere in the book is it specifically attributed to Reynolds. As in the longer work, the histories show the operation of Providence. Three of the ten stories are domestic tragedies. In the ninth, a series of seeming accidents the author ascribes to the power of God. The tenth history presents a woman whose adultery leads her to a career of prostitution. Eventually she dies "miſerably of Hunger and the Pox." [75] In these works, a disease was always considered as sent by heaven in punishment of sin. Of more interest than the commonplace operation of retributive justice is an editorial comment made on the equity of Providence who punishes a lesser crime more severely than a greater one. In explanation, the author states:

[73] *Ibid.*, p. [211], misnumbered 209.   [74] *Ibid.*, p. 21.
[75] *The Triumphs of Gods Revenge againſt the Crying and Abominable Sin of Adultery*, 1679 ed., p. 159.

The wayes of Gods Providence are unſearchable, and man is not able to penetrate into the ſacred obſcurity of his hidden Actions. We are not to judge ill of outward appearances, and to think that Heaven is not ſo exact in his punishments, as we could wiſh him, or to believe that it was more ſevere than requiſite, in taking away the life of an acceſſory, and more merciful than he ſhould be, in ſaving ſo wicked a principle. Have not ſuch unworthy thoughts of the juſtneſs, and mercy of Heaven, they are truly exact, and righteous, and God ſhews a *Decorum* in all his actions, and we are here deluded to think he more ſeverely puniſhed the leſs Criminal by death, and ſaved the greater. . . . Since the leaſt of our ſins deſerve the puniſhment of Death, none ought to tax the juſtice of Heaven in the Death of the Maid: and the life that was given to *Roſana*, as it might have proved a mercy, had ſhe made a right uſe of it, and repented her of all her paſt evils, and converted to heaven . . .[76]

It is obvious that the lessons contained in these two books are those taught in the authorized sermons of the Elizabethan times. Indeed, some of the examples in *The Triumphs of God's Revenge against Adultery* might have come from the "Sermon against Whoredom and Uncleanness," in that collection of homilies. The devices for moral teaching used in these tales were also employed, generally with more effectiveness, by the dramatists. Divine Providence was a convenient theatrical device for precipitating the crisis, but the use of providential operations had been sketched by the preachers and the earlier writers of these nondramatic works.

The naïve belief in the direct interventions of Providence to punish specific sins or to preserve individuals from danger was an essential concept in all the popular literature of the time. Works which employed examples from the lower classes of people to teach morality made crude use of providential manifestations and helped to establish a method of treatment which was used with little alteration in the domestic tragedies of the period. The ideas behind both dramatic and nondramatic literature were based on the established church theology as it found reflection in the popular mind. Playwrights found it convenient to accommodate their new genre of domestic tragedy to traditions already established in many forms of literature written for the middle and lower classes—to traditions, therefore, whose roots were embedded deep in popular thought.

[76] *Ibid.*, p. 181.

Chapter Four

MORALITY PLAYS

WHILE on the Continent humanistic ideals prevented free development of popular drama, in England the theatres remained for the most part in the hands of the people. The first English dramas to emerge from the church were the mysteries played on pageant wagons before audiences of townspeople in Coventry, York, and other large towns. The morality plays continued and developed the tradition of serious entertainment for the general populace. Through the media of allegorical and generalized characters these dramas taught moral lessons. Everyman was rich, but he was still every man, king or beggar. Gradually the abstract vices and virtues assumed the characteristics of men and women of the middle class. Even the figures of kings and nobles appeared as seen through bourgeois eyes.

The early moral dramatists had no appreciation of the difference between tragedy and comedy and took no pains to develop sympathy for their leading characters. The protagonist of a moral play was chosen to exhibit specific vices which were punishable by death and damnation unless the force of mercy intervened. In the earliest of these plays, the author made little effort to show whether a sinner was really worthy of mercy. Gradually, however, the customary steps of repentance and penance necessary for the salvation of the soul became important parts of the plays. All through the Tudor and early Stuart periods, the idea of mercy continued to appear in the morality plays and in their descendants, the domestic tragedies. The belief in an easily obtained mercy prevented the development of a real tragic spirit. Professor Farnham remarks: "So long as the moral dramatist and his audience conceive that a universal law of justice, under which a man lives and engages himself with his destiny, is dominated by the force of mercy, their recognition of tragedy must necessarily be small." [1]

[1] Willard Farnham, *The Medieval Heritage of Elizabethan Tragedy*, p. 193.

The concept of mercy similarly retarded the development of tragic feeling in Elizabethan, Jacobean, and Caroline domestic tragedies. These plays, however, whatever their artistic shortcomings, present valuable evidence of the customs and beliefs of the plain citizen of Elizabethan England. In fact, it was in the morality plays that this citizen first became recognized as a character suitable for serious drama. The moralities also first used as plots the kinds of stories which evolved into domestic tragedies.

The earliest morality play, the anonymous *Castle of Perseverance*, written about 1405,[2] established an outline followed with little alteration by the authors of the domestic tragedies. The chief character, Mankind, is born, is subjected to the importunities of his good and bad angels, accepts the counsel of the latter, and spiritually descends rapidly with the willing aid of the Seven Deadly Sins. Soon Death strikes him down, but not until he has repented his sins. Mercy and Peace intercede for Mankind, and the Father forgives him. Thus he is saved from damnation.

The outline of the action as employed in this play—sin, the intervention of Providence, and divine mercy—continued in use in domestic tragedies throughout the period covered by this book. Refinement greatly subtilized the treatment but did not seriously alter the basic concepts. Soon the writers abandoned the pageant of man's life from birth to death and the post-mortem debate between Mercy and Justice, to concentrate on the events which terminated in the deaths of their heroes. Thus, the emphasis on repentance, on earthly punishments, and on divine mercy became paramount.

The name of the principal character of *The Castle of Perseverance*, Mankind, indicates clearly the author's intention to make the story of his protagonist applicable to all men without regard to rank and social position. He meant Mankind to represent each person in the audience. Though the hero is no king, he is rich. Unfortunately, as his wealth has increased, his Christian virtue has decreased. When he least expects it, he is struck down for his sins by an intervention of Providence. He accordingly makes all realize that the greatest worldly achievements will not preserve one from the consequences of sin. Mankind may have been a character general enough to include the high as well as the low,

---

[2] Walter K. Smart, "The *Castle of Perseverance*: Place, Date, and a Source," *The Manly Anniversary Studies in Language and Literature*, p. 49.

but in essence his career particularly represented the dangers of the material success always desired and sometimes achieved by Mr. Average Man.

Mankind reappears in the title role of a play [3] in the last half of the fifteenth century. Again Mankind succumbs to the vices, repents his evil life, and dies forgiven. The play has progressed beyond *The Castle of Perseverance* in its delineation of the characters of the vices, Mischief, New Guise, Titivillus, Nought, and Now-A-Days. These figures have cast off the stiffly allegorical outlines of their predecessors and are ruled by such an irrepressible sense of mischief as might characterize the ne'er-do-wells of any community. The advance in the quality of the dialogue is illustrated in the first speech of New Guise, a complaint of his wife's ill-treatment.

> I haue fede my wyff so well tyll sche ys my mast*er*;
> I haue a grett wonde on my hede; lo! & *th*eron leyth a playst*er*.[4]

Such a farcical marital quarrel leads directly to realistic comedy, but the humanizing of the vice was one of the necessary steps on the way to domestic tragedy. In the Elizabethan murder plays the vice and the sinner were combined into one and the same character.

Mankind contains much of the conventional medieval contempt of the world:

> Of *th*e erth & of *th*e gler [clay?] we haue ow*er* propagacyon,
>   By *th*e prouydens of Gode *th*us be we deryvatt,
> To whos mercy I recome*n*de *th*is holl co*n*grygacyon;
>   I hope on-to hys blysse ye be all predestynatt!
> E*n*ery ma*n* for hys degre, I trust, xall be p*ar*tycypatt,
> Yf we wyll mortyfye ow*er* carnall co*n*dycyon
>   And ow*er* volu*n*tarye dysyres, *tha*t eu*er* be perverto*n*nat,
> To renu*n*ce *th*es & yelde ws wnd*er* God*es* provycyon.[5]

The worldly position of Mankind illustrates the clash between man's desire to succeed in mundane affairs and his hope for heavenly reward. He is expected to work. Labor is recommended by Mercy as a way of leading a Christian life and at the same time of attaining worldly success. Toil will also help man to avoid the vices.

---

[3] *Mankind*, in John Matthews Manly, *Specimens of the Pre-Shakespearean Drama*, I, 315–52.

[4] *Ibid.*, p. 324, ll. 239–40.   [5] *Ibid.*, p. 322, ll. 181–88.

Gyff them non audyence, thei wyll tell yow many a lye;
Do truly yow*er* laboure & kepe yow*er* haly-day[6]

Impressed by this good advice, Mankind becomes a farmer, but he attains little success in this career and soon decides to abandon the soil.

Now, Gode of hys mercy, sende ws of hys sonde!
I haue brought seed her to sow wi*th* my londe;
I wyll ron dylew*er*, *tha*t yt xall stonde.
   *In no*mine *Patris & Filii & Spir*[*i*]*t*us *Sancti*, now I wyll be-gyn.
Thys londe ys so harde, yt maketh wn-lusty & yrke,
I xall sow my corn at wynt*er* and lett Gode werke.
A-lasse, my corn ys lost! Her*e* ys a foull werke.
   I se well, by tyllynge lytyll xall I wyn.
Her*e* I gyf wppe my spade for now & for eu*er*.[7]

The failure of his agricultural venture having caused him to lose faith in the watchfulness and benevolence of God, Mankind falls ready prey to the call of evil. He progresses from very simple delights such as tavern frequenting and dancing to more serious sins. His lesser indiscretions illustrate how the morality play was beginning to show hospitality to realistic scenes of contemporary life. Mankind continues in his course of wrongdoing until Mercy teaches him the error of his ways. Then Mercy explains the boundlessness of God's mercy for all those who will repent their sins and turn earnestly to Him.

The Iustice of God wyll as I wyll, as hym-sylfe doth pre-cyse:
N*olo morte*m *peccator*is, *inquit*, yff he wyll [be] reducyble.

· · · ·

In *th*is presente lyfe m*er*cy ys plente tyll deth makyth hys dywysion;
But wha*n* 3e be go, *vs*que *ad minimu*m *quadra*ntem 3e scha[ll] rekyn *th*is
   ryght.

Aske m*er*cy & haue, whyll *the* body wi*th the* sow[l]e hath hys annexio*n*;
Yf 3e tarye tyl y*our* dysesse, 3e may hap of y*our* desyre to mysse;
Be repe*n*tant here, trust not *the* ow*er* of deth; thynke on *th*is lessu*n*:
*Ecce nu*nc te*m*pus *acceptabile, ecce nu*nc *dies salut*is! [8]

---

[6] *Ibid.*, p. 326, ll. 292–93.   [7] *Ibid.*, p. 335, ll. 534–41.
[8] *Ibid.*, p. 347, ll. 826–27; p. 349, ll. 854–59.

Mankind contributed to the morality the death of an English farmer as the catastrophe. This concept was of fundamental importance in the development of domestic tragedy. The use of a person from the lower classes of society for moral purposes brought to the stage the final ideological development necessary for the domestic tragedies. The history of tragedies of domestic incident up to 1642 illustrates the application and refinement of these techniques already present in the early moralities.

The best known of all morality plays, and certainly the finest in artistic conception and dramatic construction, is *Everyman*,[9] written between 1495 and 1500 and printed before 1531. Although *Everyman* is probably an adaptation of the Dutch *Elckerlijk*, it has been so thoroughly Anglicized that it plays a significant part in the development of English drama. The name, Everyman, is obviously as broad in application as Mankind. Not yet had writers come to realize that:

Before English drama could go far upon the road toward tragedy it needed to learn that the poetic discovery of life's inner nature is not dependent upon abstracting and allegorizing. It needed to learn that the dramatic poet's most severe but most rewarding task is the revelation of human universality by the very act of creating authentic human individuality, that Hamlet truly can be Hamlet magnificently and pitiably alone, yet at the same time Hamlet-Everyman.[10]

The author of *Everyman,* with a great sense for the dramatic, seized upon the crucial point in the morality plays, the approach of death. Abandoning the panorama of the entire life of man, the poet limits the action of his play to the time between Death's first approach and Everyman's departure into the grave. Everyman appears as a man of great wealth, higher in station than the protagonists of the domestic tragedies. Pleading for a respite, he offers Death an enormous bribe.

> Yet of my good wyl I gyue ye, yf thou wyl be kynde;
> Ye, a thousande pounde shalte thou haue . . .[11]

A half-century later, in 1560, Richard Shakespeare, the grandfather of William, left an estate formally valued at £38 17s.; yet he was "at least a well-to-do husbandman, occupying a respectable position

[9] *Everyman,* in Joseph Quincy Adams, *Chief Pre-Shakespearean Dramas,* pp. 288–303.

[10] Farnham, *op. cit.,* p. 212.

[11] *Everyman,* in Adams, *Chief Pre-Shakespearean Drama,* p. 290.

in the little farming community of Snitterfield." [12] When less than £40 made a man well to do, the size of Everyman's bribe must have staggered the members of the audience. Everyman, however, lacks royal prerogatives and may perhaps best be described as a member of the landed gentry of England—certainly not one of the princes whose tragic falls Lydgate described. Everyman illustrates once more the vanity of the material gains so dear to the middle-class heart. In *Everyman* the conflict is still between the good and evil in man. The forces of mercy eventually triumph, for Everyman atones for his evil ways by confession and repentance, thus giving strength to Good Deeds so that she may follow him beyond the grave.

An interesting parallel to *Everyman* exists in a moral tract by William Bullein, printed in 1564 and again in 1575, called *A Dialogue Both Pleasant and Pitiful Wherein Is a Goodly Regiment against the Fever Pestilence*. Although in dialogue form, it was not intended for theatrical performance. It offers essentially the same situation as *Everyman*, but on a lower social plane, and it exploits the family relationships usually neglected in the morality plays. After much discussion of the plague, its cause and cure, the wife (Vxor) and her husband (Ciuis), in an effort to escape the disease, flee to the country. On their way they are met by a strange, ominous figure, Mors. As in *Everyman*, Mors allows Ciuis time to settle the affairs of his soul, even offering him theological instruction.

Thus do I ende bothe good and badde, but precious in the sight of the lorde is the death of his sainctes, and many be the scourges of wicked men. . . . The paines of helle doe follow me to swallowe vp al fleshe that doth not repent them of their wickednesse.[13]

Ciuis receives consolation from Theology and dies in peace. The work approaches domestic tragedy because of the concern Ciuis expresses over the fate of his wife and child. Insistence on repentance for the salvation of the soul appears here, as it does in all homiletic literature.

Enough Is as Good as a Feast (c. 1580), by W. Wager, added to the familiar tale of the man tempted by vices a remonstrance against the abuses of grasping landlords and harsh masters, in what is perhaps the

---

[12] Joseph Quincy Adams, *A Life of William Shakespeare*, p. 10.

[13] William Bullein, *A Dialogue Both Pleasant and Pitiful Wherein Is a Goodly Regiment against the Fever Pestilence*, reprinted by Early English Text Society, LII, 118.

first expression of social protest in English drama. Mr. Worldly Man, through the aid of the vices, has risen to a position of affluence. His moral sense has not kept pace with his material gains; he has become a miser. Two pathetic scenes in which an old tenant and a servant seek redress from Mr. Worldly Man enlist the sympathies of the audience. These suppliants appeal to Covetousness, the vice who acts as agent for Worldly Man. He reports to his employer.

> *Covetousness:* And beholde Sir as I traueled in the Street:
> With thefe two fellowes I chaunced for to meet.
> Who tolde me that they had an earneft fute to you
> One for his houfe that he dwelleth in now.
> Wherin (he faith) you go about to doo him much wrong:
> For he faith that he hath dwelt in it very long.
> The other faid, you owe him a peece of money:
> he wrought with you half a yeer & had never a peny
> And thus they tooke on with me before you did come:
> And now haue I fhowed you the whole circumftance & fome.
> *Vvorldly man:* Mary hang them Villains haue I nought to doo:
> But to ftand and reafon matters with them two?
> Hear you tenãt, in few woords you knowe my minde
> According as I haue tolde you, fo you fhall me finde.
> Other [*sic*] prouide money your lease to renue:
> Or els you fhall out incontinent this ts [*sic*] true.
> *Tenant:* Oh Landlord me thinks this is to much extremitie:
> Alas upon mine age take you fome pittye.
> Cham olde & haue many children and much charge:
> I truft landlord ich fhall vind you better at large.
> *Vvorldly man:* I cannot tel what I fhould doo more beleeue me:
> Many Landlords would not do as I doo by thee.
> For I am cõtent for money yᵘ fhouldft haue it before an other:
> I can doo no more for thee if thou wert my brother.[14]

Worldly Man refuses the servant's request in a manner even more highhanded.

These characters can be considered as pathetic but not as tragic figures. They vanish from the play, but the sympathy aroused for them helped to prepare the citizens in Elizabethan audiences to accept as tragic heroes members of their own social class. The presence of such

[14] W. Wager, *A Comedy or Enterlude Intitled, Inough Is as Good as a Feaft*, pp. [38–39], Henry E. Huntington Facsimile Reprints.

scenes indicates a sympathetic interest in these disturbed economic conditions. The swindling of the servant and the tenant was viewed as the most damning of the sins of Mr. Worldly Man. The victims might be regarded as remote ancestors of the heroes of the social-protest dramas.[15]

The rebuff of the servant and the tenant is followed by one of the most fully elaborated death scenes in all these moral plays. Worldly Man complains of illness; then God's Plague, obviously an agent of Divine Providence, claims him.

> I am the plague of God properly called,
> Which commeth on the wicked ſudainly:
> I go through all townes and Cittyes ſtrongly walled,
> Striking to death and that without all mercy.
> Héer thou wicked couetouſe perſon I doo ſtrike,
> Which once on the plowe hadſt taken holde:
> But willingly again thou ranneſt in the Dike:
> Therfore thy plague ſhalbe doubled ſeuen folde.[16]

A physician solicitously suggests an appeal to God's mercy. For his pains, he is sent away without his fee. Worldly Man devotes his efforts to arranging his temporal, not his spiritual, affairs. While dictating a letter to his wife, he falls dead. Since he has wasted the time given him for repentance, he is claimed by Satan, who chortles gleefully.

> How cunningly put he his money to uſury?
> Yea, and that without offence of any law:

---

[15] Another play by Wager, *The Cruel Debtor* (c. 1565), treated the sin of covetousness from a slightly different viewpoint. Only a few pages of the text have survived. Greg has discovered that the play is a dramatization of the parable in Matthew 18:23–35. In this parable, a servant owes his king ten thousand talents. Since the servant could not pay his debt, the king forgave him the amount owed. The same servant was owed "an hundred pence" by one of his fellows who was unable to pay. Thereupon the wicked servant had his debtor cast into prison. Then the king "was wroth and delivered" his servant "to the tormentors, till he should pay all that was due unto him." The text of the surviving drama breaks off at the point where the king is about to forgive the servant his debt. The complete play might have been an interesting dramatic exemplum of the miseries wrought by covetousness on two members of the servant class. See W. Wager, *The Cruell Debtter*, ed. Walter W. Greg, Malone Society Collections.

All for Money, by Thomas Lupton, written about 1577, employs satire for the purpose of social protest. Throughout the play, elements of pathos are mingled with satiric comedy.

[16] Wager, *Enough Is as Good as a Feast*, p. [42].

He was not to learne any kinde of bribery.
Wherby wicked gaines to him he might draw.

Satan then congratulates Covetousness for a job well done in per-
verting the soul of Worldly Man.

Thou teacheſt the worldly man, a leacemonger to be,
To oppreſſe the poore and of his riches him to defraud:
Wickedly to vſe the lawes he learned of thee,
Therefore indeed thou art worthy of much lawd.
All you worldly men, that in your riches doo truſt,
Be mery and iocund, builde Palaces and make luſty cheer:
Put your money to Uſury, let it not lye and ruſt,
Occupye your ſelues in my lawes while ye be here,
Spare not, nor care not, what miſcheef you frequent.
Uſe drunkennes, deceit, take other mens wiues:
Paſſe of nothing, one houre is inough to repent,
Of all the wickednes you haue doon in your liues.
Oh, if you wil thus after my Lawes behaue,
You ſhall haue all things as this worldly man had:
Be bolde of me what you wil to craue,
And dout you not but with you I wil play the loouing lad.
Yea, and after death I wil prouide a place,
For you in my kingdome for euer to reign:
You ſhall fare no wurſe then dooth mine own grace,
That is to lye burning for euer in pain.[17]

Especially significant in the progression of the morality plays toward
domestic tragedy is the secularization here presented of the effects of

---

[17] *Ibid.*, pp. [49–50]. Another play by Wager, *The Longer Thou Livest the More
Fool Thou Art* (c. 1568), presents an additional example of the fate which awaited
unregenerate sinners. The hero, Moros, leads a riotous life under the guidance of
Idleness, Incontinence, and Wrath. At length, God's Judgement condemns him to hell:

> *Moros:* Go with thee ill favoured knave,
> I had lever thou wert hanged by the necke,
> If it pleaſe the Deuill me to haue,
> Let him carry me away on his backe.
> *Confuſion:* I will carry thee to the Deuill in déede,
> The world shalbe well ridde of a foole.
> *Moros:* Adew to the Deuill, God ſend us good ſpeede,
> An other while with the Deuill I muſt go to ſchool.
>   —*A Very Mery and Pythie Commedie, Called The Longer
> Thou Liueſt, the More Foole Thou Art*, p. [52], Tudor Fac-
> simile Texts.

sin. The earlier plays had, as a rule, been content to exhibit the effect of sin on a sinner and the consequent peril to his soul, but seldom displayed the results of his greed on the innocent bystander. In this work, the action motivated by covetousness reflects the contemporary economic woes of England. Nevertheless, punishment is given by God through the action of His Providence. The device of showing earthly punishment for sins by immediate reaction of natural or human forces rather than by dramatically obvious supernatural manifestations of Providence seldom appeared in the morality plays, but had already been used in the prodigal-son plays and in the interludes. The two operations of Providence, immediate worldly punishment by poverty, sickness, and the like and death by supernatural agencies, found expression in the domestic tragedies. Usually, however, each intervention of Providence aided the human agencies of justice.

II

Worldly grief as a penalty for sin is exploited in Ulpian Fulwell's interlude, *Like Will to Like, Quoth the Devil to the Collier* (c. 1562–68.[18] The interlude was usually a shorter play than the morality, frequently performed indoors before a limited audience. Professor Tucker Brooke suggests "the interlude . . . is throughout its career an essentially aristocratic species." [19] He seems to be thinking especially of the early interludes and perhaps of their probable manner of presentation on small stages in private houses.[20] The later interludes clearly dedicated themselves to the instruction of audiences made up of essentially the same kinds of persons who saw the moralities and who subsequently came to the theatres. The change in emphasis resulted from the drifting of the interlude into the hands of men whose primary purpose was moral, a development which helped to cement the alliance between domestic tragedy and theological propagandizing. Professor Brooke partly contradicts his earlier statement as he notes the change which took place in the interlude.

The most conspicuous feature of the last interludes is their pronounced tendency, when free from outside influence, to revert to the general form

---

[18] *An Enterlude Entituled Like Wil to Like, Quod the Deuil to the Colier,* in *The Dramatic Writings of Ulpian Fulwell,* ed. John S. Farmer, p. 4.

[19] C. F. Tucker Brooke, *The Tudor Drama,* p. 71.

[20] Edmund K. Chambers, *The Elizabethan Stage,* III, 21–27.

and tone of the early morality. As the species lost its hold upon the fashionable public, it passed naturally out of the hands of non-moral, professional entertainers like Heywood into those of unprogressive, leisurely poetasters, who appear to have belonged largely to the clerical profession, and whose object was more frequently edification than amusement.[21]

Fulwell's play combined the familiar moral framework with scenes of realistic comedy. This union is of importance in the present study because a tradition of realism had to be established before domestic tragedy could be written. This realism found its most natural expression in comedy, but a plot the principal episode of which was the death of a commoner inevitably presented scenes full of homely details. Each of the evil characters, comic as he may be in early portions of the play, comes to grief in a manner intended to shock and instruct if not to arouse pity and terror. English or quasi-allegorical names furnish additional evidence of the effort to make the work amusing and instructive through the exploitation of familiar scenes, persons, and episodes. The appellations Tom Tosspot, Cuthbert Cutpurse, Pierce Pickpurse, and Ralph Roister illustrate as well as did the old allegorical names the characteristics of their owners; likewise, they suggest the crowd of hangers-on at a county fair or a village gathering in sixteenth-century England. The names of other characters, such as Philip Fleming and Tom Collier, have no moral significance. A few allegorical personages represent the virtues, and their dullness may serve to explain the extraordinary influence wielded by the vice, Nichol Newfangle, and his followers.

Nichol's successful endeavors to attract converts to lives of vice are so entertainingly presented that they have given the piece a comic reputation. From Nichol's point of view, the play is a comedy. After work well done, he departs on the Devil's back for a vacation in hell. In the eyes of his unfortunate victims, the results of his actions are far from amusing, for two become beggars and two are hanged. The last scenes reveal the serious purpose of the work. In this play the "scaffold speeches" make their first appearance on the English stage. This device was common in nondramatic literature and was to become a popular feature of certain types of plays for the next two hundred years. In these speeches, as previously indicated, the condemned criminal repents his evil way of life, warns all who are near by to eschew

[21] Brooke, *The Tudor Drama*, p. 110.

vice, and begs God to show him mercy. That he will receive divine forgiveness for his sins is taken for granted. The penance for his crimes is death at the hands of human agencies, a fate willingly borne by the now pious sinner. In this play all four culprits deliver these speeches. The beggars presumably have not transgressed sufficiently to deserve death or are perhaps given additional time for repentance; but their fates are warnings of God's power and justice. Tom Tosspot says:

> O all ye parents, to you I do say:
> Have respect to your children and for their education,
> Lest you answer therefor at the latter day,
> And your meed shall be eternal damnation.
> If my parents had brought me up in virtue and learning,
> I should not have had this shameful end;
> But all licentiously was my up-bringing,
> Wherefore learn by me your faults to amend.
> But neither in virtue, learning, or yet honest trade,
> Was I bred up my living for to get:
> Therefore in misery my time away must vade;
> For vicious persons behold now in the net.
> I am in the snare, I am caught with the gin;
> And now it is too late, I cannot again begin.[22]

This admonition to parents was a favorite theme both in the plays and in the nondramatic works. It recurs in the prodigal-son plays and also in some of the Elizabethan murder plays.

Cuthbert Cutpurse, condemned to the gallows, expatiates on his situation in the following edifying fashion:

> O cursed caitiff, born in an evil hour,
> Woe unto me that ever I did thee know.
> For of all iniquity, thou art the bow'r;
> The seed of Satan thou dost alway sow.
> Thou only hast given me the overthrow.
> Woe worth the hour, wherein I was born!
> Woe worth the time that ever I knew thee!
> For now in misery I am forlorn;
> O, all youth take example by me:
> Flee from evil company, as from a serpent you would flee;
> For I to you all a mirror may be.

---

[22] Fulwell, *op. cit.*, p. 44.

> I have been daintily and delicately bred,
> But nothing at all in virtuous lore:
> And now I am but a man dead,
> Hanged I must be, which grieveth me full sore.
> Note well the end of me therefore;
> And you that fathers and mothers be,
> Bring not up your children in too much liberty.[23]

Pierce Pickpurse, as he stands on the steps of the scaffold, adds the final point of the play.

> Sith that by the law we are now condemned,
> Let us call to God for his mercy and his grace;
> And exhort that all vice may be amended,
> While we in this world have time and space.
> And though our lives have licentiously been spent,
> Yet at the last to God let us call;
> For he heareth such as are ready to repent,
> And desireth not that sinners should fall.
> Now we are ready to suffer, come when it shall.[24]

"Scaffold speeches" become tiresomely familiar in the domestic tragedies. Nearly all such plays written before 1642 have some version of the speech given above. Confession was considered one of the required parts of repentance, and writers lost no opportunity of making the repentance scenes realistic.

George Wapull's *The Tide Tarrieth No Man* appeared the year the Theatre opened. Wapull reveals the same interest in the plight of the tenant and the moneyless person that Wager had displayed in *Enough Is as Good as a Feast. The Tide Tarrieth No Man* shows the evil effects of greed on the innocent and guilty alike. The vice, Courage, who might better have been named Recklessness, teaches courageousness in foolish matters and in greed.

> Now you may fée how Corage can worke,
> And how he can encorage, both to good and bad:
> The Marchaunt is incouraged, in gredineffe to lurke
> And the Courtyer to win worfhip, by Corage is glad.
> The one is good, no man will denay,
> I meane corage to win worfhip and fame: .

---

[23] *Ibid.*, p. 49.   [24] *Ibid.*, pp. 49–50.

So that the other is ill, all men will fay,
That is corage to gréedineſſe, which getteth ill name.[25]

Courage is not one of the theological vices. Courage might be applied, the author is careful to note, to good as well as to evil ends. Wapull follows the Aristotelian scheme of virtue and vice. To Aristotle, courage would be the virtue between the two extremes of cowardice and foolhardiness. Wapull uses courage to refer both to the mean and to the extreme of foolhardiness. Money, in this work, is in a similar ambiguous position. Money in itself is not evil; only its misuse leads to the revelation of its fearful potentialities.

The punishment meted out to Courage is an obvious case of God's retributive justice. The character of Greediness, the merchant, however, represents something new. He is a contemporary Londoner, a moneylender and a landlord. Though he is from the merchant class, his death forms the major catastrophe of the play. The dramatic importance of a man of this social station is a further step toward realistic dramas and domestic tragedy.

A subplot recounts the rash marriage of Wastefulness with the Maid Wantonness. Wastefulness soon comes to economic grief. Tempted to take his own life, he is prevented by Faithful Few. The story, reminiscent of *The Disobedient Child*, marks the intrusion of a purely domestic problem into the framework of a morality play.

III

Because it provided a useful plot which had long been employed for didactic drama, the prodigal-son story offered a natural base upon which to build domestic tragedy. In the prodigal-son plays, the situation was domestic, the treatment realistic, the attitudes serious. A few of these plays departed from the Biblical parable by bringing the tale to a tragic conclusion and in this way became the first real domestic tragedies.

Continental humanist writers dramatized the prodigal-son story many times between 1490 and 1550. Seeking in classical antiquity for a model for their writing, these men found it in the comedies of Terence. In a typical Terentian comedy, a son endeavors to conceal his licentious way of life from his father. The plot grows so tangled that there is no possible natural resolution of all the complications

[25] George Wapull, *The Tyde Taryeth No Man*, p. [20], Tudor Facsimile Texts.

except forgiveness by the father. The benevolent *pater ex machina* and the indolent, obstreperous youth employed by the Roman playwright fitted perfectly into the outlines of the prodigal-son parable.

Castellani Castellano's *Del figliuol prodigo*, written sometime between 1490 and 1500, is one of the earliest vernacular dramatizations of the story. Neither Gnapheus, the Dutch scholar, in his *Acolastus*, printed in 1529 but probably written much earlier, nor Macropedius (George Langveldt), another Dutchman, in his *Asotus* [c. 1510], *Rebelles* [c. 1535], and *Petriscus* [c. 1536], made any substantial change in the conclusion of the story. *Rebelles*, as Bond points out, is the first adaptation of the prodigal-son drama to contemporary Dutch school life.[26] All these plays were written in Latin. In Germany, in Holland, and elsewhere on the Continent, authors of prodigal-son plays carefully followed classical models, interpreting them in the light of Reformation thought. Cicero's statement that comedy is a mirror of human life [27] was especially influential upon authors of these plays, for these writers understood the phrase to mean that the mirror should reveal life as it ought to be lived.

The continental plays, with one exception, closely follow the outline of the story of Luke.[28] The one exception is an anonymous French play of 1540 entitled *La Moralité de l'enfant de perdition*. It is a crude production telling the story of a prodigal whose repentance comes too late. Having become a highwayman, he kills his father and mother, both of whom exhibit, at death, deep Christian piety. The son's share of loot is stolen by his associates; he suffers terrible remorse and abandons his soul to perdition, giving his head and brains to Lucifer, his skin to Satan, his arms to Astoroth, and other parts of his body to lesser devils.[29] The play was extraordinarily popular, having had a theatrical life of over half a century.[30] The presence of such a work in the literature of France indicates that the popular drama of that coun-

---

[26] R. Warwick Bond, *Early Plays from the Italian*, p. xcix.

[27] *Pro Sex. Roscio Amerino*, quoted by Adolf Schweckendieck, "Bühnengeschichte des verloren Sohnes in Deutschland," *Theatergeschichtliche Forschungen*, XV, 12. "Comoediam esse humanae vitae speculum." See above, Chapter I.

[28] Cf. Schweckendieck, *op. cit.*; Kurt Michel, *Das Wesen des Reformationsdramas entwickelt am Stoff des verloren Sohns.*

[29] *Moralité novvelle tres-frvctvévse, de l'infant de perdition qui pendit fon pere, & tua fa mere*, p. [38], misnumbered 30, reprinted in facsimile.

[30] Ernest Bernbaum, *The Drama of Sensibility*, p. 31.

try might have led to a development of domestic tragedy, had it not been for the codifying and regularizing influence of the Pléiade.

In England, the prodigal-son play, subject to no such restrictions, came to its fullest development. In its frequent use of tragic ending, it approached domestic tragédy. *Nice Wanton*,[31] an anonymous play of about 1550, is the earliest worthy of analysis. It presents the disruption of a middle-class family and the death of two of its members as a result of their prodigal living. Xanthippe is the mother of three children: Barnabas, a righteous prig, and Ismael and Dalila, who are the prodigals. Barnabas blames the waywardness of his brother and sister on his mother's neglect of them in their childhood. Ismael and Dalila embark on their evil courses by running away from school. When they meet Iniquity, they are well established in the prodigal way of life. Ismael has become a gamester and Dalila a whore. Dalila and Iniquity fleece Ismael and he runs off saying:

> Tis no matter; I wyll haue money, or I wyll swete.
> By Gog's bloud, I wyll robbe the next I mete!
> Yea, and it be my father! [32]

Iniquity and Dalila come to blows over the division of their loot.

After a long interval, Dalila appears again on the stage. Diseased and poor, miserable and forlorn, she has lost her beauty but has regained her conscience. She laments in the following instructive manner:

> Alas, wreched wretche that I am!
> Most miserable caitife that euer was borne!

---

[31] *A Preaty Interlude Called, Nice Wanton.*
>   Wherein ye may see
>   Three braunc[h]es of an yll tree:
>   The mother and her chyldren three,
>   Twoo naught, and one godlye.
>
>   Early sharpe, that wyll be thorne;
>   Soone yll, that wyll be naught;
>   To be naught, better vnborne;
>   Better vnfed, then naughtely taught.

Ut magnus magnos, pueros puerilia decent. . . . Anno Domini, MDLX, in Manly, *Specimens of the Pre-Shakespearean Drama*, I, 457.

[32] *Ibid.*, p. 467, ll. 229–31.

> Full of payne and sorow, croked and lame
> Stuft with diseases, in this world forlorne!
>
> .   .   .   .
>
> Where I was fayre and amiable of face,
> Now am I foule and horrible to se:
> Al this I haue deserued for lacke of grace,
> Iustly for my sinnes God doth plague me.
>
> My parentes did tidle me,—they were to blame,—
> In-steade of correction, in yll did me maintain.
> I fell to naught, and shall dye with shame! [33]

Barnabas, the virtuous brother, meets her in a scene which ignores the emotional possibilities of the reunion of a brother and sister in order to stress the Christian moral. With no show of fraternal affection, Barnabas dutifully assumes the care of Dalila for the few remaining months of her life.

Ismael, the erring brother, is next seen in court where he is "indited by xij men of felony, burglary and murdre." [34] Condemned to death, he accuses Iniquity of leading him into a life of crime and has the satisfaction of seeing the latter sentenced to share his fate.

Master Worldly Shame blames Xanthippe for the death of Ismael and Dalila, because of her lack of care in their training. As the mother contemplates suicide, Barnabas rebukes her, saying:

> By maintenaunce they grew to mischief and yll;
> So, at last, Gods iustice did them both spill.
>
> In that God preserued me, small thanke to you!
> If God had not geuen me speciall grace
> To auoyd euil and do good,—this is true—
> I had liued and dyed in as wretched case
> As they did, for I had both suffraunce and space. [35]

He offers the conventional solace.

> Yet in this we may al take comfort:
> They toke great repentaunce, I heard say;
> And, as for my sister, I am able to report

---

[33] *Ibid.*, p. 468, ll. 261–64; p. 469, ll. 273–79.
[34] *Ibid.*, p. 473, ll. 374–75.   [35] *Ibid.*, p. 477, ll. 501–7.

She lamented for her sinnes to her dy[i]ng-day.
To repent and beleue I exhorted her alway.
Before her death she beleued that God, of his mercy,
For Christes sake, would saue her eternally.[36]

The work concludes with an appeal to parents to be circumspect in bringing up their children and an admonition to children to obey their parents.

Nice Wanton follows the customary teaching of the preachers that by repentance and divine mercy can the soul be saved from perdition. Human forgiveness may even be a trap to sinners, to keep them from theological repentance. The operations of Divine Providence in the fate of Ismael and in the plague which strikes Dalila bring this play nearer the developing English tradition than to the continental prodigal-son story. On the other hand, *Nice Wanton* is superior in characterization to many of the moralities. The characters are in-dividualized human beings. Even the abstract personages, Iniquity and Worldly Shame, have become English country people. Iniquity is a cleverer Ismael. He is lusty, sly, and quick witted. Like any crim-inal in the plays, he pays for these human characteristics with his life. Worldly Shame resembles a nagging neighbor bleating "I told you so," more than he does his cousins in the morality plays.

Quite obviously this drama does not approach tragedy. There is considerable doubt as to which of four characters is the protagonist, Xanthippe, Barnabas, Dalila, or Ismael. The deaths of Dalila and Ismael take place off stage, and no effort is made to arouse tragic pity for either. Repentance and divine mercy rob the play of any effect of tragic catastrophe. The situation of Xanthippe, however, creates in the audience an emotion almost tragic. Her lax discipline disrupts her home and indirectly brings two of her children to disgraceful deaths. However, moralizing spoils the scene in which she becomes aware of her guilt. The development for its own sake of such a family situation in domestic tragedy had to wait for many years until the theological ends had ceased to be primary.[37]

---

[36] *Ibid.*, pp. 477–78, ll. 510–16.

[37] Thomas Ingeland, in *The Disobedient Child* (c. 1560), carried on the prodigal-son tradition in a more orthodox fashion than that of *Nice Wanton*. Although the play is not a tragedy, the author seems to have been dissatisfied with the sentimental reconciliation characteristic of his continental predecessors. Instead of welcoming his

In George Gascoigne's *The Glass of Government* (1575), the development of the prodigal-son play took a step backward. Closely imitating the continental playwrights, Gascoigne abandons any pretense of realism. The deaths of two of the principals, however, relate the work to domestic tragedy. Latin names are used for the characters, and the drama is set "as it were, in Antwerpe." The argument of the play is, in the words of the author:

Tvvo riche Citizens of Andvverpe (beeing nighe neighboures, & hauing eche of them tvvo fonnes of like age) do place them togither vvith one godly teacher. The foolemafter doth briefly inftruct them in their duetie tovvards God, their Prince, their Parents, their cuntrie, and all magiftrates in the fame. The eldeft being yong men of quicke capacitie, do (Parrotte like) very quickly learne the rules vvithout booke: the yonger, beeing fomewhat more dull of vnderftanding, do yet engraue the fame within their memories. The elder, by allurement of Parafites and levvde company, beginne to incline themfelues to concupifence. The parents (to preuent it) fend them all togither to the Vniverfitie of *Dowaye,* vvhereas the yonger in fhort fpace be (by painful ftudie) preferred, that one to be Secretarie vnto the *Palfgraue,* that other becommeth a famous preacher in *Geneua.* The eldeft (turning to their vomit) take their carriage with them, and trauaile the worlde. That one is apprehended and executed for a robbery (euen in fight of his brother) in the *Palfgraues* courte: that other vvhipped and banifhed *Geneua* for fornication: not vvithftanding the earneft fute of his brother for his pardon.[38]

---

son with open arms, the father gives him a little money and, with the following admonition, sends him back to the wife he has deserted:

> If that at the first thou wouldst have been ordered,
> And done as thy father counselled thee,
> So wretched a life had never chanced,
> Whereof at this present thou complainest to me;
> But yet come on, to my house we will be going,
> And there thou shalt see what I will give:—
> A little to help thy need living,
> Since that in such penury thou dost live;
> And that once done, thou must hence again,
> For I am not he that will thee retain.

The nonfatal conclusion puts this work in the category of "drama," that heterogeneous middle form that has, since the inception of domestic tragedy, vied with it for public approval. *A Pretie and Mery Trew Enterlude: Called the Difobedient Child,* in W. C. Hazlitt, *Dodsley's Old Plays,* II, 315–16.

[38] George Gascoigne, *The Glaffe of Gouernement,* p. [111], Tudor Facsimile Texts.

Although Gascoigne says he plans to instruct the citizens of England, none of the scenes makes contact with real English life.

> Content you then (my Lordes) with good intent,
> Graue Citizens, you people greate and ſmall,
> To ſee your ſelues in Glaſſe of Government
> Beholde raſhe youth, which dangerouſly doth fall
> On craggy rockes of ſorrows nothing ſofte,
> When ſober wittes by Vertue clymes alofte.[39]

In artistic conception, this play is a decided retrogression from *Nice Wanton*. Gascoigne has returned to a narrow imitation of his Dutch masters, retaining only the fatal conclusion of his English predecessor. Long, tedious passages of didactic dialogue in pedestrian prose and the artificially contrived plot with its paired brothers, one good and one bad in each family, unite to deprive the play of interest and also render it unimportant in the history of either the prodigal-son story or the development of domestic tragedy. Professor Boas says: "His [Gascoigne's] departure from the spirit of the original story in St. Luke's Gospel was a sign that the day of the Prodigal Son dramatic cycle was passing." [40]

The prodigal-son story passed as the basis for an independent dramatic group, but the theme long remained as a useful source of plots. The story appeared in Elizabethan times, occasionally with a fatal conclusion. In its early history, it aided the development of English domestic tragedy and helped to prepare English drama to withstand the growing influence of the humanistic idea that only a king could be a hero of tragedy.

Domestic tragedy developed rapidly after 1576, yet it borrowed many of its most effective dramatic devices and its most important conventions from the morality plays. Had it not been for the moralities, domestic tragedies could not have come into being, for the early homiletic dramas accustomed audiences to dramatic traditions necessary for domestic tragedy.

The most important of these traditions was the use of the common man as protagonist for a tragic story. In the early moralities, the hero, for purposes of instruction, was made as general as possible, since "Everyman" could mean "Any Man." As their protagonists acquired

---

[39] *Ibid.*, p. [iv].
[40] Frederick S. Boas, *An Introduction to Tudor Drama*, p. 41.

individual characteristics, poets found that the shopkeepers, merchants, and others who made up the audiences became, when transferred to the stage, the most effective instruments for moral teaching. Later dramatists discovered that spectators responded actively to the pathetic appeal of misfortunes which overtook members of their own class.

Realism, as it developed in the morality plays, was important to domestic tragedy. A serious application of the realistic method was employed in the catastrophes of such plays as *Like Will to Like*, in the tenant scenes in *Enough Is as Good as a Feast* and *All for Money*, and in Dalila's repentance scene in *Nice Wanton*. No comic element remains in any of these dramas; the hard earthy facts are stressed for didactic emphasis. Serious realism developed to a great extent in the later plays, not as an end in itself, but as a method of emphasizing the moral lesson. Realism and moral emphasis led the moralities, the interludes, and the prodigal-son plays to tragic conclusions. Through the last group, domestic tragedy really became established, for in these dramas the moral framework was combined with a story of human rather than of abstract characters.

The theology in the morality plays became increasingly orthodox. All the steps of theological procedure for the correction of sin were provided with dramatic equivalents. The device of repentance prevented the intrusion of sentimental pity by its insistence that all sinners of whatever sort accept the earthly consequences of their folly. Civil authorities were pleased if a man could make his peace with heaven. But that important matter was really outside their province; theirs it was to see only that he paid his debt to society. The agency of Divine Providence, on the other hand, insured the ends of both earthly and heavenly justice.

Many morality plays continued to be presented after the opening of the theatres in 1576, but the murder plays and other domestic tragedies took over the didactic mission of the moralists and applied the religious message directly to life. As dramatists gained in technical skill, theatrical managers discovered that playwrights in devising exciting plays of human characters could combine moral instruction with economic success.

Chapter Five

PLAYS FROM LEGEND AND HISTORY

A NUMBER of plays based on legend and history are, in essence, domestic tragedies, for their protagonists are commoners who meet death during the action of the drama. Such a tragedy is *The Life and Death of Jack Straw* (1591). Its plot is based on the orthodox belief that a commoner who foolishly attempts to rise above the station to which God has called him is filled with wicked presumption, which makes him a victim of Nemesis or, in more strictly Christian terms, exposes him to the danger of God's wrath. This play seasons its moral instruction with the excitement of the rise and defeat of a rebellion. In others of these plays, such as the two dramatizations of the story of Appius and Virginia and the Jane Shore parts of *Edward IV*, the emotional basis is formed by the pathetic appeal of a harassed woman of low degree.

Appius and Virginia (c. 1564),[1] by R. B., clearly indicates the dependence of the early domestic tragedy on the morality. While the story is a classic one, and so might be considered outside the limits of domestic tragedy, the family of Virginius is plebeian. Virginius is merely a centurion, one of the lowest officers in the Roman armies. The appeal lies in the helplessness of the poor but honest father and the innocence of the daughter. Only a contemporary English setting is lacking to make this play a domestic tragedy, and the rule of proximity of milieu is violated again and again by writers whose dramas are accepted examples of this form.[2]

The story originally told in Livy iii. 44 ff. was repeated in the *Ro-*

---

[1] R. B., *A New and Tragicall Comedie of Apius and Virginia*, in W. C. Hazlitt, *Dodsley's Old Plays*, IV, 107.

[2] Even in this ostensibly Roman play, the author made frequent references to the English countryside, for one character mentions in rapid succession "half-acre," "Gaffer Miller's stile," and "Carter's hay-rick" (*ibid.*, p. 136). For another English domestic tragedy set in Italy, cf. the Italian plot of Yarington's *Two Lamentable Tragedies*.

man de la Rose, in Chaucer's *Physician's Tale,* in Painter's *Palace of Pleasure,* before it was finally put in dramatic form by R. B.

The description of the play as a "Tragicall Comedie" indicates the author's intention of presenting lives of citizens in a tragic manner. In *Appius and Virginia,* neither the plot nor the dramatic conception, but only the rank of the protagonists warrants the use of the word "comedy." R. B., obviously feeling that term misleading, characterized his play as a "Tragicall Comedie." [3] This term he used in a sense directly opposite to that of Plautus in *Amphitruo,* where the Roman playwright meant a comedy in which kings take part.[4] Here "Tragicall Comedie" is used to describe a tragedy of the common people. In the prologue, the word "tragedy" alone is employed.[5]

Appius and Virginia, as previously indicated, preserves certain elements of the morality play. In minor roles appear Haphazard, Conscience, Justice, Rumor, and other allegorical abstractions. The vice, Haphazard, induces Appius to attempt to gain the custody of Virginia. Rumor discloses the scheme to Virginius, and Comfort prevents the bereaved father from taking his own life after the death of his daughter. Haphazard, for his sins, goes to the scaffold with Appius and Claudius. Even the abstract characters possess a fair amount of human individuality. The real action, however, results from the conflict of the human characters: Virginius, the centurion; Virginia, his daughter; Appius, the judge; and Claudius, the henchman of Appius. Through them, the author attempts to give psychological motivation to the action. In addition, he shows the clash of two opposed ethical forces. He uses the characters to embody, not to personify, good and evil. Virginia, as a tragic heroine, makes a definite appeal to the sympathies of the audience. Stilted as she may sound when she pleads for death at her father's hand, she displays a much more natural and attractive pathos when her courage momentarily fails her. She first asks for death rather than dishonor:

> Thou knowest, O my father, if I be once spotted
> My name and my kindred then forth will be blotted:

---

[3] He might have called it a comedy in the sense that moral justice is done in the end, but under such a usage no play of the Elizabethan period can be called a domestic tragedy.

[4] *T. Macci Plauti comoedia,* ed. W. M. Lindsay (Oxford, Oxford University Press, 1903), I, 58.

[5] R. B., *Appius and Virginia,* in W. C. Hazlitt, *Dodsley's Old Plays,* IV, 109.

> And if thou, my father, should die for my cause,
> The world would accompt me guilty in cause.
> Then rather, dear father, if it be thy pleasure,
> Grant me the death; then keep I my treasure
> My lamp, my light, my life undefiled,
> And so may Judge Appius of [my] flesh be beguiled.[6]

She then anticipates the pathos of the eighteenth-century "she-trage-dies."

> The gods forgive thee, father dear! farewell, thy blow do bend.
> Yet stay a while, O father dear, for flesh to death is frail:
> Let first my wimple bind my eyes, and then let thy blow assail.
> Now father, work thy will on me, that life I may enjoy.
>   [*Here tie a handkercher about her eyes,*
>   *and then strike off her head.*[7]

Appius and Virginia is the first of the English domestic tragedies to exploit the pathetic possibilities of a death scene. The authors of morality plays were accustomed to use death to illustrate God's retributive justice, but it remained for the classical influence to add the notion of tragedy as an art form, rather than as only a moral treatise. In the conclusion of the present play, Divine Providence operates in an original way. When Appius realizes the trick played on him, he calls loudly for justice. A personification of Justice appears, sentences Appius to death, and elevates Virginius to the position formerly held by the wicked judge. Claudius and Haphazard are likewise condemned. The dramatic technique involved here is far in advance of the crude schemes of the morality plays. In expert hands, and without the religious connotations, this same dramatic device is used in *The Merchant of Venice*, where Shylock insists on obtaining all that the letter of the law allows, and then finds that he is caught in his own legal trap.

When he set his play in ancient Rome, R. B., apparently realizing that his characters would not be Christian, has them speak of Jupiter and "the gods." Yet he roots the play firmly in the theology of sixteenth-century England. Operations of Divine Providence mete out punishments and rewards to sinners and virtuous characters. The evil-doers all learn the error of their ways and repent. In the conclusion of his work, R. B. departed from his source to emphasize the moral pur-

[6] *Ibid.*, p. 144.   [7] *Ibid.*, pp. 145–46.

pose. In the original, Virginius leads a successful rebellion against Appius. According to sixteenth-century theology, rebellion was a sin. God's Providence was a certain and the only righteous instrument of punishment of a wicked ruler for injustice. This play illustrates such an operation of heavenly intervention. Virginius, who has lived a virtuous life and had meekly submitted to what heaven sent him, is raised by Providence to rule. Appius, who has misused for his own selfish ends the power God had vested in him, is punished for his transgressions. The death of the innocent Virginia serves the purpose of assuring the audience that the sin of Appius is great enough to call for drastic operation of Providence. Virginia is sacrificed so that Rome may be freed from a tyrant. The reason for her own death is left unstated. It may be that the innocent girl had lived out her allotted days, or that destiny calls for her, or that she has some unrevealed sin. Possibly she is taken to prevent her from committing future sin. The question is never answered on theological grounds. The dramatic purpose is self-explanatory.

In 1608, John Webster again dramatized the story of the Roman centurion and his daughter, in *Appius and Virginia*.[8] Webster rejected the obviously moral but dramatically ineffective ending of R. B.'s play and returned to the conclusion employed by Livy. In the early drama, in spite of her superiority to the heroines of the interludes, Virginia impresses one as being something of a prig, colorless in her great virtue. In Webster's play she is made a healthy girl, eager, alert, and about to be married to Icilius, a soldier. Virginius, although he has risen to become a leader in the army, is still a plebeian.

> *App*[*ius*]. Come, y'are a proud *Plebian*.
> *Virg*[*inius*]. True, my Lord.
> Proud in the glory of my Ancestors,
> Who have continued these eight hundred years:
> The Heralds have not knowne you these eight months.[9]

---

[8] In *The Complete Works of John Webster*, ed. F. L. Lucas, Vol. III. Some doubt exists as to the authorship of this play, for it bears traces of Heywood's style. If Heywood's, it has probably been revised by Webster. However, in tracing the development of these plays as a type, the authorship of any one is of small importance. See Felix E. Schelling, *Elizabethan Playwrights*, p. 165; Edmund K. Chambers, *The Elizabethan Stage*, III, 514–15.

[9] Webster, *op. cit.*, III, 206; IV, i, 294–98.

The fate of Virginia is far more effectively presented by Webster than by his predecessor. Webster did not make R. B.'s mistake of giving no preparation for the death scene. Early in the tragedy the possibility is suggested that she will seek death at her father's hands. Suspense mounts as the trap closes around her. After alternating scenes of hope and despair, Virginius is ordered by the court to give his daughter into the custody of Claudius. He asks permission to bid her farewell and, at the end, dramatically stabs her.

> Farewel, my sweet *Virginia;* never, never
> Shall I taste fruit of the most blessed hope
> I had in thee. Let me forget the thought
> Of thy most pretty infancy, when first
> Returning from the Wars, I took delight
> To rock thee in my Target; when my Girl
> Would kiss her father in his burganet
> Of glittering steel hung 'bout his armed neck;
> And viewing the bright mettal, smile to see
> Another fair *Virginia* smile on thee:
> When first I taught thee how to go, to speak:
> And when my wounds have smarted, I have sung
> With an unskilful, yet a willing voice,
> To bring my Girl asleep. O my *Virginia,*
> When we begun to be, begun our woes,
> Increasing still, as dying life still growes.
> *App[ius].* This tediousness doth much offend the Court.
> Silence: attend her Sentence.
> *Virg[inius].* Hold, without Sentence I'l resign her freely,
> Since you will prove her to be none of mine.
> *App[ius].* See, see, how evidently Truth appears.
> Receive her, *Clodius.*
> *Virg[inius].* Thus I surrender her into the Court
>   , [*Kills her.*
> Of all the Gods. And see, proud *Appius,* see
> Although not justly, I have made her free.
> But if thy Lust with this Act be not fed,
> Bury her in thy bowels now shee's dead.[10]

This speech pathetically depicts the contrast between the tranquillity of family life and the corruption of the official cruelty of Appius and

[10] *Ibid.,* pp. 207–8; IV, i, 321–47.

Claudius. After the death of Virginia, Virginius flees to the country. There he finds his soldiers, who urge him to lead an army against the wicked judges. In this way, Webster seems to indicate that since Virginius had been appointed to overthrow the tyrant, he could escape the consequences of the sin of rebellion.

The revolt soon succeeds, and Appius and Claudius are tried for the murder of Virginia. When they are brought before Virginia's body, it bleeds,[11] and Appius realizes his guilt, confessing in a "scaffold speech" which closes thus:

> Judges are term'd
> The Gods on earth; and such as are corrupt
> Read me in this my ruine. Those that succeed me
> That so offend, thus punish. This the sum of all,
> *Appius* that sin'd, by *Appius*' hand shall fall.
>   [*Kils himself.*[12]

The conclusion of this play, in which the actions of the protagonist vitally affect affairs of state, resembles orthodox more than domestic tragedy. Four acts of the play, however, present a family situation whose outcome only by chance involves affairs of state.

In *Appius and Virginia,* Webster reveals an aristocratic viewpoint, for at the end Appius, who is a true Roman, dies bravely. The lowborn Marcus Claudius, lacking courage to use the proffered sword, comes to a coward's end on the scaffold. Webster indicates that persons who rise above their stations are often prey to passions of the lowborn; it takes a great character like Virginius to withstand the temptation to abuse power. While Appius as nominal hero allows the play to conform roughly to the classical ideas of tragedy, Virginia has only nobility of character on her side, so that the work is equally a tragedy of the people. Quite probably there was no very clearly formed aesthetic theory in Webster's mind as he wrote this play, which contained elements of both domestic and orthodox tragedy. It seems clear, however, that this story would, from the classical point of view, have been an extremely dubious if not impossible subject for tragedy.

II

A story which violated all the classical rules for tragedy is the German legend of Fortunatus and his sons. Dekker, who employed the

---

[11] *Ibid.,* p. 221; v, ii, 98–103.   [12] *Ibid.,* p. 222; V, ii, 140–44.

story in his *Old Fortunatus* (1599),[13] made from it a comedy, light-hearted, fanciful, and gay. As a comedy it was entered in the Stationers' Register. However, the basic story of the fall of Fortunatus and his children is almost pure domestic tragedy. The early versions clearly recognize this fact. Dekker's source was a story in the German *Volksbuch* of 1509. Of this account, the German Meistersinger, Hans Sachs, had made a tragedy in 1553.[14] In Sachs's version, Fortunatus, the son of a nobleman, has by his prodigal existence reduced himself to penury. The goddess Fortune offers him the choice of wisdom, strength, health, beauty, long life, or riches. He chooses the last and receives an enchanted purse. By a trick he wins a magic hat which has the power to transport the wearer anywhere in the twinkling of an eye. After several adventures, he dies without regret for the life he has led. His two sons quarrel for the possession of the purse and the hat, and the one who gets both speedily loses them and his life as well.

In Dekker's version, Fortunatus has always been a beggar. Suddenly Fortune, out of sheer caprice, raises him to riches. Since he has chosen the most worldly of all the gifts, his punishment is as inexorable as that in any of the morality plays. Dekker's interest in common men enabled him to draw an understanding portrait of the beggar bedazzled by the turn of fate, but he does not allow this understanding to soften his condemnation of the man for having chosen badly. Fortunatus, cast down by Fortune at the peak of his happiness, is hardly a ludicrous figure, for he realizes his folly and repents his error. His last thought is to save his sons from a similar fate. His efforts are unsuccessful, however, for his children quickly come to grief. Ampedo, the more intelligent of the two sons, burns the wishing hat, saying:

> . . . as this doth perish,
> So shall the other [the magic purse]; count what good and bad
> They both have wrought, the good is to the ill
> As a small pebble to a mighty hill.[15]

Andolecia, the other son, at the time of his death realizes his errors and repents fervently in a scene not intentionally comic.

[13] The 1599 edition may be a revision of a two-part *Fortunatus* play, possibly by Greene, which the Admiral's Company put on in 1596. See Chambers, *op. cit.*, III, 291.

[14] Hans Sachs, *Tragodia*, mit 22 Personen, der Fortunatus mit dem Wünschsackel und hat, VII Actus, in *Hans Sachs*, ed. Johann Gustav Büsching, II, 73–124.

[15] Thomas Dekker, *Old Fortunatus*, ed. Oliphant Smeaton, p. 114; V, ii, 77–80.

Fortune, forgive me! I deserve thy hate;
Myself have made myself a reprobate.
Virtue, forgive me! for I have transgressed
Against thy laws; my vows are quite forgot,
And therefore shame is fallen to my sin's lot.
Riches and knowledge are two gifts divine.
They that abuse them both as I have done,
To shame, to beggary, to hell must run.
O conscience, hold thy sting, cease to afflict me.
Be quick, tormentors, I desire to die;
No death is equal to my misery.
Cyprus, vain world and vanity, farewell.
Who builds his Heaven on earth, is sure of hell.[16]

The play continues the purposes and improves the methods of the old moralities. In these homiletic dramas, the bitter philosophic pill is covered with clowning, buffoonery, and other trappings whose entertainment value surpasses their instructive worth. In the final judgment scene, as Virtue ousts Vice and relegates Fortune to her proper sphere, the moral is directed to the audience.

Although *Old Fortunatus* is a conglomeration of many elements, the basic story of the fall of Fortunatus and his sons is essentially a domestic tragedy, even though Dekker chose to call the play a comedy. So carefully are the moral and serious elements worked into the structure of the comedy that they can easily be missed in a casual reading. Although the work may appear comic to the reader, its intellectual outline follows that developed in the moralities and carried on in the Elizabethan tragedies of domestic incident.

III

The history of England with its chronicles of rebels and popular heroes furnished several dramatists with materials for tragedies of common life. Occasionally the king who gives his name to a chronicle-history play has less dramatic importance than other members of the cast. The everyday characteristics of all classes of persons are presented appealingly. In these plays, historical verisimilitude is disregarded as citizens talk and act like Elizabethan Londoners; the kings themselves frequently slough the dignity, the pomp and circumstance, which in-

---

[16] *Ibid.*, p. 118; V, ii, 185–97.

variably attend them in classic plays. In such a commonplace world, the tragic fate of a person of low degree is as much a matter of course as any other circumstance of life.

Seldom do chronicle-history plays present a sustained and integrated plot either of comic or tragic proportions. The life of a king is used as the framework for a series of events which may or may not be related in cause and effect, but which took place in his reign. Comedy, tragedy, pathos, court intrigue, mingle without coherence of plot structure. Among the elements which made up this haphazard jumble were rudimentary domestic tragedies—specimens of the form highly significant in its development which have been generally overlooked by previous investigators in the field. Singer [17] makes no mention of any of these plays, although he discusses works which have less claim to be called domestic tragedy than several of the chronicle histories.

A popular story was that of the commoner who misguidedly attempted to redress his wrongs by armed rebellion. An early example of this kind of play is the anonymous *The Life and Death of Jack Straw* (1591). The play tells of a rebellion which took place in the reign of Richard II. Jack Straw is represented as a peaceful citizen provoked by an overzealous tax-collector. Jack enlists the sympathy of the audience by telling the officious agent,

> For I am sure thy office doth not arm thee with such authority,
> Thus to abuse the poor people of the country.[18]

Words pass quickly to blows, and the officer is slain. Jack, as fugitive from justice, leads a rebellion to right the wrongs of himself and his class, but he soon loses the sympathy of the audience by his highhanded conduct, his arrogance, and his unwillingness to listen to reason. He becomes wild with ambition and filled with pride, only to fall cringing. The action follows the familiar pattern of presenting the disaster which overcomes anyone who dares to revolt against God's agent, the king.

The story of Jack Cade has been considered in the discussion of *The Mirror for Magistrates*. It is told again, unsympathetically, in the second part of Shakespeare's *Henry VI*,[19] where Cade is presented as an errant knave who richly deserves his fate. The moral and political

---

[17] Hans Wolfgang Singer, *Das bürgerliche Trauerspiel in England.*

[18] *The Life and Death of Jack Straw*, in W. C. Hazlitt, *Dodsley's Old Plays*, V, 380; I, i, 14–15.

[19] 2 *Henry VI*, IV, ii–x.

lesson is identical with that in *The Mirror*. Shakespeare's treatment of the rebel contains nothing remotely resembling the tragic. In order to reinforce the moral, he made Cade a loutish, swaggering bully. Shakespeare shows contempt for Cade only because he is a common man endeavoring to usurp political functions. His ready sympathy for the misfortunes of ordinary citizens is well revealed in *3 Henry VI* where he depicts the grief of a son who has killed his father and of a father who has killed his son.[20]

A play by Robert Daborne entitled *A Christian Turn'd Turk; or, The Tragical Lives and Deaths of the Two Famous Pirates, Ward and Dansiker*, of 1610, described the lives of figures notorious in popular history. The work deals with the entire career of a man, rather than merely the end of his life. The author makes some effort to emphasize the tragic features, and in the prologue he attempts to justify the material as being, after all, worthy of tragedy.

> All faire content dwell here, & may our straines
> Giue you that choice delight which crownes our paines.
> Our subiect's low, yet to your eyes presents
> Deeds high in bloud, in bloud of Innocents.[21]

The close of the play contains a moral admonition of the sort rarely lacking in domestic tragedies. Daborne realized that his hero, Ward, had lived too unusual a life to make an effective example for his audience, so he was careful to make the moral general in application. Ward says:

> All you that liue by theft and Piracies,
> That sell your liues and soules to purchase graues,
> That dye to hell, and liue farre worse than slaues,
> Let dying *Ward* tell you that heauen is iust.
> And that dispaire attends on bloud and lust.[22]

The hero of the story, although his adventures were remarkable, was a man drawn from the common people. His recognition of the operation of divine justice reinforces the author's lesson.

A story of more interest to writers than the lives of notorious pirates was that of the famous Jane Shore, the mistress of Edward IV. Her

[20] *3 Henry VI*, II, v, 55–122.

[21] Robert Daborne, *A Christian Turn'd Turk*, ed. A. E. H. Swaen, in *Anglia*, XX, 189.

[22] *Ibid.*, p. 255.

tragedy, appearing in the 1563 edition of *The Mirror for Magistrates*, relates how Jane was "required" by the king and how on his death she was constrained by Richard III to do public penance. Her repentance was used to emphasize the moral of the story.

The events of Jane Shore's life were dramatized in part or in full several times during the Elizabethan period. Usually her feminine charm, her kindliness, her homely virtues (except the one of chastity), are all stressed to win sympathy for her. She so fascinated Heywood that she, more than anyone else, is the central character of his *Edward IV*.

Her story makes its first appearance in literature in Sir Thomas More's *The History of King Richard the Third*.

Now then by and by, as it were for anger not for covetise, the Protector sent into the house of Shore's wife . . . and spoiled her of all that ever she had, above the value of two or three thousand marks, and sent her body to prison. . . . And for this cause (as a goodly continent prince, clean and faultless of himself, sent out of heaven into this vicious world for the amendment of men's manners) he caused the Bishop of London to put her to open penace, going before the cross in procession upon a Sunday with a taper in her hand. In which she went in countenance and pace demure so womanly, and albeit she were out of all array save her kirtle only, yet went she so fair and lovely, namely while the wondering of the people cast a comely rud in her cheeks . . . that her great shame won her much praise, among those that were more amourous of her body than curious of her soul. And many good folk also that hated her living, and glad were to see sin corrected, yet pitied they more her penance, than rejoiced therein, when they considered that the protector procured it, more of a corrupt intent then any virtuous affection. This woman was born in London, worshipfully friended, honestly brought up, and very well married, saving somewhat too soon, her husband an honest citizen, young and goodly and of good substance. But forasmuch as they were coupled ere she were well ripe, she not very fervently loved for whom she never longed. Which was happely the thing that the more easily made her incline unto the king's appetite when he required her. Howbeit, the respect of his royalty, the hope of gay apparel, ease, pleasure, and other wanton wealth, was able soon to pierce a soft tender heart. But when the king had abused her, anon her husband (as he was an honest man and one that could his good, not presuming to touch a king's concubine) left her up to him all together. When the king died, the Lord Chamberlain took her. Which in the kings days, albeit he was sore enamored upon her, yet he forbare her. . . . Proper she was and fair; nothing in her body that you would have changed, but if you would have wished her somewhat higher. Thus say they that knew her in her youth. Albeit some that now see her (for yet she liveth) deem her never to have been well visaged. Whose judgement seemeth me somewhat like as though men should guess the beauty of one long before departed by her scalp taken out of the charnel house; for now is she old, lean, withered, and dried up, nothing left but riviled skin and hard bone. And yet being even such whoso well advise her visage, might guess and divise which parts how filled, would make it a fair face. Yet delighted not men so much in her beauty, as in her pleasant behaviour. For a proper wit had she, and could both read well and write, merry in company, ready and quick of answer, neither mute nor full of babble, sometimes taunting without displeasure and not without disport. . . . she never abused to any man's hurt, but to many a man's comfort and relief; where the king took displeasure, she would mitigate and appease his mind; where men were out of favour, she would bring them in his grace. For many that had highly offended, she obtained pardon. Of great forfeitures, she got men remission. And finally in many weighty suits, she stood many men in great stead, either for none or very small rewards, and those rather gay than rich, either for that she was content with the deed's self well done, or for that she delighted to be sued unto, and to show what she was able to do with the king, or for that wanton women and wealthy be not always covetous. I doubt not some shall think this woman too slight a thing to be written of and set among the remembrances of great matters, which they shall specially think, that happely shall esteem her only by that they now see her. But me seemeth the chance so much the more worthy to be remembered, in how much she is now in the more beggarly condition, unfriended and worn out of acquaintance, after good substance, after as great favour with the prince, after as great suit and seeking to with all those that those days had business to speed, as many other men were in their times, which be now famous, only by the infamy of their ill deeds. Her doings were not much less, albeit they be much less remembered, because they were not so evil. For men use if they have an evil turn, to write it in marble; and whoso doth us a good turn, we write it in dust which is not worst proved by her, for at this day she beggeth of many at this day living, that at this day had begged if she had not been.[23]

Holinshed repeated this version of the story almost verbatim in his *Chronicles*. More's apology for including the story of Jane Shore in

---

[23] *The Hiſtory of King Richard the Thirde (Vnfiniſhed) Writen by Maſter Thomas More*, in *The English Works of Sir Thomas More*, reproduced in facsimile from William Rastell's edition of 1577, ed. W. E. Campbell and A. W. Reed, pp. 56–57. The text in this quotation has been modernized for ease of reading.

his history shows that he, as a good humanist, felt that historical and tragic persons should possess a proper dignity and prominence. He finally admits her because he pities her weakness and because he feels that her story is a good moral example. His treatment of her as a woman whose good deeds offset her sins and whose great troubles win her universal pity sets the pattern for the subsequent versions of her story. The tale as told by More and as repeated by Holinshed appears to have been the source of the plays dealing with Jane Shore. Later dramatists drew freely on their imaginations to fill in the details of the outline as given by Sir Thomas More.

Jane Shore is mentioned in several plays in which she is not the protagonist. In a few of these her story serves as an interlude to draw tears from the audience, to give them a respite from the grim machinations of Richard the Third, to intensify his villainy by giving him a helpless victim whom he persecutes for spite, or to enforce the lesson that riches won by sin and lust will vanish in time and that good deeds will not, in the end, save one from the consequences of sin. None of the works denies Jane spiritual salvation; all suggest she may achieve it, partly because of her kindliness, but primarily because of her repentance and public penance.

The earliest play to contain Jane Shore as a character is a university Latin play, *Richardus Tertius*, by Thomas Legge, acted at St. John's College, Cambridge, in March, 1579 / 80. Here she appears only once. Clad in a white sheet and carrying a candle in token of her repentance, she plods her doleful way across the stage as part of the ceremony of public penance. Several times characters mention her in terms of greatest contempt,[24] but no effort is made to arouse pity for her. Her death is not even shown, for after the procession she disappears, to be heard of no more.

In the anonymous play, *The True Tragedy of Richard the Third* (c. 1590), famous as the basis for Shakespeare's *Richard III*, Jane appears as a character deserving sympathy. She comes on stage twice, once when she learns of the death of Edward IV and again after the proclamation of Richard III ordering the imprisonment of any man who should give her charity. On her first appearance she is obviously intended to win the favor of the audience, for she is now alone, unpro-

---

[24] Thomas Legge, "*The True Tragedy of Richard the Third*," *to Which Is Appended the Latin Play of "Richardus Tertius,"* ed. Barron Field, pp. 102, 105, 107.

tected, and at the mercy of Richard. Her second entrance shows the
depth to which she has fallen. She regrets that she has caused her husband pain and hopes that he will eventually forgive her. She then seeks
aid from those she has helped. Lodowick, whose lands she had saved
from confiscation by Edward IV, spurns her. So does a citizen whose
son she had saved from the gallows. Even servants refuse to help her;
at last a page calls her a whore, and she says:

> And all such vsurping kings as thy Lord is, may come
> to a shamefull end, which no doubt I may liue yet to see. Ther-
> fore sweet God, forgiue all my foule offence:
> And though I haue done wickedly in this world,
> Into hell fire, let not my soule be hurld.[25]

Her death is not presented in the play. The author rather chooses to
follow history in emphasizing the misery of her life. In spite of the
lack of immediate punishment, the familiar devices of moral literature
all appear. Jane confesses her fault, repents her evil life, asks for forgiveness, and goes to suffer her fate as decreed by Providence. The
authors of later plays deviated from history to present her death as a
result of the action of the play. The death scene served both dramatic
and moral purposes, providing an emotional climax and affording a
complete example of God's retributive justice. In Heywood's play the
moral element is suggested by the phrase in the title, "an example for
all wicked women." Although emotionally the reader is invited to feel
sorry for Jane, intellectually he is reminded that she must suffer for
the heinous sin of adultery.

IV

Jane Shore's story received its most extended treatment in Thomas
Heywood's *Edward IV*, a chronicle history. In a fashion characteristic
of this type of play, the tale of Shore's wife is interspersed with many
episodes of state and of humble life. Mistress Shore's part, however,
is more than episodic, for she first appears early in the play and finally
disappears only in the last act of the second part. Thus for ten acts she
remains a prominent person in the minds of the audience. After the
first act of Part II, her story dominates the action. Heywood seems to
have exerted every effort to make her a tragic heroine. His departure
from history to show her death filled the double purpose of providing

[25] *The True Tragedie of Richard the Third*, ll. 1184–88, Malone Society Reprints.

a pathetic death scene and reinforcing the moral lesson of the play. In
An Apology for Actors (1612), Heywood insisted on the moral purpose of art, a view consistent with his dramatic practice.

. . . because playes are writ with this ayme, and carried with this methode,
to teach their subjects obedience to their king, to shew the people the untimely ends of such as have moved tumults, commotions, and insurrections.
. . . If a morall, it is to perswade men to humanity and good life, to instruct them in civility and good manners, shewing them the fruits of honesty,
and the end of villainy. . . .

Briefly, there is neither tragedy, history, comedy, morrall, or pastorall,
from which an infinite use cannot be gathered. . . . We present men
with the ugliness of their vices to make them the more to abhorre them. . . .
The unchaste are by us shewed their errors in the persons of Phryne, Lais,
Thais, Flora; and amongst us Rosamond and Mistresse Shore.[26]

Like many of Heywood's plays, *Edward IV* contains praise of the
citizen class of England. When London is attacked by the rebel Falconbridge, the citizens called upon to rally to its defense reveal qualities
of heroism not customarily accorded to anyone below the peerage. An
apprentice tells the lord mayor of London:

> Nay, ſcorn vs not that we are prentices.
> The Chronicles of *England* can report
> What memorable actions we haue done,
> To which this daies achieuement ſhall be knit,
> To make the volume larger than it is.[27]

Heywood earnestly condemns the traitors who rise against their king,
but he praises the ordinary citizens who attempt to lead upright lives
in obedience to the laws of church and state.

Although Heywood's dramatic technique in parts of this play is indeed slipshod, he exhibits much skill in his manner of introducing Jane
Shore. The rebel, Falconbridge, has heard of her beauty and hopes to
make her his personal prize. With superb dramatic irony, Heywood
has her turn to her husband when she hears the remarks of Falconbridge and promise:

> Were I by a thouſand ſtormes of fortune toſt,
> And ſhould indure the pooreſt wretched life,

---

[26] Thomas Heywood, *An Apology for Actors*, ed. J. P. Collier, pp. 53–57.
[27] *The Firſt and Second Parts of King Edward the Fourth*, in *The Dramatic
Works of Thomas Heywood*, 1874 ed., I, 18.

> Yet *Jane* will be thy honeſt loyal wife.
> The greateſt prince the Sunne did euer ſee,
> Shall neuer make me proue vntrue to thee.[28]

Master Shore has performed so valiantly in the defense of London that the king offers him a knighthood. Shore declines, preferring not to be raised so far above his station. The king then congratulates him on his fair wife and says that he will remember the Shore family. Matthew and his wife both have cause to regret the excellence of the king's memory. The special pains taken with the dramatic preparation indicate the importance to Heywood's mind of the Jane Shore story.

After the defeat of Falconbridge and the subsequent visit of the king to Hob, the Tanner, the story of Jane Shore gets under way. Heywood devotes much time to the efforts of King Edward to bend Mistress Shore to his will. A neighbor, Mistress Blague, from whom Jane seeks advice, paints a tempting picture of the pleasures and power that will be hers if she accedes to the king's desire, but ends each statement with the refrain:

> Yet I will not be ſhe ſhall counſel ye:
> Good Miſtriſs *Shore*, do what ye will for me.[29]

These lines serve the dramatic purpose of implanting Mistress Blague's unworthiness in the minds of the audience and of preparing them to accept her repudiation of Jane and her theft of the money which Jane has brought from the court.

When Jane agrees to accept the king's favors, she is represented not as a creature of lust or pleasure, but as one caught by forces beyond her control. Fully conscious of her sin, she bows to the will of her sovereign.

> *King.* But, leauing this our enigmatick talke,
> Thou muſt ſweete *Jane*, repaire vnto the Court.
> His tongue intreates, controuls the greateſt peer:
> His hand plights loue, a royall ſceptre holds;
> And in his heart he hath confirmd thy good,
> Which may not, muſt not, ſhall not be withstood.
> *Jane.* If you inforce me, I haue nought to ſay;
> But wiſh I had not liued to ſee this day.
> *King.* Blame not the time. Thou ſhalt haue cauſe to joy!

---

[28] *Ibid.*, p. 24.   [29] *Ibid.*, p. 74.

> *Jane*, in the euening I will fend for thee,
> And thou and thine fhall be aduanced by me:
> In fign whereof, receiue this true-loue kiffe.
> Nothing ill meant, there can be no amiffe.   *Exit.*
>   *Jane.* Well, I will in; and ere the time beginne,
> Learne how to be repentant for my finne.[30]

This reason for the yielding of Jane is not presented in the earlier plays on the subject, and there is only a hint of it in *The Mirror for Magistrates*. It receives more extensive development in Heywood's version than in any other. However, even here, the circumstances do not extenuate her fault, for stern Christian morality demands harsh punishment for adultery. Jane soon begins to reap the consequences of her sin, for her husband spurns her and casts her off. He decides to leave England lest anyone say he is benefiting by his wife's dishonor. He deeds his property to his brother-in-law, saying:

> *Franke Emerfley!* my wife thy fifter was;
> Lands, goods, and all I haue, to thee I paffe,
> Saue that poor portion, muft along with me,
> To beare me from this badge of obloquy.
> It neuer fhall be faid that *Matthew Shore*
> A kings difhonor in his bonnet wore.[31]

By a fortuitous dramatic coincidence, as Matthew Shore is about to embark on his voyages, he meets Jane, who has come to help various petitioners who have sought her aid. This scene serves the double purpose of dramatizing Jane's Christian charity and kindliness and of becoming the *scène à faire* of Part I of the play. She pleads with her husband to accept her as his wife once again, vowing to give up the riches and pomp she has won and to be true to him from that time forward. Matthew, however, refuses to take back a king's concubine, although he is quite willing to pray for her soul's salvation. He remains steadfast in his resolution to leave England.

The first act of Part II is devoted to Edward's conquest of France; that disposed of, the play picks up the story of Jane, using the device of a chorus to make the transition.

> King *Edward* is returned home to *England*,
> And *Lewis*, King of *France*, foon afterward

---

[30] *Ibid.*, p. 76.   [31] *Ibid.*, p. 79.

> Surprized both his ſubtil enemies,
> Rewarding them with traiterous recompence.
> Now do we draw the curtain of our Scene,
> To ſpeake of *Shore* and his faire wife againe,
> With other matters thereupon depending.
> You muſt imagine ſince you ſaw him laſt
> Preparde for trauaile, he hath been abroade,
> And ſeene the ſundry faſhions of the world,
> *Vlyſſes*-like, his countries loue at length,
> Hoping his wiues death, and to ſee his friends,
> Such as did ſorrow for his great miſhaps,
> Come home is hee; but ſo vnluckily,
> As he is like to looſe his life thereby.
> His and her fortunes ſhall we now perſue,
> Gracde with your gentle ſufferance and view.[32]

After various adventures in the war, Matthew Shore finds himself in an English prison. He had taken passage on an English ship which captured a French vessel as a prize of war. On arriving at port, he and his shipmates were dumbfounded to learn that a peace had been concluded and that in capturing this ship they were guilty of piracy. He has chosen Matthew Flood as a *nom de guerre,* and his identity is unknown to his associates. Jane, pursuing her good works, comes to the prison to seek to ameliorate the condition of the prisoners. The release of these unfortunates is the last favor she is able to win from the king, for the news quickly follows that Edward is seriously ill. At his death, Jane, realizing full well the strength of her enemies in court, spends little time in vain weeping, but quickly arranges to have most of her property transported to Mistress Blague's "Flower-de-Lice" Inn in Lombard Street. Mistress Blague receives her with every evidence of affection and good will, assuring Jane that she will always look after her. She also gives her false news of her husband's death.

In the meantime, still under the alias of Flood, Shore has been injured in the defense of the princes in the Tower and has sought refuge with Mistress Blague. As Jane is tending his wounds, still not recognizing him, the news comes of the sentence imposed on her by Richard III.

> The King, in euery ſtreet
> Of London and in euery borough town

---

[32] *Ibid.,* pp. 119–20.

Throughout this land, hath publikely proclaimed,
On paine of death, that none fhall harbour you,
Or giue you foods or clothes to keepe you warme;
But hauing firft done fhameful penance here,
You fhall be then thruft forth the city-gates
Into the naked cold, forfaken field.[33]

From this point, Jane's fall is rapid. Mistress Blague appropriates the goods left in trust with her. At the same time she upbraids the unfortunate woman for having pursued the very course which she herself had recommended. She freely admits that she is an opportunist when taxed by Jane for inconsistency.

Bla[gue]. I but you haue been a wicked liuer,
And now you fee what tis to be vnchafte:
You fhould haue kept you with your honeft hufband:
'Twas neuer other like but that fuch like filthineffe
Would haue a foule and detestable end.
Jane. Time was that you did tell me otherwife,
And ftudied how to fet a gloffe on that,
Which now you fay is vgly and deformde.
Bla[gue]. I told you then as then the time did ferue,
And more, indeed, to try your difpofition,
Than any way to encourage you to finne.
But when I faw you were ambitious,
And faintly ftood on tearmes of modefty,
I left you to your own arbiterment.
Can you deny it was not fo? how fay you?[34]

Mistress Blague, however, fails to enjoy her ill-gotten gains, for the money is quickly confiscated. Jane, moved by Christian spirit, forgives her.

From the time of her debasement to her death, Heywood seizes every opportunity to win sympathy for his heroine. The extremity of her penalty, her past generosity, her fortitude in adversity, her Christian forgiveness of those who have brought about her downfall, her very real repentance for her sin, her realization that she must be punished, her humility, her graciousness and kindliness—all those are exploited to their fullest extent. Matthew Shore undergoes a similar process of elevation in dramatic importance. At the end of the play,

[33] *Ibid.*, p. 158.   [34] *Ibid.*, p. 160.

three persons of common station all meet death: Jane, her husband, and Ayre, whom Jane had befriended and who had bravely succored her in her time of need. Ayre and Matthew Shore are apprehended for their acts of Christian charity and are condemned. When Shore reveals his identity, he is pardoned, but Ayre's sentence is confirmed. Ayre is willing to die, he says, for Mistress Shore has saved his life. Before his wife's death, Matthew reveals himself to her and forgives her. The dramatist implies that by her repentance, rather than by her good works, she is saved.

  Shore. Jane, be content. Our woes are now alike.
With one felf rod thou feeft God doth vs ftrike.
If for thy fin, ile pray to heauen for thee,
And if for mine, do thou as much for me.
  Jane. Ah, *Shore* ift poffible thou canft forgiue me?
  Shore. Yes, *Jane*, I do.
  Jane. I cannot hope thou wilt.
My faults fo great, that I cannot expect it.
  Shore. Ifaith, I do, as freely from my foule,
As at Gods hands I hope to be forgiuen.
  Jane. Then God reward thee, for we now muft part:
I feel cold death doth feize vpon my heart.
     . . . .

  Shore. Oh, happy graue! to us this comfort giuing!
Here lies two liuing dead! here one dead liuing!
Here for his fake, lo! this we do for thee!
Thou lookft for one, and art poffeft of three.
  Jane. Oh, dying marriage! oh, fweet married death
Thou graue, which only fhouldft part faithful friends,
Bringft vs togither, and doft joine our hands.
Oh, liuing death! euen in this dying life,
Yet, ere I go, once, *Matthew* kifs thy wife.
     He kiffeth her, and fhe dies.
  Shore. Ah, my fweet *Jane* farewell, farewell, poor foul!
Now, tyrant *Richard* do the worft thou canft.
She doth defie thee. Oh, vnconftant world,
Here lies a true anatomie of thee,
A king had all my ioy, that her enioyed,
And by a king again fhe was deftroyed.
All ages of my kingly woes fhall tell.

> Once more, inconſtant world farewell, farewell.
>   *He dyes.*[35]

The deaths of Matthew and his wife really conclude the play, although another scene follows to complete the affairs of state. This seems tacked on as an afterthought. Even a portion of this scene returns to the Shore situation, reporting to Richard the deaths of Matthew, Jane, and Ayre. There is no doubt that, from the point of view of dramatic emphasis, the deaths of Jane and Matthew Shore are intended to be the catastrophe of the play. The last moments of Matthew and his wife are given far more emotional emphasis than even the strangling of the princes in the Tower.

Throughout the play, emphasis is laid on the gentle virtues of Jane, virtues of common humanity. Her kindliness, consideration, and generosity, all established before she leaves her husband's house, are continued through the days of her affluence, during her poverty, and to the moment of death. Her behavior is contrasted favorably with that of higher-born court favorites and with citizens of her own social rank. Her good qualities, in other words, are personal attributes, not those characteristic of any particular class. By these virtues Jane stands apart from the common herd of people as surely as though she had come of a long lineage of noble ancestors. It is because she possesses virtues in a higher degree than other persons of any social class that she meets many of the requirements of a tragic heroine. Heywood has learned how to replace eminence of birth with eminence of character.

Professor Brooke points out that in their divergence from the realities of history the two parts of this play present minor figures and events to the exclusion of important national personages and happenings. "To enroll the former works [the two parts of *Edward IV*] among serious history plays would be as great an impertinence as to catalogue 'A Tale of Two Cities' among the histories of the French Revolution." [36] The cavalier treatment of nationally significant events of the reign of Edward IV resulted from the author's desire to stress domestic affairs, the activities of the common people, rather than the affairs of state. In addition to employing Jane Shore, king's mistress and wife of a goldsmith, as protagonist of a ten-act play, Heywood has, whenever possible, stripped the king of his royal trappings in

---

[35] *Ibid.*, pp. 182–83.   [36] C. F. Tucker Brooke, *The Tudor Drama*, p. 344.

order to depict him primarily as a man. However, he does not maintain this point of view consistently. He represents the king's campaign in France, for example, by employing all the familiar paraphernalia of the drum and trumpet chronicle-history play. But throughout much of the action, he emphasizes the qualities which make Edward the king a human being. The audience saw a king who laughed, joked, made merry, reveled, bussed a wench, and sang a lusty song in a manner they could relish. During the first scene of the play, in which his mother reproaches him for marrying beneath him, Edward refuses to consider matters of state. He jokes in a slightly bawdy fashion calculated to gain the approval of the groundlings. Though most of the characters speak blank verse, he rambles on in lighthearted prose. In his dealings with Hob, the Tanner, he is accepted without question as a butler; no trace of the king's regal majesty shines through his humble livery. Similarly in his wooing of Jane, the fact that he is the king gives him power to exact her compliance, but does not give him the charm to win her affection.

One of the characteristics of early domestic tragedy was that the fate of its protagonist seldom affected the larger social and political world to which he belonged. This is often made the distinction between domestic and orthodox tragedy. In the latter, the demise of the protagonist is fraught with consequences to the nation, to the world, and to the gods; in the former, the death of the hero affects only himself and those within his domestic circle. Although *Edward IV* is ostensibly a history play, it possesses many characteristics of domestic tragedy. To be sure, Heywood could not avoid the political consequences of the death of Edward; but the fate of Jane Shore, purely a domestic matter, is given more attention. To see these events in proper historical perspective, it is only necessary to examine Shakespeare's *Richard III*, which presents the death of Edward IV, but almost completely omits Jane Shore from consideration.[37]

In his treatment of Jane Shore's story, Heywood departed from historical fact in several ways significant for the development of domestic tragedy. The most obvious change was the presentation of the deaths of Jane and her husband. Actually she lived until about 1527, many years after the deaths of the other personages of the story, becoming the mistress of several men and remaining unregenerate to the

[37] Shakespeare, *Richard III*, III, iv, 72.

end of her days. Heywood's alteration of the story as he found it in More, in Holinshed, and in his dramatic predecessors indicates that he was willing to suppress any facts which might cost her the sympathy of the audience. It shows his acceptance of the stern morality which demanded death for her sin, but which allowed the salvation of her soul if she would repent. Heywood implies that her good works did not offset her sin, but that her contrite repentance saved her. In accordance with his moral purpose, he causes her to turn to religion as soon as she has been cast out of the court.

> Maſter Lieutanant! in my heart I thank ye
> For this kind comfort to a wretched ſoul.
> Welcome, ſweet prayer-book, food of my life,
> The ſoueraign balm for my ſick conſcience.
> Thou ſhalt be my ſouls pleaſure and delight,
> To wipe my ſins out of *Jehovaes* ſight.[38]

Shore, after he has revealed himself, tells her:

> *Jane*, be content. Our woes are now alike.
> With one ſelf rod thou ſeeſt God doth vs ſtrike.
> If for thy ſin, ile pray to heauen for thee,
> And if for mine, do thou as much for me.[39]

Jane's death following her reconciliation with her husband carries out the moral intention of the play. Shore, by refusing to take her once more as his wife, forgoes the chance to save both Jane and himself. What he could forgive in a dying woman he could not pardon in a living wife. Morality required that she die forgiven and penitent in order that her soul might be saved in the next world. Heywood avoids the sentimentality of an easy forgiveness in the interests of Christian justice.

The presence of Matthew Shore helps to hold this play on the plane of domestic tragedy. He is the strictest moralist in the drama, for he will accept no favors won through his wife's new-found influence; he will have nothing to do with her during the time of her prosperity. In this respect Heywood followed his source. But Shore's return, Jane's saving of his life, his eventual care of her, and his death at her side are all inventions of Heywood. The reconciliation between Shore

---

[38] *Edward IV*, in *The Dramatic Works of Thomas Heywood*, 1874 ed., I, 167.
[39] *Ibid.*, p. 182.

and his wife was the obligatory scene in the moral play, for as a good Christian Matthew could not withhold pardon when it was earnestly and penitently sought. Their deaths gave a conclusion satisfactory both to the average theatergoer and to the moralist.

Thus in *Edward IV*, Heywood wrote a chronicle-history play in which he devoted little attention to matters of state. He selected as the central interest of this involved ten-act play the fortunes and misfortunes of Jane Shore, the wife of a commoner, the mistress of the king. Neither the death of Edward IV nor the murder of the princes in the Tower, but the last moments of Mistress Shore and her husband form the catastrophe of the drama. The theme of the work is based, not on policies of state or lessons of political conduct, but on Christian morality. The religious doctrine and the aesthetic ideas that underlie this play are those at the root of the other domestic tragedies of Tudor and Stuart times.

The authors of these plays taken from history and legend may have made little conscious effort to write domestic tragedy. In many cases, for the sake of dramatic contrast, the playwrights chose a hero from the ranks of the common people. The rebels, Jack Straw and Jack Cade, are presented without sympathy. "It goes without saying that the downtrodden multitude is never allowed the right to revolt against bad government; the poet condemns rebellion in the sternest manner, even when it has been brought about, as in the anonymous play of *Jack Straw*, by the pressure of unendurable tyranny." [40] Royal tyranny explained but did not justify Jack Straw's revolt. The rebellion was both a crime against one's king and a sin against God.

Plays of folk origin, such as *Old Fortunatus*, through homely examples offer moral lessons to unsophisticated people. The story of Jane Shore effectively combined pathos, human interest, entertainment, and moral instruction. Previous discussions of domestic tragedy have included none of the plays considered in this chapter. For several reasons, however, they have a place in the history of the development of the genre. First, the protagonists of all of these works come from the humbler ranks of society. Second, the plays continue and develop the moral instruction characteristic of both dramatic and nondramatic homiletic literature. This moralizing, directed so plainly at the middle

---

[40] Wilhelm Creizenach, *The English Drama in the Age of Shakespeare*, translated [by Cécile Hugon] from *Geschichte des neueren Dramas*, p. 131.

classes of England, while rare in the orthodox tragedies, exists in high degree in all domestic tragedies of the Elizabethan, Jacobean, and Caroline periods. Third, the fate of the protagonist in these plays is usually unrelated to great affairs of state. His death is important only to his own limited society. The one exception to this rule occurs in Webster's *Appius and Virginia;* nevertheless, the drama displays a sufficient number of the characteristics of domestic tragedy to deserve analysis here. Fourth, the domestic tragedies, for the most part, express a sympathy for the common people, a realization of their good qualities, and an understanding of their problems. This practice is far removed from that of authors of orthodox tragedies, who gave scant consideration to any except their noble heroes. Fifth, these dramas frequently contain realistic elements drawn from the common life of London. Realism applied to serious moral, ethical, and theological purposes had been developed in the moralities and interludes. Writers of domestic tragedy seized upon this technique and continued its development, while authors of traditional tragedy consistently ignored it. For all these reasons, the plays discussed in this chapter deserve a place in any complete history of Tudor and Stuart domestic tragedies.

Chapter Six

SIXTEENTH-CENTURY MURDER PLAYS

THE TERM "murder play" might be applied with some degree of accuracy to practically all of the great tragedies of the Elizabethan times. It is ordinarily used, however, to designate a specific kind of domestic tragedy which appeared in the late sixteenth and early seventeenth centuries. Murder plays realistically dramatized sensational crimes of violence committed in England. These plays narrated events similar to the ones which the pamphleteers had employed for moral purposes. To the bald facts found in their sources, playwrights added characterization, motivation, theatrical skill, and poetic imagination. They retained most of the moral and homiletic devices characteristic of the pamphleteers. The best known of these plays, *Arden of Feversham, A Yorkshire Tragedy*, and *A Warning for Fair Women*, have long been recognized as outstanding dramas. The first two reveal so much dramatic power that they have been attributed to Shakespeare, though few modern scholars of note support this view.

Many murder plays have been lost. Henslowe's *Diary* and the Stationers' Register preserve a few titles, and it seems not unlikely that others have vanished leaving no trace. A sufficient number remain, however, to establish the distinguishing characteristics of the group. Devices and conventions common to the surviving domestic murder plays, but used to a lesser extent in the orthodox tragedies of the time, may indicate the attributes of the genre. The dramatic instruments of Divine Providence, repentance, oaths, and the like, employed so frequently in the popular literature of Elizabeth's reign, appear again and again in the realistic murder plays.

The most famous of all Elizabethan domestic tragedies, and unquestionably the best, is the anonymous *Arden of Feversham* (1591–

92). [1] It is based on the account in Holinshed's *Chronicle* of a murder committed February 15, 1551/2. Although the historian devoted six pages to the tale, he apologizes for including it with matters of greater moment:

About this time there was at Feuersham in Kent a gentleman named Arden, most cruellie murthered and slaine by the procurement of his owne wife. The which murther, for the horriblenesse thereof, although otherwise it may séeme to be but a priuate matter, and therefore as it were impertinent to this historie, I haue thought good to set it foorth somewhat at large, hauing the instructions deliuered to me by them, that haue vsed some diligence to gather the true vnderstanding of the circumstances.[2]

Holinshed spared no gory details that would enhance the effect of his story. The author of *Arden of Feversham* imitated this realistic approach, producing effects quite at variance with most Elizabethan romantic tragedies and with those of the cold, measured, classical tradition. The dramatist realized that he was offering his public unusual fare and in the last words of the play attempted to justify this procedure.

> Gentlemen, we hope youle pardon this naked Tragedy,
> Wherin no filed points are foisted in
> To make it gratious to the eare or eye;
> For simple trueth is gratious enough,
> And needes no other points of glosing stuffe.[3]

Some critics find in these lines an apology for failing to present, in a work called a tragedy, the catastrophe of a king or other person of political importance. Actually the playwright is attempting to justify,

---

[1] *The Lamentable and Trve Tragedie of M. Arden of Feversham in Kent,* in C. F. Tucker Brooke, *The Shakespeare Apocrypha,* pp. 1–35. Ascription of this play, by one Edward Jacob, to Shakespeare nearly two centuries after its appearance has given it a place in *The Shakespeare Apocrypha.* Few modern scholars accept this attribution, the only real bases of which are that the play is a good one and that Shakespeare was in London at the time it was produced. Kyd, who had written the pamphlet, *The Murder of John Brewen,* has always seemed a likely person to nominate as the writer of *Arden of Feversham.* If the author of *Arden* was not Kyd, he was someone profoundly influenced by Kyd's style. The introduction to *The Shakespeare Apocrypha* gives a convenient summary of critical opinion on the question of authorship of *Arden of Feversham* (see pp. xiii–xv).

[2] *Holinshed's Chronicle of England, Scotland, and Ireland,* III (1808), 1024.

[3] *Arden of Feversham,* in Brooke, *The Shakespeare Apocrypha,* p. 35; Epilogue, ll. 14–18.

not the humble rank of the characters, but his stark realism. In later Elizabethan times, writers of domestic tragedy recognized the violence they had done to critical dogma, but excused themselves on the grounds of emotional and moral effectiveness. However, the author of *Arden of Feversham* took for granted his right to produce a domestic tragedy.

Holinshed and the writer of the play are in substantial agreement about the facts of the murder. Both the historian and the playwright present the action as follows: Master Arden, a landholder of Feversham, has a wife, Alice, who has fallen in love with Mosbie, a tailor. That they may continue to enjoy their illicit love, Mosbie and Alice plot to murder Arden. Alice's attempt to poison her husband fails when he pours out the poisoned broth she has prepared, complaining of its offensive taste. Greene and Michael join the conspiracy— Greene because Arden has despoiled him of his land and Michael because he loves the sister of Mosbie. For ten pounds Greene hires Black Will and Shakbag, two highwaymen, to commit the murder. Fortuitous circumstances foil several attempts on the life of Arden. At last, as he is lured into playing at tables with Mosbie, he is struck down from behind by Black Will, whom Alice and Mosbie have secreted in a closet in the game room. Black Will having been recompensed, the conspirators carry the body to a field and with the aid of Susan, Mosbie's sister, obliterate the blood stains. That evening, while entertaining guests whom Arden had invited, Alice pretends to be worried over the absence of her husband. The guests accompany her in search of him and quickly discover his body. The conspirators are promptly charged with the murder, convicted, and led away to suffer death.

The action of the play, the details of the crime, the characteristics of the countryside, and Arden's home are all presented in a straightforward, realistic manner. Only in the dialogue evidences of romantic drama creep in. The two murderers occasionally speak poetry which startles the hearers by the effectiveness of its imagery. Shakbag observes:

> Black night hath hid the pleasures of ye day,
> And sheting darknesse ouerhangs the earth
> And with the blacke folde of her cloudy robe

> Obscures vs from the eiesight of the worlde,
> In which swete silence such as we triumph.[4]

In contrast, the scenes in Arden's house are full of local color. Although the dialogue is occasionally heightened by brilliant imagery and poetic fancy, the calculated realism of most of the play led the author to make the apology already quoted.

Arden's almost miraculous escapes from death arouse tremendous excitement in a reader or spectator. For this effective management of the action, the dramatist was indebted to Holinshed. In his variations from the source, the playwright rearranged events to stress the ethical implications of the story. The entire construction of the play is that of a moral demonstration, and at every stage of the action, the hand of Providence can be discerned. The treatment of Arden gives the key to the author's employment of the dramatic device of the agency of Providence.

Arden is not an attractive figure at any time. The idea of showing him as essentially a vicious character the dramatist owed to Holinshed, for in the *Chronicle,* Arden appears as a land-grabber and, worse, as a man willing, for the monetary gain, to wink at his wife's adultery.

. . . yet because he would not offend hir, and so loose the benefit which he hoped to gaine at some of hir fréends hands in bearing with hir lewdness, which he might haue lost if he should haue fallen out with hir: he was contented to wincke at hir filthie disorder, and both permitted, and also inuited Mosbie verie often to lodge at his house.[5]

In the play, Arden's character remains so black that Professor Moorman in *The Cambridge History* is unable to account for the dramatic purpose of the author.

Apart from the work of mere journeymen playwrights, there is no play in the whole range of Elizabethan dramatic literature which disregards tragic *katharsis,* alike in its terror and its pity, so completely as *Arden of Feversham.*

But are we to ascribe this neglect of tragic *katharsis* to obtuseness of dramatic vision? The marvellous power which the playwright reveals in the handling of certain situations and the deftness with which he introduces,

---

[4] *Ibid.,* p. 16; III, ii, 1–5.   [5] *Holinshed's Chronicle,* III, 1024–25.

now a touch of grim humour and now a gleam of tragic irony, are sufficient indications that his treatment of the story was deliberate.[6]

When regarded from the point of view of dramatic practice, the treatment of Arden is inexplicable. When the religious conceptions of the sixteenth century are applied to the play, not only the treatment of Arden, but also the reasons for the changes from the source are obvious.

Throughout the action, the fortunes of Arden correspond to his state of grace. Early the playwright shows him to be guilty of sin, but not in great enough degree to warrant punishment by death. To keep him from deserving the greatest penalty, he removes from his hero the sin of being a pander to his wife's dishonor. Such a sin would have been mortal, and the playwright was not ready to allow Arden to suffer for the extremities of sin. Instead, he attributes to his protagonist the lesser evil of land stealing, for which there was a precedent in the source and for which Arden could easily make restitution should he so desire. It is the covetousness for land which starts the operation of the intrigue. Arden's underhand methods have added Greene to the list of conspirators.

> Pardon me, mistres Arden, I must speake,
> For I am toucht. Your husband doth me wrong
> To wring from me the little land I haue:
> My liuing is my lyfe, onely that
> Resteth remainder of my portion.
> Desyre of welth is endles in his minde,
> And he is gredy gaping still for gaine,
> Nor cares he though young gentlemen do begge,
> So he may scrape and hoorde vp in his poutche.[7]

Because Greene is using unlawful means to attain his ends, interventions of Providence preserve Arden's life in order to give him a final opportunity to repent his evil ways and to turn to righteousness. The chance to make restitution comes to him through one Richard Reede, who begs Arden to return the land

> . . . which wrongfully you detaine from me:
> Although the rent of it be very small,

---

[6] *The Cambridge History of English Literature*, ed. A. W. Ward and A. R. Waller, V (1910), 270.

[7] *Arden of Feversham*, in Brooke, *The Shakespeare Apocrypha*, p. 9; I, i, 471–79.

> Yet will it helpe my wife and children,
> Which here I leaue in Feuershame, God knowes,
> Needy and bare: for Christs sake, let them haue it! [8]

Thus Arden, though given an opportunity to restore the land he has unlawfully acquired, refuses to do so. He answers this plea with threats, and Reede replies:

> What, wilt thou do me wrong & threat me, too?
> Nay, then, Ile tempt thee, Arden, doo thy worst.
> God, I beseech thee, show some miracle
> On thee or thine, in plaguing thee for this.
> That plot of ground which thou detaines from me,
> I speake it in an agony of spirite,
> Be ruinous and fatall vnto thee!
> Either there be butchered by thy dearest freends,
> Or els be brought for men to wonder at,
> Or thou or thine miscary in that place,
> Or there runne mad and end thy cursed dayes! [9]

This prayer, prompted by Arden's lack of Christian charity, brings immediate answer. After this interview, one further attempt on the life of Arden fails because it is made in broad daylight in a public street. As soon as Arden returns home, Reede's curse begins to work. He is "butchered" by his "dearest freends," and his body lies unburied in the field which he had stolen from Reede. Clearly the author intended the audience to realize that Arden had paid for his sins as surely as if he had been struck down by a thunderbolt. Although his sin was not carnal, he was as guilty of evil living as were Alice and Mosbie. As in the grimmest of the homiletic plays, the wages of sin is death. Thus the murderers appear in the role of the "scourge of God," [10] but, in accordance with the accepted traditions of the time, this does not prevent them from paying the extreme penalty for murder. In Holinshed the account of Reede's part in the tragedy appears at the end of the narrative, seemingly added as an afterthought.

Which field he had . . . most cruellie taken from a woman . . . to the great hinderance of hir and hir husband the said Read: for they long inioied it by a lease which they had of it for manie yeares, not then expired: neuer-

---

[8] *Ibid.*, p. 25; IV, iv, 13–17.   [9] *Ibid.*, ll. 28–38.   [10] See above, Chapter II.

thelesse, he got it from them. For the which, the said Reads wife not onlie exclaimed against him, in sheading manie a salt téere, but also curssed him most bitterlie euen to his face, wishing manie a vengeance to light vpon him, and that all the world might woonder on him. Which was thought then to come to passe, when he was thus murthered, and laie in that field from midnight till the morning: and so all that daie, being the faire daie till night, all the which daie there were manie hundreds of people came woondering about him.[11]

Holinshed thus recognized the providential operation of divine justice. The playwright laid additional stress on the incident, however, by incorporating it cleverly in the plot. Reede, who serves no other dramatic purpose, must be considered as the one who seals the fate of Arden. His interview with Arden, far from being extraneous to the plot, precipitates the catastrophe, for at that point divine protection is withdrawn from Arden.

At the end of the play, the perpetrators of the murder suffer death for their sins. Providence is content to reveal the murderers to the authorities of the law, who are the agents of God's justice. The magistrates lead Mistress Arden before the corpse of her husband. As blood wells forth from his wounds, everyone, even Alice, accepts the obvious significance.

> *Ales.* Arden, sweete husband, what shall I say?
> The more I sound his name, the more he bleedes;
> This bloode condemnes me, and in gushing foorth
> Speakes as it falles, and askes me why I did it.
> Forgiue me, Arden: I repent me nowe,
> And, would my death saue thine, thou shouldst not dye.
> Ryse vp, swete Arden, and enioy thy loue,
> And frowne not on me when we mete in heauen:
> In heauen I loue thee, though on earth I did not.[12]

Execution comes as punishment to Alice, Mosbie, Michael, and Susan, Mosbie's sister. Faced with death, the characters who hope for salvation repent their misdeeds and believe that God will forgive them. Alice says:

---

[11] *Holinshed's Chronicle*, III, 1030.
[12] *Arden of Feversham*, in Brooke, *The Shakespeare Apocrypha*, pp. 33–34; V, iii, 3–11.

> Leaue now to trouble me with worldly things,
> And let me meditate vpon my sauiour Christ,
> Whose bloode must saue me for the bloode I shed.[13]

Susan makes a similar speech. Neither Mosbie nor Michael repents his part in the affair, nor do they hope for everlasting mercy. The author wishes to impress upon the audience that no one in the plot escaped his just deserts, for in an epilogue he tells how each met his death. The final scene is so cursorily dramatized that it seems a sketch rather than a full scene, although it serves well enough the dramatic and moral purpose.[14]

Arden of Feversham combined with elements of excitement and suspense a didactic purpose inherited both from the morality plays and from the pamphlets of hack writers. The application of popular theology appears in the design of the plot to show Arden struck down by Providence in answer to a curse of one to whom he has refused pity. The popular religious beliefs are the bases of other providential manifestations as well as the contrition and formal repentances of the principals in the crime. *Arden of Feversham's* dramatic and poetic power has strengthened the case of advocates of Shakespearean authorship of the play. Swinburne wrote:

Either this play is the young Shakespeare's first tragic masterpiece, or there was a writer unknown to us then alive and at work for the stage who excelled him as a tragic dramatist not less—to say the very least—than he was excelled by Marlowe as a narrative and tragic poet.[15]

---

[13] *Ibid.*, p. 34; v, v, 9–11.

[14] Moral justice is far from perfectly executed in this play, for an innocent man goes to the scaffold along with the murderers of Arden. Bradshaw, as this man was named, had known Black Will in days when they were soldiers. In all innocence, Bradshaw points out his erstwhile companion to Greene, and the latter seizes the first opportunity to enlist the aid of Black Will in killing Arden. Although Bradshaw has no knowledge of the plot, a letter from Greene to Alice mentions his name, and so he dies with the rest. There is no explanation of this miscarriage of justice. In every other case, human justice and theological judgment are in complete agreement. It seems likely that when Bradshaw was taken over from the source, the author considered that his dramatic importance and pathetic appeal outweighed the dangers of possible theological misunderstanding.

[15] Quoted in John Addington Symonds, *Shakspere's Predecessors in the English Drama*, p. 333.

Most critics now hold it to be the work of Kyd,[16] and some go so far as to call it his finest drama,[17] although it is much less well known than *A Spanish Tragedy*. It appears to have had considerable popularity, for in addition to the quarto of 1592, there was another in 1599, and yet a third in 1633.[18] The earliest of the well-known domestic tragedies, it remains the finest.

II

The second of the extant murder plays, Robert Yarington's *Two Lamentable Tragedies*, printed in 1601, was probably written much earlier, possibly in 1594, to take advantage of the notoriety of the murder of Thomas Beech, which occurred on August 23, 1594.[19] The identity of Robert Yarington is a complete mystery, for no further mention of him is made in Elizabethan times. His failure to attract attention in his own day is not surprising, if this play is a fair example of his work. The drama is characterized by incoherence, awkward construction, and naïve psychology. It was apparently intended to be a sermon cast in dramatic form.

The work has no main plot, for in alternating scenes it depicts two distinct actions. The story of Beech is set in London; the murder of Pertillo is laid in Italy. A general prologue employs the allegorical figures of Homicide, Avarice, and Truth. In his treatment of the murder of Beech by Thomas Merry, Yarington places great emphasis on realistic presentation. The motivation of the crime is economic. Merry kills his friend Beech for his money. Rachael, Merry's sister, helps him to conceal the crime. Thomas Winchester, a boy in the service of Beech, and Harry Williams, an assistant to Merry, know the identity of the murderer. Williams promises to keep the crime secret, and Merry silences the boy, Thomas, by breaking his skull with a hammer. The dismembered corpse of Beech is soon found, and Williams, tormented by conscience, reveals the facts to the authorities. Merry, Rachael, and Williams are arrested, but Williams, pleading benefit of clergy, escapes with branding. Rachael and Merry both repent their sins and are hanged.

[16] See Charles Crawford, "The Authorship of *Arden of Feversham*," *Shakespeare Jahrbuch*, XXXIX (1903), 74–86.

[17] C. F. Tucker Brooke, *The Tudor Drama*, p. 356.

[18] Brooke, *The Shakespeare Apocrypha*, p. xiii.

[19] Edmund K. Chambers, *The Elizabethan Stage*, III, 518.

The elements of realism are not so strongly emphasized in the Italian as in the English tale. Pertillo is left to the care of his uncle, Fallerio, who is trustee of his estate. The idea that the property he now controls will pass from his hands is repugnant to Fallerio, and he plots the death of his nephew. He hires two ruffians to murder the boy. One of the murderers, conscience-stricken, attempts to avert the crime, but without avail. He lives long enough to reveal the perfidy of Fallerio to the count and to clear the name of Pertillo's friend Alenso, the son of Fallerio. Alenso, seeking death for grief at the loss of his friend, offers to take his father's place in court while the latter escapes in disguise. The father agrees, believing that a boy would not be severely punished. When the deception is revealed, however, Alenso is condemned. His father, overcome with new-found rectitude, gives himself up, and both are hanged.[20]

The dramatist in both stories lays great emphasis on moral and theological instruction. He frankly presents the fates of the murderers as the fruits of covetousness, so that each of the tragedies becomes a dramatized sermon on avarice. They emphasize two ideas over and over again: the evil consequences of greed and the efficacy of sincere repentance.

In the prologue, Homicide and Avarice are presented as working hand in hand. Homicide complains that he has had no employment because his companion has been unsuccessful in England.

> I have in vaine past through each stately streete,
> And blinde-fold turning of this happie towne,
> For wealth, for peace, and goodlie government,
> Yet can I not finde out a minde, a heart
> For blood and causelesse death to harbour in;
> They all are bent with vertuous gainefull trade,
> To get their needmentes for this mortall life,
> And will not soile their well-addicted harts
> With rape, extortion, murther, or the death
> Of friend or foe, to gaine an Empery.[21]

In this speech may be noted a blending of theological and middle-class virtues. The tradesman is coming into his own. Such a phrase as

[20] For the relationship of this play to *Beech's Tragedy*, *The Orphan's Tragedy*, and *The Tragedy of Merry*, see Appendix A.

[21] Robert Yarington, *Two Lamentable Tragedies*, in A. H. Bullen, *A Collection of Old English Plays*, p. 7.

"bent with vertuous gainefull trade" would have been absurd to a world-scorning ascetic of the early sixteenth century.

This play differs from *Arden of Feversham* in that none of the persons murdered shows any moral guilt. Since no man but Christ ever lived without sin, death may here be punishment for secret vice. On the other hand, the fate of the innocents may possibly be laid to blind chance operating even in a world controlled by Providence. Or the whole problem may readily be explained in terms of dramatic necessity. The playwright needed his corpses, and as he stressed the moral of the punishment for vice, he could easily skip the lesser matter of the rewards for virtue.

There is no doubt that vice in these dramas is always punished. None of the criminals is allowed to enjoy his ill-gotten gains. Each plot makes this point so many times that it must be considered the basic thesis of the author. The mother of Pertillo, on her deathbed, at the time when the gift of prophecy is usually given, says:

> If you deale ill with this distressed boye,
> God will revenge poore orphants iniuries,
> If you deale well, as I do hope you will,
> God will defend both you and yours from ill.[22]

Although Fallerio then pays little attention to these words, at his death he recalls them vividly. He is so bold as to trifle with Divine Providence and forswear himself in God's name. To deceive his son concerning his intentions toward Pertillo, he says:

> If ought betide him otherwise than well,
> Let God require due vengeance on my head,
> And cut my hopes from all prosperitie.[23]

The dangers of swearing unlawful oaths impress even the murderers and cause them to ask if Fallerio really wishes the death of Pertillo.

After Fallerio's sins have brought him to the scaffold, he realizes that his blasphemies are being punished and that the dying prayers of the innocent have been heard. This demonstration of God's power causes him to pray for mercy, and, as he is truly contrite, he may hope to win forgiveness.

> *Fall[erio]*. Ah sister, sister, now I call to minde,
> Thy dying words now prov'd a prophesie,

---

[22] *Ibid.*, p. 17.   [23] *Ibid.*, p. 43.

If you deale ill with this distressed childe,
God will no doubt revenge the innocent.
I have dealt ill, and God hath tane revenge.

. . . .

And now thou doest indevor to incite
Me to make my parting peace with God and men.
I do confesse, even from my verie soule,
My hainous sinne and grievous wickednesse
Against my maker manie thousand waies:
Ab imo cordis I repent my selfe
Of all my sinnes against his maiestie;
And, heavenly father, lay not to my charge
The death of poore *Pertillo* and those men
Which I suborn'd to be his murtherers,
When I appeare before thy heavenlie throne
To have my sentence or of life or death.
Vesu[vio]. Amen, amen and God continue still
These mercie-moving meditations.
Allen[so]. And thou, great God, which are omnipotent,
Powerfull enough for to redeeme our soules
Even from the verie gates of gaping hell,
Forgive our sinnes and wash away our faults
In the sweete river of that precious blood
Which thy deare sonne did shed in *Galgotha*,
For the remission of all contrite soules.[24]

Alenso and Fallerio stand as equals when faced with death, for both
are repentant sinners, and though Fallerio's crime is the greater, the
mercy of God can save him. The play teaches that no sin, even avarice
or murder, is so black as to be beyond the hope of divine grace. At the
same time, divine justice employs the agency of Providence to keep
a man from enjoying his ill-gotten gains in his earthly life. By paying
for a sin with suffering, the wrongdoer learns to turn with repentance
to God and so to escape everlasting damnation.

The murder of Beech by Thomas Merry is used in a similar way
to illustrate the dreadful extremities of sin and the retribution that
will come to the wrongdoer. After the murder, Merry is warned:

The Lord is just, and will revenge his blood,
On you and yours for this extremitie.

[24] *Ibid.*, pp. 91–92.

> I will not stay an hower within your house,
> It is the wickedest deed that ere was done.[25]

Merry, stricken by conscience, laments to the audience and to himself that his sin is not concealed from omniscient and omnipotent God.

> Desire to gaine began this desperate acte;
> Now plaine apparance of destruction,
> Of soule and body, waights upon my sinne.
> Although we hide our sinnes from mortall men
> Whose glasse of knowledge is the face of man,
> The eye of heaven beholdes our wickednesse,
> And will no doubt revenge the innocent,[26]

Rachael shares her brother Merry's fears and introduces the theme of repentance, saying to him:

> I feare thy soule will burne in flames of hell
> Unless repentance wash wash [sic] away thy sinne
> With clensing teares of true contrition.[27]

Even Merry, stained with double murder, wishes for grace.

> Rach[ael]. But God will overpasse this greevous sinne,
> If you lament with true unfained teares
> And seeke to live the remnant of your yeares
> In Gods true feare with upright conscience.
> Mer[ry]. If it would please him pardon this amisse
> And rid my body from the open shame
> That doth attend this deed, being brought to light,
> I would endevour all my comming dayes
> To please my maker and exalt his praise.[28]

The pious intention of the dramatist shows clearly in this scene. Williams, the only one, except Merry and his sister, who knew of the crime, has "beene to heare a Sermon." [29] It is after religious exercise that he decides to reveal the crime to the authorities. The inference is obvious. The sermon was the instrument which turned the erring Williams to a better way of life. Though it required the further persuasions of a friend to complete the conversion, the sermon prepared him to return to God's ways.

[25] *Ibid.*, p. 23.
[26] *Ibid.*, p. 36. The original concludes with a comma as indicated.
[27] *Ibid.*, p. 47.   [28] *Ibid.*, p. 70.   [29] *Ibid.*, p. 70.

When the murder comes to light, both Merry and his sister, Rachael, are condemned to death. Rachael, although she is guiltless of murder, was an accessory after the fact and, for this reason, was executed. Each of them makes the conventional "scaffold speech" in which the sinner asks forgiveness and in which the dramatist drives home his point. Merry speaks thus:

> . . . thy [Rachael's] conscience is at peace,
> And feels no terror for such wickedness;
> Mine hath beene vexed but is now at rest,
> For that I am assur'd my hainous sinne
> Shall never rise in judgement gainst my soule,
> But that the blood of *Jesus Christ* hath power
> To make my purple sinne as white as Snowe.
> One thing, good people, witness here with me,
> That I do dye in perfect charitie,
> And do forgive, as I would be forgiven
> First of my God and then of all the world.[30]

Rachael, intimating that vice breeds vice, makes her confession, directing the moral to the audience.

> Let him [Williams] and me learn all that hear of this
> To utter brothers or their masters misse;
> Conceale no murthers, lest it do beget
> More bloody deeds of like deformitie.
> Thus God forgive my sinnes, receive my soule!
> And though my dinner be of bitter death,
> I hope my soule shall sup with Jesus Christ,
> And see his presence everlastingly.[31]

This play is even more clearly a dramatized sermon than other domestic tragedies and more obviously is only indirectly popular entertainment. Yarington made concessions to the bloodthirsty tastes of London audiences, but his purpose was emphatically moral instruction. Although other playwrights used homiletic devices in domestic tragedies, the excessively lengthy theological discussions in this play, the lack of dramatic skill, and crude, unprofessional stage directions all indicate that the work was not that of a professional playwright.

[30] *Ibid.*, p. 93.

[31] *Ibid.*, p. 95. The word "learn" in the first line is obviously used in the sense of "teach."

The absence of the name of Yarington from any records of the time implies that this play was a sporadic excursion into the drama. While there is no evidence for this theory, it seems not altogether unlikely that Yarington may have been more closely connected with the Church than with the theatre. At least his chief interests were theological in character. He based his play more closely on an outmoded form of drama than was the practice of men who earned their livings by writing for the theatres, for he continued the tradition of the morality plays, substituting human characters for abstractions and concrete sins for generalities. The presence of the allegorical characters in the prologue and in the choruses emphasizes the descent of the domestic tragedies from the moralities.

III

A Warning for Fair Women, like *Two Lamentable Tragedies,* preserves some of the framework of a morality play, for among its *dramatis personae* several allegorical figures appear. In each play there is insistence on Christian morality and careful illustration of the manner in which interventions of Divine Providence punish sin. However, the author of *A Warning for Fair Women* far surpassed Yarington in dramatic skill and in psychological insight into the characters.

A Warning for Fair Women dramatizes a murder which took place in 1573,[32] the principal facts of which Munday recorded in his pamphlet, *A View of Sundry Examples.*[33] The action of the play can be briefly summarized as follows. George Browne loves Anne, the wife of George Sanders. To aid in his wooing, he enlists the help of Anne Drury and her servant Roger. When Mistress Drury's efforts prove successful, the lovers decide to murder Master Sanders. After two vain attempts, Browne kills Sanders and also a boy who had the misfortune to be present. The boy, however, does not succumb at once, but lives to send the pursuers after Browne and later to accuse him of the murder. Captured and brought back, Browne pleads guilty. His attempts to shield Anne Sanders are fruitless, for her conscience moves her to confess her part in the crime. The conspirators are then condemned to death.

[32] Brooke, *The Tudor Drama,* p. 357.
[33] See above, Chapter III. It also appears in Stow's *Chronicle.*

The opening of the tragedy is an evident imitation of the beginning of Yarington's play. History, Comedy and Tragedy dispute over
the right to hold the stage for the day. Comedy, attempting to crush
one of her rivals, satirizes the contemporary fashion in tragedy.

> How ſome damnd tyrant, to obtaine a crowne,
> Stabs, hangs, impoyſons, ſmothers, cutteth throats,
> And then a Chorus too comes howling in,
> And tels vs of the worrying of a cat,
> Then of a filthie whining ghoſt,
> Lapt in ſome fowle ſhéete, or a leather pelch,
> Comes ſtreaming like a pigge halfe ſtickt,
> And cries *Vindicta*, reuenge, reuenge:
> With that a little Roſen flaſheth forth,
> Like ſmoke out of a Tabacco pipe, or a boyes ſquib:
> When comes in two or three like to drouers,
> With taylers bodkins, ſtabbing one another . . .[34]

Tragedy makes no reply, but becomes a kind of chorus and proceeds
to set the stage for the action of the play. She explains that the scene
is London and the subject native. She returns at the end of each act
to resume the role of commentator. By means of dumb show, she
signifies the events of the coming act, using allegorical figures which
have nothing to do with the dramatic action. The first of these dumb
shows illustrates the author's method:

The Furies goe to the doore and meete them: firſt the Furies enter before
leading them, dauncing a ſoft daunce to the ſolemne muſicke: next comes
Luſt before *Browne*, leading miſtris *Sanders* couered with a blacke vaile:
Chaſtitie all in white, pulling her backe ſoftly by the arme: then *Drewry*,
thruſting away Chaſtitie, *Roger* following: they march about, and then ſit
to the table: the Furies fill wine, Luſt drinks to *Browne*, he to Miſtris
Sanders, ſhee pledgeth him: Luſt imbraceth her, ſhe thruſteth Chaſtity from
her, Chaſtity wrings her hands, and departs: *Drury* and *Roger* imbrace one
another: the Furies leape and imbrace one another.[35]

The figures of Chastity and Lust have been imported from the
morality plays, and the action in this dumb show resembles scenes in
the early homiletic dramas. The remaining pantomimes reveal simi-

[34] *A Warning for Faire Women*, pp. [2–3], Tudor Facsimile Texts.
[35] *Ibid.*, p. [23].

lar methods, although the symbolism becomes slightly more complicated.

The action of the play, as usual, exemplifies the operations of Divine Providence. Like Yarington, the dramatist absolves the victim from moral guilt. In order to blacken the sin of the culprits and possibly to sound a sentimental note, the playwright presents Master Sanders as a loving husband and father: an upstanding merchant, a generous creditor, and a good citizen. Sanders is, perhaps, short-sighted in failing to tell his wife that he is hard pressed for money at a time when she has bought new clothes. She thinks his objections to her purchases pure stinginess and, while alienated from him, is peculiarly susceptible to Browne's importunings. Sanders is, of course, not guilty of covetousness, for he is willing, when his affairs will again be in order, to buy his wife all the clothes she needs. She recognizes her husband's good qualities, as does Mistress Drury, who praises him as follows:

> . . . her hufband
> Is one that I am much beholding to,
> A man both louing, bountifull and iuft,
> And to his wife, in all this cittie, none
> More kinde, more loyall harted, or more firme,
> What finne were it to doe him then that wrong? [36]

At the end of the second act, Tragedy remarks that it is not sin but destiny that causes the end of Sanders's life. The power of Divine Providence has hitherto preserved him, but to all an end must come.

> *Trag[edy]*. Twice (as you fee) this fad diftreffed man,
> The onely marke whereat foule *Murther* fhot:
> Juft in the loofe of enuious eager death,
> By accidents ftrange and miraculous,
> Efcap't the arrow aymed at his hart.
> Suppofe him on the water now for Woolwich,
> For fecrete bufineffe with his bofom friend,
> From thence, as fatal deftinie conducts him,
> To Mary-Cray by fome occafion cald:
> Which by falfe *Druries* meanes made knowne to *Browne*,
> *Luft*, *Gaine*, and *Murther*, fpurd this villaine on,
> Still to purfue this unfufpecting foule,

---

[36] *Ibid.*, p. [15].

> And now the dreadful houre of death is come,
> The difmal morning when the deftinies,
> Do fhere the labouring vitall thréed of life,
> When as the lambe left in the woods of Kent,
> Unto this rauenous woolfe become a pray,
> Now of his death the generall intent,
> Thus *Tragedie* doth to your eyes prefent.[37]

Even at the moment of death, Sanders shows himself to be an upright Christian and a good man. He seeks to arrange his spiritual affairs before the moment of doom.

> *San[ders].* Heare me a word, you are a gentleman,
> Soile not your hands with blood of innocents.
> *Bro[wne].* Thou fpeakeft in vaine.
> *San[ders].* Then God forgiue my finne,
> Haue mercie on me, and vpon thée too,
> The bloudie author of my timeleffe death. . . .
> Jefu receiue my foule into thy hands.[38]

Divine Providence manifests itself almost as soon as the crime is committed. At the moment of the murder, Providence causes Browne to suffer delusions. Believing Sanders already dead, he thinks his victim's dying appeal to Jesus a supernatural voice.

> *Bro[wne].* What found was that? it was not he that fpake,
> The breath is vanifht, from his noftrils,
> Was it the other? no, his wounds are fuch
> As he is likewife paft the vfe of fpéech.
> Who was it then that thundred in mine eares,
> The name of Jefu? Doubtleffe twas my confcience,
> And I am damn'd for this vnhallowed déede.
> O finne how haft thou blinded me til now,
> Promifing me fecuritie and reft,
> But giueft me dreadful agonie of foule?
> What fhal I do? or whither fhal I flie?
> The verie bufhes wil difcouer me.
> See how their wounds do gape vnto the fkies,
> Calling for vengeance.[39]

The most striking instance of the intervention of Divine Providence is the following. When Browne murders Sanders, he also stabs Sanders's companion, a young boy named John Bean. Although the

[37] *Ibid.*, pp. [35–36]. [38] *Ibid.*, p. [39]. [39] *Ibid.*, pp. [39–40].

boy has received ten wounds, "each of them mortal," he lives ten days until his murderer has been captured. When John Bean again sees Browne, he denounces him as the murderer and then, his miraculous service accomplished, quickly expires. Lest the audience miss the significance of this incident, Barnes, Bean's master, says:

The wondrous worke of God, that the poore creature not ſpeaking for two days, yet now ſhould ſpeake to accuſe this man, and preſently yeeld vp his foule.[40]

The same idea is repeated later when some lords are discussing the incident:

> *1 Lord.* T 'is [*sic*] a wondrous thing
> But that the power of heauen ſuſtained him,
> A man with nine or ten ſuch mortal wounds,
> Not taking foode ſhould liue ſo many daies,
> And then at ſight of *Browne* recouer ſtrength,
> And ſpeake ſo chéerely as they ſay he did.
> *4 Lord.* I, and ſoone after he auouch'd the fact
> Unto *Brownes* face then to giue vp the ghoſt.
> *2 Lord.* T 'was [*sic*] Gods good wil it ſhould be ſo my Lord.[41]

All the characters recognize the magnitude of the sin of murder; and guilty and innocent alike believe in the everlasting damnation which will result from the deed unless penance and expiation win divine mercy for the guilty. The motivating force which drives the killer is not economic as in *Two Lamentable Tragedies*. Although the medieval practice, following the precepts of Aristotle, was to rank incontinence as the least serious of the sins, the sexual desire in *A Warning for Fair Women* is mentioned in more opprobrious terms than was avarice in Yarington's play. The character Tragedy indicates how lust infects and weakens the soul, so that crime follows crime as the natural warnings of conscience become weakened. This is an illustration of the popular idea of a "chain of vice," which dramatists had adopted from the preachers. A person who committed a small sin, they believed, lost grace and weakened his conscience in proportion to the gravity of the offense. Thus, each succeeding moral lapse became easier. As a man fell from God, God withdrew from him.[42]

---

[40] *Ibid.*, p. [56].   [41] *Ibid.*, p. [58].
[42] *Certain Sermons, or Homilies, Appointed to Be Read in Churches, in the Time of the Late Queen Elizabeth of Famous Memory,* 1852 ed., p. 74.

From petty misdemeanors, the road to cardinal sins was easy—indeed, almost inevitable. Thus, many of the murderers in these plays blame their great crimes on youthful waywardness. In a later appearance, Tragedy indicates the end result of evil.

> Thus finne preuailes, fhe drinkes that poyfoned draught,
> With which bafe thoughts henceforth infects her foule,
> And wins her free confent to this foule deed,
> Now bloud and *Luft,* doth conquer and fubdue,
> And *Chaftitie* is quite abandoned:
> Here enters *Murther* into al their hearts,
> And doth poffeffe them with the hellifh thirft
> Of guiltleffe bloud . . .[43]

The idea of the chain of vice is better expressed in another speech by Tragedy when she says:

> Preuailing Sinne hauing by three degrees,
> Made his afcenfion to forbidden deedes,
> As firft, alluring their vnwary mindes
> To like what fhe propofde, then practifing
> To draw them to confent: and laft of all
> Miniftring fit meanes and opportunitie
> To execute what fhe approoued good:
> Now fhe vnuailes their fight, and lets them fee
> The horror of their foule immanitie
> And wrath that al this while hath bin obfcurde,
> Steps forth before them in a thoufand fhapes
> Of gaftly thoughts, and loathing difcontents:
> So that the reft was promift; now appeares
> Unreft and deepe affliction of the foule,
> Delight prooues danger, confidence difpaire . . .[44]

Browne enjoys none of the fruits of his crime. He is soon arrested and brought to trial. He pleads guilty, and exhibits some generosity in attempting to shield Anne Sanders. When sentence is pronounced, the lord justice offers him the conventional hope of divine mercy held out even to the worst of sinners.

> *Browne* thou art here by the Law condemnd to die,
> Which by thine own confeffion thou deferu'ft.

---

[43] *A Warning for Fair Women,* p. [24].   [44] *Ibid.,* pp. [50–51].

All men muſt die, although by diuers meanes,
The maner how is of leaſt moment, but
The matter why, condemns or iuſtifies:
But be of comfort, though the world condemne,
Yea, though thy conſcience ſting thée for thy fact,
Yet God is greater than thy conſcience,
And he can ſaue whom al the world condemnes,
If true repentance turne thee to his grace.
Thy time is ſhort, therefore ſpend this thy time
In praier and contemplation of thy end,
Labour to die better than thou haſt liu'd,
God grant thou mai'ſt.[45]

That Browne has profited from the admonition of the lord justice is indicated by his bearing at his execution, which immediately follows the courtroom scene. His "scaffold speech" reveals the dangers of neglecting care for one's soul. Echoing the prodigal-son plays, Browne places the blame for his woeful end on the evil courses of his youth.

Vile world how like a monſter come I ſoyld from thee?
How haue I wallowed in thy loathſome filth,
Drunke and beſmeard with al thy beſtial ſinne?
I neuer ſpake of God, vnleſſe when I
Haue blaſphemed his name with monſtrous oathes:
I neuer read the ſcriptures in my life,
But did eſtéeme them worſe then vanitie:
I neuer came in church where God was taught,
Nor euer to the comfort of my ſoule
Tooke benefite of Sacrament or Baptiſme:
The Sabboth dayes I ſpent in common ſtewes,
Unthrifite gaming, and vile periuries:
I held no man once worthy to be ſpoke of
That went not in ſome ſtrange diſguiſde attire,
Or had not fetcht ſome vile monſtrous faſhion,
To bring in odious deteſtable pride:
I hated any man that did not doe
Some damned or ſome hated filthie déede,
That had béene death for vertuous man to heare,
Of all the worſt that liue, I was the worſt,
Of all the curſed, I the moſt accurſed,

---

[45] *Ibid.,* pp. [62–63].

> All careleſſe men be warned by my end,   .
> And by my fall your wicked liues amend.
> > *He leapes off.*[46]

In the case of Anne Sanders, the playwright again employs supernatural devices. She early suffers qualms of conscience over the
murder and berates Browne bitterly when he suggests that the crime
may not come to light, saying:

> Shall I feare more my ſeruants, or the world,
> Then God himſelfe? He heard our treacherie,
> And ſaw our complot and conſpiracie:
> Our hainous ſinne cries in the eares of him,
> Lowder than we can crie vpon the earth:
> A womans ſinne, a wiues unconſtancie,
> Oh God that I was borne to be ſo vile,
> So monſtrous and prodigious for my luſt.
> Fie on this pride of mine, this pamperd fleſh,
> I will reuenge me on theſe tiſing eies,
> And teare them out for being amourous.[47]

Her belief in the immanence of Divine Providence makes doubly
impressive its intervention in her own case. As she stands before the
bar, she wears a white rose in token of her innocence.[48] After she has
perjured herself by swearing her freedom from all guilt in the
murder, the lord justice tells her to look at the rose, saying, "His
colour now is of another hue," [49] although he does not specify its new
color.

Even after she has been sentenced, Anne attempts to persuade
Mistress Drury to exonerate her. Mistress Drury, however, having
repented of her part in the crime, refuses to endanger her soul with
perjury.

> Should I, to purchaſe ſafety for another,
> Or lengthen out anothers temporall life,
> Hazard mine owne ſoule euerlaſtingly,
> And looſe the endleſſe ioyes of heauen,
> Preparde for ſuch as wil confeſſe their ſinnes?
> No miſtris *Sanders*, yet there's time of grace,
> And yet we may obtaine forgiuenes,

---

[46] *Ibid.*, pp. [69–70].   [47] *Ibid.*, p. [44].
[48] *Ibid.*, p. [64].   [49] *Ibid.*, p. [66].

> If we wil feeke it at our Sauiours hands.
> But if we wilfully fhut vp our hearts
> Againft the holy fpirit that knockes for entrance
> It is not this worlds punifhment fhal ferue,
> Nor death of body, but our foules fhal liue
> In endleffe torments of vnquenched fire.[50]

This argument convinces Anne Sanders, and to the doctor of divinity who comes to urge her to consider her evil ways, she declares herself truly repentant. The doctor welcomes her confession, telling her:

> Done like a chriftian and the childe of grace,
> Pleafing to God, to angels, and to men,
> And doubt not but your foule fhall finde a place
> In *Abrahams* bofome, though your body perifh.[51]

Having repented, Anne spends her last hours in Christian contemplation and in efforts to teach her children the paths of virtue.

> And God I thanke that found out my fin,
> And brought me to affliction in this world,
> Thereby to faue me in the world to come.
> Oh children learne, learne by your mothers fall
> To follow vertue, and beware of finne,
> Whofe baites are fwéete and pleafing to the eie,
> But being tainted, more infect than poyfon,
> And are farre bitterer than gall it felfe,
>
> . . . .
>
> Beholde (my children,) I will not bequeath,
> Or gold or filuer to you, you are left
> Sufficiently prouided in that poynt,
> But here I giue to each of you a booke
> Of holy meditations, *Bradford's* workes,
> That vertuous chofen feruant of the Lord,
> Therein you fhalbe richer than with gold,
> Safer than in faire buildings: happyer
> Than al the pleafures of this world can make you.
> Sleepe not without them when you go to bed,
> And rife a mornings with them in your hands.
> So God fend downe his bleffing on you al:
> Farewel, farewel, farewel, farewel, farewel.[52]

---

[50] *Ibid.*, p. [72].　　　　[51] *Ibid.*, p. [73].
[52] *Ibid.*, p. [75]. See above, Chapter II.

Perhaps even John Bradford would be forced to admit that the distressed woman overrated his powers of persuasion to virtue, but the earnestness of her advertisement leaves no doubt as to the ultimate purpose of this play. As in the earlier domestic tragedies, the author puts theological considerations first and dramatic effectiveness a poor second; for there is no doubt that these long exhortations bring the action of the play to a standstill. The central dramatic issue, the murder of George Sanders, struggles for attention against the primary interest of the writer, which is the conversion to faith of the sinners. The emotional climax comes early, while the intellectual peak is reached in the final repentance scenes. The conflict between the two purposes of the author causes the action to halt while he harangues and exhorts his audience. The excitement of the murder story probably enticed the people into the theatre, and they accepted the lecture which came with the play as a necessary part of the dramatization of a thrilling tale of homicide. There is, however, some evidence that the audience may have found this moralizing a little hard to stomach. At the end of the play, Tragedy remarks that perhaps tomorrow the company may act a play in a more usual and popular vein.

> Here *Tragedie* of force must needes conclude.
> Perhaps it may feeme ftrange vnto you al,
> That one hath not reuengde anothers death,
> After the obferuation of fuch courfe:
> The reafon is, that now of truth I fing,
> And fhould I adde, or elfe diminifh aught,
> Many of thefe fpectators then could fay,
> I haue committed error in my play.
> Bear with this true and home-borne Tragedie,
> Yéelding fo flender argument and fcope,
> To build a matter of importance on.
> And in fuch forme as happly you expected,
> What now hath faild, to morrow you fhall fée
> Perform'd by *Hyftorie* or *Comedie*.[53]

The author took as great pains to depict realistically the everyday lives of the characters as he had taken to present the facts of the murder accurately. John Bean, his lass, Joan, and Anne Sanders's

[53] *A Warning for Fair Women*, p. [73].

young son are drawn from life. In the Sanders home before the murder, the domestic details give the reader the illusion of reality. Anne's quarrel with her husband over money for clothes is a common sort of family squabble.

One of the most unusual bits of realism comes to light in the court scene, which appears to be an almost literal transcript of an Elizabethan court in action. Notice the charge of the clerk as he reads the accusation of the crown against Browne. Certainly no playwright would think of including such a detail as the price of a sword unless he had heard such a bit in similar arraignments.

To the barre *George Browne,* & hold vp thy hand. Thou art here indited by the name of George Browne, late of London Gentleman, for that thou vpon the xxv. day of March in the xv. yeare of the raigne of her ſacred Maieſtie whom God long preſerue, betweene the houres of vii. and viii. of the clocke in the forenoone of the ſame day, néere vnto Shooters hill, in the countie of Kent, lying in wait of purpose and pretended malice, hauing no feare of God before thine eies, the perſons of *George Sanders* Gentleman, and *Iohn Bean* yeoman, then and there iourneying in Gods peace and the princes, feloniouſly did aſſault, and with one ſword, price ſixe ſhillings, mortally and wilfully, in many places diddeſt wound vnto the death againſt the peace, crown and dignitie of her maieſtie. How ſaieſt thou to theſe fellonious murders, art thou guiltie or not guiltie? [54]

The authors of domestic tragedies employed realism as a means to an end. They hoped thus to convince the audience that the persons in the play were real. Once this idea was implanted, the spectators, most of them common people, would feel the moral lesson of the action brought home to their own lives. What had happened to men and women like themselves could happen to them also, unless they avoided the errors which had brought about the catastrophe of the play.

A Warning for Fair Women, then, illustrates how completely dedicated domestic tragedy was to moral instruction. The central theme is religious, showing that the punishment for sin is death, that a murderer will not live to enjoy what he has gained by his crime. Although a malefactor may, for a time, conceal his guilt from man, God is omniscient and by His Providence intervenes to punish the evildoers. In the present play, the prolonged life of John Bean and

[54] *Ibid.,* p. [61].

the color change of Anne Sanders's rose give two obvious examples of the dramatic use of providential interventions. Hope of grace is held out to the repentant sinner. While it is sure that punishment follows sin, it is not indicated that prosperity always follows godly living, for the death of Sanders would vitiate such an idea. The author, in an effort to account for operations of chance in a universe ostensibly ruled by Divine Providence, made destiny the reason for the end of life.

The realism in *A Warning for Fair Women* is used mainly because of its power to emphasize the moral lesson. While the author had a keen eye and ear in the observation of people about him, his primary purpose was not photographic but didactic.

The language of the play is not as powerful or as well chosen as that of *Arden of Feversham*, but is superior in poetic and dramatic power to that of *Two Lamentable Tragedies*. The author of *A Warning for Fair Women*, obviously a man of far more theatrical experience than Yarington,[55] missed several dramatic opportunities that he might have developed, had his interest not been so severely moral. The acquiescence of Anne Sanders to the advances of George Browne, the obligatory scene of the first part of the play, is not presented. Nor is the equally important one in which she agrees to the murder of her husband. Her conversion to Christian faith at the end of the play comes too quickly when judged in terms of modern dramaturgy and credible psychology. Perhaps to audiences accustomed to the easy shifts of love and hate in the drama of the period, this weakness was not so noticable as it would be now. The author overlooked a chance to make a psychological study of murder like that undertaken in *Macbeth*, probably because he lacked the imaginative power to conceive such an approach to a murder story and because such a method would not have been so obviously moral. The combination of psychological and theological approach failed to occur to the writer, and thus *A Warning for Fair Women* alternates action with didacticism, while the excuse for the action is that the didacticism may be palatable to the audience.

[55] Joseph Quincy Adams conjectures that the play may be from the pen of Thomas Heywood. The Christian morality of this play is not unlike that of Heywood in his other works. *Edward IV*, *The English Traveller*, and *A Woman Killed with Kindness* prove that he was interested in domestic tragedy. Mr. Adams's article is "The Authorship of *A Warning for Fair Women*," *Publications of the Modern Language Association*, XXVIII (1913), 594–620.

Chapter Seven

SEVENTEENTH-CENTURY MURDER PLAYS

AFTER the turn of the century, murder plays in general related wilder and more extravagant crimes than had the similar dramas of the sixteenth century. The popularity of the genre was fading, and before the Puritans closed the theatres in 1642, the realistic murder play had largely vanished from the repertories. The surviving records show no example of this dramatic form after the first quarter of the seventeenth century.

A Yorkshire Tragedy (c. 1606) has, from the time of its first publication, been associated with the name of Shakespeare. It was entered as his in the Stationers' Register; his name appeared on the title pages of the 1608 and the 1619 quartos, and the work was included in the Third and Fourth Folios of Shakespeare's works in 1664 and 1685 respectively. In spite of the contemporary evidence, modern scholars are inclined to doubt the authenticity of the ascription.[1]

In the original edition, *A Yorkshire Tragedy* was headed by the superscription, "All's One, or, one of the Foure plaies in one, Called

---

[1] Professor Brooke sums up the opinion on Shakespeare's authorship of *A Yorkshire Tragedy* as follows: "The authenticity of the *Yorkshire Tragedy* has been allowed by Steevens, Ulrici, Hopkinson, Ward, and others; but the case which has been made out for the negative by Malone, Tyrrell, Knight, Halliwell-Phillips, Symonds, and Swinburne seems much the stronger. The barbaric force of the play and the splendour of some of the prose it contains cannot fail to impress the reader; but the late date (1605–8) is in itself an almost conclusive argument against the possibility of Shakespeare's authorship.

"Neither in characterization, nor in plot, nor in metrical peculiarities have the most ardent defenders of the *Yorkshire Tragedy's* authenticity pretended that there is any approach to Shakespeare's manner subsequent to 1605." *The Shakespeare Apocrypha*, pp. xxxiv–xxxv. Halliwell-Phillips suggests that the publisher took advantage of Shakespeare's absence from London to bring out a play with his name on the title page. J. O. Halliwell-Phillips, *Outlines of the Life of Shakespeare*, 8th ed., I, 224.

A York-Shire Tragedy." [2] It was evidently a part of a program of one-act plays. *A Yorkshire Tragedy* is the sole survivor of this group.

The murder which formed the basis for this work and for the play, *The Miseries of Enforced Marriage*, by George Wilkins,[3] took place in 1605. Walter Calverley (or Caverley) had plighted his troth to Clare Harcop. His father insisted that he marry Katherine, for whom he felt no affection. However, after sending a sorrowful message to Clare, he reluctantly obeyed his father. On receipt of the note, she committed suicide. When Calverley heard of her death, he began a career of unrestrained drinking and gambling. His extravagance soon involved his family, for his brother was sent to prison for a debt of the prodigal, and Calverley continually urged his wife to obtain money for him by any means, fair or foul. At length, remorse for his brother's fate obsessed him with the wild idea that he must exterminate his family. Stow's *Chronicle* describes his crimes thus:

Walter Caluerly of *Caluerly* in Yorke ſhire, Eſquier, murthered 2. on his yong children ſtabbed his wife into the body with full purpoſe to haue murthred her, and inſtantly went from his houſe to haue ſlain his yongeſt child at Nurſe, but was preuented. For which fact at his tryall in Yorke, he ſtood mute, and was iudged to be preſt to death, according to which iudgement hée was executed at the Caſtell of Yorke, the fift of August.[4]

The Miseries of Enforced Marriage dramatized the events of the first part of the story. Beginning with Calverley's wooing of Clare, it depicts their vow of trothplight, his marriage to Katherine, his wild excesses, and his abject misery. Wilkins's play departs from history, however, by supplying a happy ending, in which Calverley swears to reform. A wealthy friend dies opportunely, leaving them his property. Since it omits the murder, *The Miseries of Enforced Marriage* does not belong in this chapter and will be considered in Chapter Nine.

A Yorkshire Tragedy moves swiftly in the presentation of the crime and in the punishment of the murderer. The opening scene refers briefly to the events which are depicted fully in Wilkins's play, but which are not germane to the present drama. Either *A Yorkshire Tragedy* assumes that the audience will have the necessary back-

[2] Brooke, *The Shakespeare Apocrypha*, p. 251.
[3] See above, Chapter III, and below, Chapter IX.
[4] John Stow, *Annales; or, A Generall Chronicle of England*, 1631 ed., pp. 870–71.

ground knowledge, or this information had been presented in one of the earlier plays of the "Foure plaies in one." It is sufficient for the purposes of the plot that the husband be established as a rake, although it would have been better dramaturgy to have given reasons for his dissipation. In her opening lines, the wife describes her husband's character.

> My husband neuer ceases in expence,
> Both to consume his credit and his house;
> And tis set downe by heauens iust decree,
> That Ryotts child must needs be beggery.
> Are these the vertues that his youth did promise?
> Dice, and voluptuous meetings, midnight Reuels,
> Taking his bed with surfetts: Ill beseeming
> The auncient honor of his howse and name!
> And this not all: but that which killes me most,
> When he recounts his Losses and false fortunes,
> The weaknes of his state soe much deiected,
> Not as a man repentant but halfe madd,
> His fortunes cannot answere his expence:
> He sits and sullenly lockes vp his Armes,
> Forgetting heauen looks downward, which makes him
> Appeare soe dreadfull that he frights my heart,
> Walks heauyly, as if his soule were earth:
> Not penitent for those his sinnes are past,
> But vext his mony cannot make them last:—
> A fearefull melancholie, vngodly sorrow.[5]

As in *Nice Wanton*, the author shows the agency of Divine Providence operating to punish addiction to sin. The husband's wild, half-mad career has brought him only misfortune, misery, and nearbeggary. Divine Providence has acted to "make those vile affections and that unrighteousness their punishment which they make their pleasure." [6] The play also illustrates the idea of the "chain of vice" already mentioned in Chapter Six. The husband's relatively innocent faults of gaming and midnight revels lead him inexorably to the crimes which form the catastrophe of the drama.

[5] *A Yorkshire Tragedy*, in Brooke, *The Shakespeare Apocrypha*, p. 252; sc. ii, ll. 2–21.

[6] *Discourses on Divine Providence*, in *The Complete Works of Stephen Charnock*, ed. Rev. James M'Cosh, I, 28.

The religious doctrine common to all domestic tragedy receives less emphasis than usual in *A Yorkshire Tragedy*. Nevertheless, the moral lies hidden in both the lines and the action of the drama. The husband boasts that he has always scorned religious observances, for in answer to his wife's suggestion that he beg at court for money to pay his debts, he says:

Shall I that Dedicated my selfe to pleasure, be nowe confind in seruice to crouch and stand like an old man ith hams, my hat off? I that neuer could abide to vncover my head ith Church? [7]

In this speech, the husband shows himself to be a "scorner," one of that "sort of men whose hearts are so stuffed with malice, that they are not contented to dwell in sin, and to lead their lives in all kinds of wickedness; but also they do contemn and scorn in other all godliness, true religion, all honesty and virtue." [8] The orthodox belief was "that never any yet [of these scorners] converted unto God by repentance, but continued still in their abominable wickedness, heaping up to themselves damnation, against the day of God's inevitable judgment." [9] For this reason, the husband makes no formal religious repentance in prison, and no hope of divine mercy is held out to him.

The master of his brother's college brings the husband to a realization of the enormity of his sins. The brother, "who profited in his diuine Imployments, mighte haue made ten thousand soules fit for heauen," [10] has been imprisoned for a debt of the husband. The master remonstrates with the wayward youth, and the latter replies in a fashion quite different from the insults with which he answered a gentleman who sought to reason with him earlier.

Sir, you haue much wrought with mee. I feele you in my soule, you are your artes master. I neuer had sence til now; your sillables haue cleft me. Both for your words and pains I thank you: I cannot but acknowledge grieuous wronges done to my brother . . .[11]

---

[7] *A Yorkshire Tragedy*, in Brooke, *The Shakespeare Apocrypha*, p. 255; sc. iii, ll. 57–61.

[8] *Certain Sermons, or Homilies, Appointed to Be Read in Churches, in the Time of the Late Queen Elizabeth of Famous Memory*, 1852 ed., pp. 348–49.

[9] *Ibid.*, p. 349.

[10] *A Yorkshire Tragedy*, in Brooke, *The Shakespeare Apocrypha*, p. 256; sc. iv, ll. 22–24.

[11] *Ibid.*, p. 256; sc. iv, ll. 40–46.

After the master has left, the husband shows that he has been sincere in all that he said. He soliloquizes:

Oh thou confused man! thy pleasant sins haue vndone thee, thy damnation has beggerd thee! That heauen should say we must not sin, and yet made women! giues our sences waie to finde pleasure, which being found confounds vs. Why shold we know those things so much misuse vs?—oh, would vertue had been forbidden! wee should then haue prooued all vertuous, for tis our bloude to loue what were forbidden. . . . what is there in three dice to make a man draw thrice three thousand acres into the compasse of a round little table, & with the gentlemans palsy in the hand shake out his posteritie thieues or beggars? Tis done! I ha dont, yfaith. . . .

In my seede fiue are made miserable besides my selfe: my ryot is now my brothers iaylor, my wiues sighing, my three boyes penurie, and mine own confusion.[12]

He has fallen so far from divine grace that the rebuke which should have turned him to a better life starts him on a career of crime. His mad idea is that he must kill all of his family to save them from the abject misery which engulfs him. He seems possessed of the Devil, so wild is his frenzy. He stabs his wife, kills two of his children and a manservant who attempts to prevent him, and rushes off on horseback to murder his third child who is lodged twelve miles away. As in the nondramatic accounts of this murder,[13] an intervention of Providence foils his plan. The stage direction reads, *"Enter Husband as being thrown off his horse, And falls.*[14] This accident enables the officers to overtake and arrest him. As he is brought before the bar of justice, he continues to rail and to curse because he has not been able to complete his series of crimes. He is then confronted with his wife, and the contemplation of her virtue and love causes him to repent his evil ways. She accuses him of unkindness and he replies:

> Faith, and so I thinke I haue:
> I did my murthers roughly, out of hand,
> Desperate and suddaine, but thou hast deuiz'd
> A fine way now to kill me, thou hast giuen mine eies
> Seauen woonds a peece; now glides the deuill from mee,
> Departes at euery ioynt, heaues vp my nailes.
> Oh catch him new torments, that were near inuented,

[12] *Ibid.,* pp. 256–57; sc. iv, ll. 65–98.   [13] See above, Chapter III.
[14] *A Yorkshire Tragedy,* in Brooke, *The Shakespeare Apocrypha,* p. 259; sc. viii.

> Binde him one thousand more, you blessed Angells,
> In that pit bottomlesse; let him not rise
> To make men act vnnaturall tragedies,
> To spred into a father, and in furie,
> Make him his childrens executioners:
> Murder his wife, his seruants, and who not?
> For that man's darke, where heauen is quite forgot.[15]

After this orthodox repentance speech, the wife answers, "Oh my repentant husband," and forgives him. Her forgiveness is thus withheld until he has made his confession and repentance.

The idea of demonic possession was popular in the literature of the period. It is after the Devil has been driven out of the husband that he comes to a full understanding of the consequences of his crimes. In spite of the fact that he has "sat in the seat of the scornful" and therefore has no hope of grace, he makes a "scaffold speech" in the approved manner.

> Oh, were it lawfull that your prettie soules
> Might looke from heauen into your fathers eyes,
> Then should you see the penitent glasses melt,
> And both your murthers shoote vpon my cheekes;
> But you are playing in the Angells lappes,
> And will not looke on me,
> Who void of grace, kild you in beggery.
> Oh that I might my wishes now attaine,
> I should then wish you liuing were againe,
>
> . . . .
>
> Oh, would you could pray heauen me to forgiue,
> That will vnto my end repentant liue.
>
> . . . .
>
> Farewell, ye bloudie ashes of my boyes!
> My punishments are their eternall ioyes.
> Let euery father looke into my deeds,
> And then their heirs may prosper, while mine bleeds.[16]

The author, by denying the hope of last-minute divine forgiveness and salvation through the means of a hurried penitent speech, points a sterner moral example than did the previous writers of murder

---

[15] *Ibid.*, p. 260; sc. x, ll. 15–28.   [16] *Ibid.*, p. 260; sc. x, ll. 38–63.

plays. Except for the difference in the ultimate goal of the sinner, this play follows the intellectual pattern of its predecessors.

A Yorkshire Tragedy has undoubted dramatic power. It is an extremely brief play, approximately eight hundred lines in length. Most of it is in rugged prose, some of which expresses exceedingly well the speech of ordinary life, as can be noted in the following:

Boy, look you walk my horse with discretion; I haue rid him simply. I warrand his skin sticks to his back with very heate: if a should catch cold & get the Cough of the Lunges I were well serued, were I not? [17]

The previously quoted monologue of the husband before he starts on his murders offers another example of effective prose.

In contrast, much of the verse is pedestrian, particularly in the moralizing scenes, where the husband repents in rhymed couplets. For example, he says:

Ile kiss the bloud I spilt and then I goe:
My soull is bloudied, well may my lippes be so.
Farewell, deere wife, now thou and I must parte,
I of thy wrongs repent me with my harte.[18]

Throughout, the characterization is weak. The husband appears as a monster of vice, unredeemed by any saving virtues, and the wife could be the sister of Patient Griselda. The other characters merely serve their essential dramatic functions. The power of the play lies, not in the characterization, but in the rapidly developing dramatic situation, as the action speeds quickly to the catastrophe. At crucial points, the language rises to the heights necessary for the dramatic purposes. In the author's ability to handle the plot and in the surety of his technique at the critical moments in the story lie the excellences of the play.

II

The writers of the last of the extant domestic murder plays, William Rowley, Thomas Dekker, and John Ford, returned in *The Witch of Edmonton* (1621) to a more orthodox treatment of the homiletic devices employed in *A Yorkshire Tragedy*. The setting of *The Witch of Edmonton* is Edmonton and London. The printed

---

[17] *Ibid.*, p. 251; sc. i, ll. 21–25.   [18] *Ibid.*, p. 260; sc. x, ll. 54–57.

text, which did not appear until 1658, supplied a distich purporting to give the whole argument.

> Forc'd marriage, murder; murder blood requires;
> Reproach, revenge; revenge, hell's help desires.[19]

The title is taken from the subplot, which is connected only superficially with the main part, a murder play of the type already treated. Although the story of Mother Sawyer, the witch of Edmonton, properly belongs in a later chapter, it will be considered here to avoid discussing two parts of the same play in separate chapters. The servant of evil, the Black Dog, brings each story to a catastrophic conclusion, and indicates a relationship of each to the other as well as to the other domestic tragedies of the period.

The protagonist of the murder story is young Frank Thorney, formerly in the service of Sir Arthur Clarington. Frank secretly marries a fellow servant named Winnifred, who, unknown to Frank, has been the mistress of Sir Arthur. Frank is obliged to conceal his marriage from his father lest the old man disinherit him, for old Thorney is determined to have his son wed Susan, the daughter of Carter, a rich yeoman. Frank agrees to go through with a bigamous marriage in order to get control of Susan's money. A few days after the wedding, he plans to abandon her and to escape with Winnifred to a distant part of England. The Black Dog, however, incites him to murder Susan, so he stabs her, and she dies forgiving her murderer. Frank endeavors to conceal his guilt by pretending that he and Susan were victims of highwaymen. In the house of his father-in-law, his self-inflicted wounds receive careful treatment. Katherine, the sister of Susan, accidentally discovers the blood-stained knife in his pocket. Then the crime is exposed, and Frank goes to his death with a contrite heart.

The playwrights consistently stressed realism throughout the plot. Speeches skillfully locate the action in contemporary England, and the authors exercised care to employ names and titles accurately. Old Carter says:

No gentleman I, Master Thorney; spare the Mastership, call me by my name, John Carter. Master is a title my father, nor his before him, were

---

[19] William Rowley, Thomas Dekker, John Ford, *The Witch of Edmonton*, in *The Works of John Ford*, ed. William Gifford and Alexander Dyce, III, 176.

acquainted with; honest Hertfordshire yeoman; such an one am I; my word and my deed shall be proved one at all times.[20]

Four-fifths of the Frank Thorney plot is written in verse, while the story of Mother Sawyer, being concerned with persons on a lower social scale, is about two-thirds prose. However, the most effective passages in the whole play are the abusive speeches of Mother Sawyer to the officials. These speeches will be considered later.

From the first, the story of Frank Thorney stresses religious and moral instruction. In this respect, the play follows the pattern of the earlier tragedies, revealing either a similar intention or a complete acceptance of a well-established tradition. A few examples will indicate the characteristic employment of dramatic devices based on religious doctrine. Frank calls down on himself the wrath of heaven if ever he is untrue to Winnifred:

> And, Winnifrede, whenever
> The wanton heat of youth, by subtle baits
> Of beauty, or what woman's art can practice,
> Draw[s] me from only loving thee, let heaven
> Inflict upon my life some fearful ruin! [21]

His fearful tragedy is thus partly heaven's punishment for his breaking of this solemn oath. In homiletic literature, indeed in much of the literature of Shakespeare's time, a character often unwittingly brings a curse down upon his own head.[22]

A few moments later, when she is importuned by Sir Arthur, Winnifred gives dramatic emphasis to the oath sworn by Frank, replying:

> This very day
> Young Thorney vow'd, with oaths not to be doubted,
> That never any change of love should cancel
> The bonds in which we are to either bound,
> Of lasting truth: and shall I, then, for my part
> Unfile the sacred oath set on record
> In heaven's book? [23]

---

[20] *Ibid.*, p. 186; I, ii, 3–8.   [21] *Ibid.*, p. 179; I, i, 63–67.

[22] Cf. the oath of Anne in Shakespeare's *Richard III*, I, ii, 14–28, and its consequences, IV, i, 66–87, IV, iii, 38.

[23] Rowley, Dekker, Ford, *The Witch of Edminton*, in *The Works of John Ford*, III, 185; I, i, 198–204.

Frank sins not only by breaking his oath to Winnifred, but also by falsely swearing that he is unmarried so that he can wed Susan.

> What do you take me for? an' atheist?
> One that nor hopes the blessedness of life
> Hereafter, neither fears the vengeance due
> To such as make the marriage-bed an inn,
> Which * * * * travellers, day and night,
> After a toilsome lodging, leave at pleasure?
> Am I become so insensible of losing
> The glory of creation's work, my soul? [24]

Frank realizes that he is pursuing a course which will lead him to grief and that he cannot escape the power of heaven, for he says after his marriage to Susan has been arranged:

> No man can hide his shame from heaven that views him;
> In vain he flees whose destiny pursues him.[25]

When the time comes for the murder of Susan, there is further evidence that the play is based on popular religious beliefs. The Black Dog, who has become the Mephistopheles to Mother Sawyer's Faustus, or who has assumed the role of the Vice of the moralities, appears briefly in the Frank Thorney plot. As Frank and Susan are strolling in the country, Frank orders her to return home, so that he can go away with Winnifred. Then the Black Dog rubs against him. Immediately Frank is seized with the notion of murdering Susan. Before he does so, he tells her of his other marriage and his reasons for it and concludes:

> I did not purpose to have added murder.
> The devil did not prompt me till this minute;
> You might have safe return'd; now you cannot.
> You have dogg'd your own death.[26]

In spite of the bad pun in the last line, it is clear that the Devil or one of his "familiars" suggests and instigates the crime. As a contrast to the malignant atmosphere surrounding the power of evil, the last words of Susan show the customary Christian feeling of a virtuous person.

[24] *Ibid.*, p. 193; I, ii, 188–96.   [25] *Ibid.*, p. 196; I, ii, 249–50.
[26] *Ibid.*, p. 229; III, iii, 37–40.

Thou art my husband, Death, and I embrace thee
With all the love I have. Forget the stain
Of my unwitting sin; and then I come
A crystal virgin to thee: my soul's purity
Shall with bold wings ascend the doors of Mercy;
For Innocence is ever her companion.

. . . .

Now heaven reward you ne'er the worse for me!
I did not think that death had been so sweet,
Nor I so apt to love him. I could ne'er die better,
Had I stay'd forty years for preparation;
For I'm in charity with all the world.
Let me for once be thine example, Heaven;
Do to this man as I him free forgive,
And may he better die and better live! [27]

Susan's family at first believes in Frank's innocence. Then Providence, by means of an accident, reveals his guilt to the family and, by a portent, brings home to him the enormity of the crime. Katherine, Susan's sister, finds the blood-stained knife in a way that an Elizabethan audience would recognize as a manifestation of Providence. While Katherine is revealing her discovery to her father, the ghost of Susan appears to Frank. He realizes that this visitation is an unmistakable sign of heaven's anger, for he later says, "To please a father, I have Heaven displeased." [28] Overcome with remorse, he confesses his guilt to Winnifred, who has come disguised as a page to nurse him. Katherine soon reveals him as the murderer to the rest of the company.

After arraignment and sentence, Frank repents and delivers a "scaffold speech," whereupon he is at once forgiven by those whom he has offended. While everyone, including Frank, recognizes the justice of the earthly punishment, all believe that he will receive divine mercy. Frank discourses thus:

He is not lost,
Who bears his peace within him: had I spun
My web of life out at full length, and dream'd
Away my many years in lusts, in surfeits,
Murders of reputations, gallant sins
Commended or approv'd; then, though I had

---

[27] *Ibid.*, pp. 229–30; III, ii, 50–65.   [28] *Ibid.*, p. 252; IV, ii, 104.

Died easily, as great and rich men do,
Upon my own bed, not compell'd by justice,
You might have mourn'd for me indeed; my miseries
Had been as everlasting as remediless:
But now the law hath not arraign'd, condemn'd
With greater rigour my unhappy fact
Than I myself have every little sin
My memory can reckon from my childhood:
A court hath been kept here, where I am found
Guilty; the difference is, my impartial judge
Is much more gracious than my faults are monstrous
* * * * to be nam'd; yet they are monstrous.

. . . .

                        Oh, that my example
Might teach the world hereafter what a curse
Hangs on their heads, who rather choose to marry
A goodly portion than a dower of virtues!—

. . . .

[I] robb'd you of a daughter; but she is
In heaven; and I must suffer for it willingly.

To this, Carter replies:

Ay, ay, she's in heaven, and I am glad to see thee so well prepared to follow her. I forgive thee with all my heart; if thou hadst not had ill counsel, thou wouldst not have done as thou didst; the more shame for them.[29]

With these manifestations of Christian feeling on both sides, Frank is led to execution. Human justice must be satisfied, but God may substitute mercy for His justice. Thus the main story of *The Witch of Edmonton* varies in no essential respect from its prototypes.

The subplot, dealing with Mother Sawyer, the witch of Edmonton, offers a double layer of interest. Religious doctrine and moral instruction are united to protest against abuses. While *Enough Is as Good as a Feast* and *The Tide Tarrieth no Man* denounced economic injustices, the development of the theme in *The Witch of Edmonton* is more extensive.

Because of her age, poverty, and ill temper, Mother Sawyer had long been thought to be a witch by her neighbors. However, she does

[29] *Ibid.*, pp. 267–69; V, ii, 91–137.

not actually become one until, by cursing, she offers an opening to the powers of evil. At once the Black Dog comes to her.

> *Dog.* Ho! have I found thee cursing? now thou art
> Mine own.
> *Saw[yer].* Thine! what art thou?
> *Dog.* He, thou hast so often
> Impórtun'd to appear to thee, the devil.[30]

The thunder and lightning which acompany the signing of the pact indicate heaven's disapproval of such a deed. Yet Mother Sawyer is undaunted and calls on her new servant to kill Old Banks, a neighbor. The Black Dog refuses, saying:

> Fool, because I cannot.
> Though we have power, know it is circumscrib'd
> And tied in limits: though he be curst to thee,
> Yet of himself he is loving to the world,
> And charitable to the poor; now men that,
> As he, love goodness, though in smallest measure,
> Live without compass of our reach: his cattle
> And corn I'll kill and mildew: but his life—
> Until I take him, as I late found thee,
> Cursing and swearing I've no power to touch.[31]

Mother Sawyer continues her course of sin until her allotted time is up. The Black Dog then appears to her in white, as a sign that she is ready for the winding sheet. He tells her:

. . . thou art so ripe to fall into hell, that no more of my kennel will so much as bark at him that hangs thee. . . . thy time is come to curse, and rave, and die; the glass of thy sins is full, and it must run out at the gallows.[32]

After she is taken into custody and condemned to death, Mother Sawyer undergoes considerable change. She repents, and her "scaffold speech," while not so extended as that of Frank Thorney, is as carefully limited a message.

> I was well resolv'd
> To die in my repentance. Though 'tis true
> I would live longer if I might, yet since

---

[30] *Ibid.*, p. 201; II, i, 128–30. [31] *Ibid.*, p. 203; II, i, 63–72.
[32] *Ibid.*, p. 258; V, i, 61–67.

> I cannot, pray torment me not; my conscience
> Is settled as it shall be: all take heed
> How they believe the devil; at last he'll cheat you.
> *Car*[*ter*]. Thou'dst best confess all truly.
> *Saw*[*yer*]   Yet again?
> Have I scarce breath enough to say my prayers,
> And would you force me to spend that in bawling?
> Bear witness, I repent all former evil;
> There is no damnèd conjuror like the devil.[33]

The playwrights carefully avoid the question of whether Mother Sawyer can hope for grace. Although she repents, her sin is so much greater than that of murder that it would have been dangerous for anyone except a churchman or a practiced theologian to hazard a guess as to her chance of salvation. The inference is that she has committed mortal sin and so is doomed for all eternity.

While the playwrights evade the question of redemption, they do not leave Mother Sawyer's actions completely unjustified. The dramatists allowed her to present her case against the conditions which impelled her to make her pact with the Devil, although they disavowed sympathy with her sin. Her first entrance shows her gathering sticks and muttering to herself:

> And why on me? why should the envious world
> Throw all their scandalous malice upon me?
> 'Cause I am poor, deform'd, and ignorant,
> And like a bow buckled and bent together,
> By some more strong in mischiefs than myself,
> Must I for that be made a common sink
> For all the filth and rubbish of men's tongues
> To fall and run into? Some call me witch,
> And being ignorant of myself, they go
> About to teach me how to be one; urging
> That my bad tongue—by their bad usage made so—
> Forspeaks their cattle, doth bewitch their corn,
> Themselves, their servants, and their babes at nurse.
> This they enforce upon me, and in part
> Make me to credit it.[34]

Another speech attacks some of the firmly established customs of the court. Before she is finally taken into custody, Mother Sawyer is

[33] *Ibid.*, pp. 266–67; V, ii, 57–67.   [34] *Ibid.*, pp. 196–97; II, i, 1–15.

threatened with arrest. Accused of being a witch, she gives her tongue
free rein:

> *Saw*[*yer*]. A witch! who is not?
> Hold not that universal name in scorn, then.
> What are your painted things in princes' courts,
> Upon whose eye-lids lust sits, blowing fires
> To burn men's souls in sensual hot desires,
> Upon whose naked paps, a lechers thought
> Acts sin in fouler shapes than can be wrought?
> *Just*[*ice*]. But those work not as you do.
> *Saw*[*yer*].   No, but for worse.
> These, by enchantments, can whole lordships change
> To trunks of rich attire, turn ploughs and teams
> To Flanders mares and coaches; and huge trains
> Of servitors to a French butterfly.
> Have you not city-wenches who can turn
> Their husbands' wares, whole standing shops of wares,
> To sumptuous tables, gardens of stol'n sin:
> In one year wasting, what scarce twenty win?
> Are not these witches?
>
> . . . .
>
>   Reverence once
> Had wont to wait on age; now an old woman,
> Ill-favour'd grown with years, if she be poor,
> Must be call'd bawd or witch.
>
> . . . .
>
> She, on whose tongue a whirlwind sits to blow
> A man out of himself, from his soft pillow
> To lean his head on rocks and fighting waves,
> Is not that scold a witch? The man of law
> Whose honey'd hopes the credulous client draw—
> As bees by tinkling basins—to swarm to him
> From his own hive to work the wax in his;
> He is no witch, not he!
>
> . . . .
>
> Dare any swear I ever tempted maiden
> With golden hooks flung at her chastity
> To come and lose her honour; and being lost
> To pay not a denier for 't? Some slaves have done it.

> Men-witches can, without the fangs of law
> Drawing once one drop of blood, put counterfeit pieces
> Away for true gold.[35]

While the court had been a favorite butt of satire from the time of Skelton or earlier, the presence of this particular kind of satiric writing in domestic tragedy is especially significant, revealing as it does more sympathy for the common people than contempt for the ways of the court. The above lines resemble the dialogue of a modern social-problem play more than that of an Elizabethan domestic tragedy. The attention to social and economic problems as it has appeared in this and other plays remains incidental and half accidental until the time of the revolutionary dramatists at the end of the nineteenth century.

The most noteworthy characteristic of *The Witch of Edmonton* is its careful adherence to the customary practices of homiletic drama. In developing the action, the authors employed, in both plots, sin and Providence as dramatic devices. The repentance of Frank Thorney follows all the conventional steps and is greeted by every member of the cast with the orthodox response of Christian forgiveness. The story of Mother Sawyer is unusual because it leaves the impression with the reader that mortal, or unpardonable, sin has been committed and that she is, therefore, condemned for all eternity. The Black Dog, who helps to tie the two parts of the play together, obviously descends from the Vices of the sixteenth-century morality plays. In contrast with this prolongation of an old-fashioned dramatic practice, Mother Sawyer's well-chosen words against the court anticipate a development many generations in the future.

In both plots, *The Witch of Edmonton* approaches tragedy. The character of Frank Thorney is a convincing portrait of a young man who weakly drifts into an impossible situation. His attempts to extricate himself cost him his life. By attempting to please everyone, he brings unhappiness to his friends and death to himself. Other characters in the plot are well drawn. The action develops with little delay and with a sure dramatic touch.

The most effective character, however, is the woman who gives the name to the play. Her neighbors, by their malice and hatred, have forced her into a life of vice. Mean and spiteful as she has become under the insults of respectable people, in adversity she nevertheless

[35] *Ibid.,* pp. 240–41; IV, i, 118–63.

displays considerable dignity and courage. Although, in accordance with the moral practice of the time, the playwrights condemn her for being a witch, the feeling pervades the play that the onus should rest on the shoulders of the people who drove her to make a compact with the Devil.

After the appearance of *The Witch of Edmonton,* murder drama set in a domestic and bourgeois milieu seems to have lost its popularity. As theatrical styles catered more and more to the upper classes, the mode for realism, for moralizing, and for didacticism passed. In the domestic tragedies, a murder had served as a subject for teaching lessons in conduct; in the later plays, the excitement of the events surrounding a murder was excuse enough for playwrights and audiences. The authors no longer felt obligated to add moral instruction. The murder play and other kinds of domestic tragedy lost favor because of the growing popularity of tragicomedy and "drama."

All the murder plays have certain characteristics in common, attributes which set them apart from the ordinary tragedies and comedies. Most of the authors of these melodramas use a realistic method of approach quite in contrast with the romantic temper of the time. Many of the playwrights apologize for the barrenness of their themes and the directness of their language; a few even appreciated the extent of their departure from critical dogma. In most cases, however, realism made the moral lesson effective by illustrating, directly in terms of the experiences of the audience, the punishments for sin.

The relationships of these domestic tragedies to their ancestors, the morality plays, is indicated as late as 1621 in *The Witch of Edmonton,* by the use of abstract characters to impersonate vices and virtues. As in the nondramatic literature, interventions of Divine Providence appear in all the murder plays of the sixteenth and seventeenth centuries, to punish vice, to reward virtue, to protect innocence, and to aid the authorized agents of God. Normal repentance in conformity to orthodox religious doctrine appears dramatically in "scaffold speeches" in nearly all of the plays. If sinners are not "scorners," like the husband in *A Yorkshire Tragedy,* or mortal sinners, like Mother Sawyer in *The Witch of Edmonton,* they aspire to divine mercy. The budding tendencies toward social drama involving the rights of the common man and the unfairness of court prerogatives had to wait over two hundred and fifty years for full development. Such tendencies soon disappeared from English drama, for the new tastes of the Caroline age and the aristocratic temper of the Restoration were unsympathetic to social protests.

Most of the murder plays were written anonymously or by low-salaried hacks who often collaborated in groups of three or more. On the other hand, one of the difficulties of disproving Shakespeare's authorship of *Arden of Feversham* and *A Yorkshire Tragedy* is to find another dramatist great enough to have written them.

The murder plays of the sixteenth and seventeenth centuries advanced domestic tragedy far beyond its literary ancestors. In the murder plays, the high points were reached comparatively early, and the species declined with the passage of years in the early seventeenth century. Heywood's *A Woman Killed with Kindness*, the outstanding representative of the domestic tragedies whose plots depict events other than homicides, came early in the century and was followed by a similar process of decadence.

Chapter Eight

THOMAS HEYWOOD'S "A WOMAN KILLED WITH KINDNESS"

A WOMAN KILLED WITH KINDNESS, Heywood's acknowledged masterpiece and the best-known Jacobean domestic tragedy, probably reached the stage shortly after the death of Elizabeth in March, 1603. The earliest of the extant plays to deal with a situation of family life divorced from the extravagance and sensationalism of murder, *A Woman Killed with Kindness* relates the story of a false friend and an erring wife. Master Frankford, who has married the sister of Sir Francis Acton, welcomes into his home Wendoll, a gentleman of small means. Wendoll proves unworthy of the friendship and seduces Mistress Frankford. Frankford discovers their treachery. Instead of killing his wife, he sends her to live in a lonely manor house, denying her only the right to see him and her children. She soon falls prey to remorse, and on her deathbed receives the forgiveness she begs of her husband.

Most anthologies of Elizabethan drama include this play, and critics have given it generous praise. In spite of the tragedy's wide appeal, little effort has been made to examine the play in relation to its intellectual milieu. Writers have customarily studied *A Woman Killed with Kindness* from one of two points of view, both of which might tend to give an exaggerated idea of its quality. It so far surpasses Heywood's other works that a student of his dramas has difficulty in restraining his superlatives when he finds the play among the run-of-the-mill products of this playwright. The other point of departure is the treatment of this drama as a domestic tragedy. Anthologists and historians of the theatre usually review briefly the more obvious domestic tragedies and then turn to this play, which, with *Arden of Feversham* and *A Yorkshire Tragedy*, stands as far above the others of the genre as it does above the average play of Heywood's. Thus, these critics employ encomiums beyond the merits of the tragedy. Representative samples of the praises will prove instructive.

John Addington Symonds, in his introduction to the Mermaid edition of Heywood, wrote:

The play in which Heywood showed for once that he was not unable to produce a masterpiece is *A Woman Killed with Kindness*. All his powers of direct painting from the English life he knew so well, his faculty for lifting prose to the borderground of poetry by the intensity of the emotion which he communicates, his simple art of laying bare the very nerves of passion, are here exhibited in perfection. This domestic tragedy touches one like truth. Its scenes are of everyday life. Common talk is used, and the pathos is homely; not like Webster's, brought from far. Tastes may differ as to the morality or the wholesomeness of the sentiment evolved in the last act. None, however, can resist its artless claim upon our sympathies.[1]

A. W. Ward, in his *A History of English Dramatic Literature*, is almost as lavish in his praise:

The exquisite pathos of this play is not more striking than the true manliness of its tone. While we pity the weakness of the erring wife even in her fall, we are conscious that the punishment inflicted on her is true justice. In the scene where, after having been apprised of her infidelity, her husband watches her demeanour and that of her paramour, we are perhaps to some extent distracted by the cleverness of the dialogue accompanying the situation. But the subsequent scene of the actual discovery is thrilling in its power. The terrible suspense of the situation, as the husband accompanied by a faithful servant returns under cover of the night to his polluted home, there to surprise his guilty wife, has few parallels in the Elisabethan drama; it might almost be described as a "prose" reproduction of some of the terrors of *Macbeth*.[2]

Felix Schelling commented as follows:

Heywood's greatest play is *A Woman Killed with Kindness*, printed in 1607. This drama rises to the dignity and pathos of true tragedy, though free from blood and horror. . . . Whether we dwell on the execution, leisurely and complete, on the powerful situation, that of the discovery, which marks the climax of the play, or consider the charity and manliness

---

[1] *Thomas Heywood*, ed. John Addington Symonds, Mermaid edition, pp. xxvii–xxviii.

[2] Adolphus William Ward, *A History of English Dramatic Literature to the Death of Queen Anne*, 1899 ed., II, 564.

of its tone in the treatment of a theme easily degenerating into sentimentality and mawkishness, it is impossible to overpraise *A Woman Killed with Kindness* or to regard it other than as one of the choicest of Elizabethan plays.[3]

Mowbray Velte is a little more reserved in his criticism. Although he failed to develop his conclusions, he touched upon the true emphasis of the play.

There is tense dramatic power and vividness too in the scene in which Frankford and Nicholas steal into the house to discover Anne and Wendoll asleep in each other's arms, and real agony in Frankford's simple "Oh! Oh!" when he first sees them so. The dramatic effect throughout is obtained by extreme simplicity of diction. There is no bombast, no straining for effect or lengthy rhetoric, but the same straightforward, forceful narrative method that characterizes "Arden of Feversham."

. . . . .

He [Master Frankford] is patient and forgiving, a truly Christian character. Again we see Heywood the moralist at work, and there is a strain of sentimentality running through all his morality. The erring wife repents a thousand-fold, and is at last forgiven by all, dying with her wronged husband's kiss still on her lips. Thus divine justice is satisfied, for her sin receives its punishment, death; but at the same time there is compensation in that she dies forgiven. Heywood has pulled at the very heart-strings of his audience, first in his picture of the grief-stricken husband, second in his picture of the penitent wife.[4]

Observations from other sources might be quoted, but these criticisms seem representative. Nearly all writers agree that the most serious weaknesses of the play are, first, the easy acquiescence of Mistress Frankford to Wendoll's pleading and, second, Frankford's forgiveness of his wife on her deathbed. The usual explanation is that audiences expected easy emotional shifts and were not disturbed by lack of motivation. This explanation may be true, but a better interpretation is available, one which illuminates not only these two scenes, but the entire course of the action.

Like the other domestic tragedies of the period, *A Woman Killed with Kindness* has as its intellectual basis the popular understanding of theology. At every critical point in the play, religious didacticism

[3] Felix E. Schelling, *Elizabethan Drama, 1558–1642*, I, 336–37.
[4] Mowbray Velte, *The Bourgeois Elements in the Dramas of Thomas Heywood*, pp. 106–7.

and not Elizabethan psychology directs the action of the characters. From the moment Wendoll shows an interest in Mistress Frankford until the conclusion of the tragedy, Heywood consistently uses the characteristic moral and theological terminology. In fact, he so emphasizes moral instruction that he neglects or distorts human motivation the better to make clear his point.

Wendoll, after having been befriended by Master Frankford, "enters melancholy," and introduces the idea of divine punishment even as he considers the betrayal of his patron.

> I am a villain, if I apprehend
> But such a thought: then, to attempt the deed,—
> Slave, thou art damned without redemption.
>
> . . . .
>
> O God! O God! with what a violence
> I'm hurried to mine own destruction.
> There goest thou, the most perfectest man
> That ever England bred a gentleman;
> And shall I wrong his bed? Thou God of thunder!
> Stay in thy thoughts of vengeance and of wrath,
> Thy great, almighty, and all-judging hand
> From speedy execution of a villain:
> A villain, and a traitor to his friend.[5]

Although fully aware of the consequences to his soul, Wendoll pursues his intention of seducing Mistress Frankford. She says nothing of any love she might feel for Wendoll or any bitterness she might have against her husband. Instead her chief concern is for the sin she seems doomed to commit, whether she will or no, for she says:

> My soul is wandering, and hath lost her way,
> Oh, Master Wendoll! Oh!
>
> . . . .
>
> I ne'er offended yet:
> My fault, I fear will in my brow be writ.
> Women that fall, not quite bereft of grace,
> Have their offences noted in their face.
> I blush and am ashamed. Oh, Master Wendoll,

---

[5] *A Woman Kilde with Kindneffe*, in *Thomas Heywood*, ed. John Addington Symonds, Mermaid edition, p. 22; II, iii, 1–25.

> Pray God I be not born to curse your tongue,
> That hath enchanted me! This maze I am in
> I fear will prove the labyrinth of sin.[6]

In accordance with the practice of moral literature of the time, Heywood shows as little as possible of the attractiveness of vice or the emotional drive toward doing the deed. When the wrongdoer was conscious of the sin he was committing and struggled against it, but found the flesh too strong for him, he was safe from the dangers of mortal sin, for his fault was in opposition to his will. Mistress Frankford's statement that she was knowingly opposing God's ways has the dramatic purpose of keeping the sympathy with Frankford. If the love affair of Wendoll and Anne Frankford captured the interest of the audience, Heywood was in danger of weakening the force of his moral lesson.

The servant, Nicholas, discloses the faithlessness of Wendoll and Mistress Frankford to Frankford. In order to trap the lovers, Frankford pretends to be called away from home on business. Wendoll at once urges his paramour to take advantage of her husband's absence. She reluctantly agrees, hesitating not from fear of detection, but because of the peril to her soul.

Mis[*tress*] *Frank*[*ford*]. O! what a clog unto the soul is sin!
We pale offenders are still full of fear;
Every suspicious eye brings danger near,
When they, whose clear hearts, from offence are free
Despite report, base scandals do outface,
And stand at mere defiance with disgrace.
Wen[*doll*]. Fie, fie! you talk too like a puritan.
Mis[*tress*] *Frank*[*ford*]. You have tempted me to mischief Master Wendoll:
I have done I know not what. Well, you plead custom;
That which for want of wit I granted erst,
I now must yield through fear. Come, come, let's in;
Once o'er shoes, we are straight o'er head in sin.[7]

The last two lines in the above speech repeat the familiar idea of the "chain of vice." A sinner could stop his headlong course of vice only by heartfelt repentance. Repentance, however, required confession, penance, and the abandonment of the rewards of sin, three things manifestly impossible at that time to Mistress Frankford.

[6] *Ibid.*, pp. 26–27; II, iii, 154–64.   [7] *Ibid.*, p. 50; IV, iii, 103–14.

Master Frankford has shown himself up to this point to be generous, considerate, and honest. His bounty toward Wendoll illustrates his liberality, and the affection of his servants is evidence of his kindness toward them. Obviously Heywood intended him to epitomize a Christian gentleman. His actions after the final proof of his wife's adultery harmonize with the character already disclosed. His first reaction is not anger, grief, or any natural human emotion, but concern for the souls of the two sinners.

> O me unhappy! I have found them lying
> Close in each other's arms, and fast asleep.
> But that I would not damn two precious souls,
> Bought with my Saviour's blood, and send them, laden
> With all their scarlet sins upon their backs,
> Unto a fearful judgment, their two lives
> Had met upon my rapier.[8]

This is the same theological concept which prevents Hamlet from killing the king while the latter is at prayer.[9] Both Hamlet and Frankford know that a person discovered in the midst of sin and killed without any chance for repentance will inevitably be damned throughout all eternity. However, the dramatic effect in the two plays is quite different. In *Hamlet*, the scene is charged with dramatic irony, and the total impression is one of disappointment. In *A Woman Killed with Kindness*, the effect is that of breaking the tension. The audience relaxes after the emotional high peak of the discovery. The scene thus leads into the pathos and moralizing which follow. The ideas motivating the two characters are also quite different. To Hamlet, the fact that prayer may preserve his uncle's soul acts as a deterrent. Hamlet spares Claudius at a moment when he presumably could have slain him with impunity and accomplished his revenge. Master Frankford, however, is primarily a Christian gentleman and, as such, is more concerned with the preservation of the immortal souls of all people, even of those who have wronged him. For that reason, he restrains himself.

When Wendoll rushes from the bedroom, Frankford momentarily shows a human desire for vengeance. As, with drawn sword, he pursues the seducer, a maidservant stops him. This interruption, instead of arousing his anger, seems to him an act of heaven. He cries:

---

[8] *Ibid.*, p. 53; IV, vi, 8–14.   [9] Shakespeare, *Hamlet*, III, iii, 73–96.

> I thank thee, maid; thou, like the angel's hand,
> Hast stayed me from a bloody sacrifice.[10]

Allusion at such a point in the play to the Biblical story of the angel's rescue of Isaac from the sacrificial sword is significant, indicating that Master Frankford interprets the maidservant as being a similar providential agent. As he recognizes the power of God in the hand of the maid who prevents him from killing Wendoll, so does he follow a Christian course in withholding his revenge on his wife. His first reaction is purely emotional. In an orgy of sentiment, he exclaims:

> O Nan! O Nan!
> If neither fear of shame, regard of honour,
> The blemish of my house, nor my dear love,
> Could have withheld thee from so lewd a fact,
> Yet for these infants, these young harmless souls,
> On whose white brows thy shame is charactered,
> And grows in greatness as they wax in years,—
> Look but on them, and melt away in tears.
> Away with them! lest, as her spotted body
> Hath stained their names with stripe of bastardy,
> So her adulterous breath may blast their spirits
> With her infectuous thoughts.[11]

Having sought through this tirade to arouse contrition in his wife, Frankford retires to another room to consider her punishment. In a soliloquy, Anne admits her sin, but shows that she is not yet fully prepared to turn repentantly to God. She is willing to hazard her soul to regain her honor. She has still to learn that mundane honor is a trifling thing in comparison with salvation of the soul. Her husband's mercy enables her to reach an understanding of this truth. While she awaits his decision, she laments in the following speech:

> Nay, to whip but this scandal out, I would hazard
> The rich and dear redemption of my soul.
> He cannot be so base as to forgive me;
> Nor I so shameless to accept his pardon.
> O women, women you that yet have kept
> Your holy matrimonial vow unstained,

---

[10] *A Woman Killed with Kindness*, in *Thomas Heywood*, p. 54; IV, vi, 24–25. Cf. Genesis, 22:10–12.

[11] *A Woman Killed with Kindness*, in *Thomas Heywood*, pp. 55–56; IV, vi, 80–91.

> Make me your instance: when you tread awry,
> Your sins, like mine, will on your conscience lie.[12]

In sentencing his wife, Master Frankford exhibits Christian mercy.

> My words are registered in Heaven already,
> With patience hear me. I'll not martyr thee,
> Nor mark thee for a strumpet; but with usage
> Of more humility torment thy soul,
> And kill thee even with kindness.[13]

He has not designed her punishment as an act of kindness to her in this world, but as a means to save her everlasting soul. Had Frankford decided to kill her, she could not have repented, and so would have been doomed to hell. She had just shown that she was not ready to make her accounting with God, for she still had no clear conception of the value of salvation. Thus, Frankford, in ordering her to live in solitude, allows her time for contemplation so that she may attain heaven. Also, Frankford is not sure of his own judgment. While a deceived husband had the right to kill an adulterous wife, there was the feeling that " 'God will returne into their bosom the euill which they haue done.' This faith sustained the important Elizabethan doctrine that men should not for private reasons take God's revenge into their own hands." [14] After he has instructed Anne to remove herself and her possessions to the manor house he has set aside for her, he decrees that she must never again see him or their children.

> But, as thou hopest for Heaven, as thou believest
> Thy name's recorded in the book of life,
> I charge thee never, after this sad day,
> To see me.[15]

Thus Frankford exemplifies the model conduct of a Christian in extreme circumstances. His concern for his wife's immortal soul triumphs over his natural feelings. His punishment of her is designed to bring home the implications of her sin and to prepare her mind and soul for repentance. Unwilling to live with her again as her husband, he fulfills

---

[12] *Ibid.*, p. 56; IV, vi, 101–8.   [13] *Ibid.*, pp. 56–57; IV, vi, 116–21.

[14] Roy W. Battenhouse, *Marlowe's "Tamburlaine," a Study in Renaissance Moral Philosophy*, p. 113, quoted from La Primaudaye, *The French Academy* (1594), Pt. II, p. 326.

[15] *A Woman Killed with Kindness*, in *Thomas Heywood*, p. 57; iv, vi, 138–41.

his duty by supporting her and giving her opportunity to save her soul.

Mistress Frankford soon realizes that her every thought must be for the attainment of divine forgiveness. She prepares a penance which is planned to bring about her death. By abstaining from food and by many contrite tears, she hopes to win divine mercy. She says:

> So, now unto my coach, then to my home,
> So to my death-bed; for from this sad hour
> I never will nor eat, nor drink, nor taste
> Of any cates that may preserve my life:
> I never will nor smile, nor sleep, nor rest;
> But when my tears have washed my black soul white,
> Sweet Saviour, to Thy hands I yield my sprite.[16]

Wendoll meets her as she is going to the manor house and offers her worldly comforts. She recognizes him as temptation persuading her to resume her sinful life. She refuses to save her body and thus lose her hope of spiritual salvation.

> Oh, for God's sake fly!
> The devil doth come to tempt me ere I die.
> My coach! this fiend, that with an angel's face
> Conjured mine honour, till he sought my wrack,
> In my repentant eyes seems ugly black.[17]

The punishment of Wendoll falls beyond the limits of the play. The text suggests that after a brief exile he may go to court and win prosperity, but worldly success is but a snare to divert his mind from contrition. Even he admits that by the repentance of Mistress Frankford their joint sin recoils on his head. Thus he departs from the action of the play, unrepentant, but subject at any time to God's retributive justice.[18]

The repentances and the free forgiveness make the last interview between Master Frankford and his wife the obligatory scene of the drama. Master Frankford visits Anne in fulfillment of his Christian duty. Sir Francis Acton, Mistress Frankford's brother, tells her why her husband has reconsidered his decision never to see her again.

> Seeing your sorrow and your penitence,
> And hearing therewithal the great desire

---

[16] *Ibid.*, p. 67; V, iii, 106–12.   [17] *Ibid.*, p. 68; V, iii, 114–18.
[18] *Ibid.*, p. 68; V, iii, 131–43.

You have to see him ere you left the world,
He gave to us his faith to follow us,
And sure he will be here immediately.[19]

When he arrives, Anne is so worried about her great sin that she begs for his forgiveness to ensure divine mercy for herself. She pleads, not for him to take her again as his wife, but for his aid in her efforts to win salvation.

Out of my zeal to Heaven, whither I'm now bound,
I was so impudent to wish you here;
And once more beg your pardon. O good man,
And father to my children, pardon me,
Pardon, oh, pardon me! My·fault so heinous is,
That if you in this world forgive it not,
Heaven will not clear it in the world to come.
Faintness hath so usurped upon my knees
That kneel I cannot, but on my heart's knees
My prostrate soul lies thrown down at your feet
To beg your gracious pardon. Pardon, oh, pardon me! [20]

Master Frankford, as a Christian, cannot refuse her plea. With no hesitation, he replies:

As freely, from the low depth of my soul,
As my Redeemer hath forgiven His death,
I pardon thee. I will shed tears with thee, pray with thee;
And, in mere pity of thy weak estate,
I'll wish to die with thee.

. . . .

Even as I hope for pardon at that day
When the Great Judge of Heaven in scarlet sits,
So be thou pardoned. Though thy rash offence
Divorced our bodies, thy repentant tears
Unite our souls.[21]

Clearly their union has become exclusively spiritual, for she dies after he has given her a kiss of forgiveness. Morality and Christian duty have been satisfied. Joy at the salvation of her soul ameliorates the grief at her death. Sir Francis Acton justifies and explains the course pursued by Master Frankford, saying:

[19] *Ibid.*, p. 71; V, vi, 10–14. [20] *Ibid.*, p. 72; V, vi, 44–54.
[21] *Ibid.*, p. 72; V, vi, 55–69.

> Brother, had you with threats and usage bad
> Punished her sin, the grief of her offence
> Had not with such true sorrow touched her heart.[22]

This scene is, then, no sentimental appeal for reconciliation, but a dramatization of the necessary steps of Christian repentance and forgiveness. The basis for the Frankford plot is the familiar contrast between lust and virtue. The victim falls prey to vice, and pays for her error when lust proves to be an empty pleasure and also a threat of eternal damnation. When the sinner is truly repentant and has met with earthly forgiveness, his soul may be saved by divine mercy. Master Frankford embodies the gentleman who never swerves from his Christian duty.

These points are fundamental in the story and serve as the keystones in the action. Although other characteristics such as pathos, sentiment, and emotionalism may occasionally appear, they are embellishments of the central theme. A sentimental interpretation of this play leaves the last scene unexplained, while from the point of view of religious doctrine, the action is charged with meaning. As a Christian, Master Frankford would like to forgive his wife, but, as a Christian, he cannot condone vice. When penance has been made, when repentance is sincere, then forgiveness may be given. In the stern Renaissance code, death was the only penance which could atone for adultery. Frankford, though careful to withhold his pardon until his wife's dying moment, gives it then as the duty of a merciful Christian.

In the subplot of *A Woman Killed with Kindness,* Heywood made the first alliance between domestic tragedy and that species later to be called "drama." This term had not then been developed to refer specifically to a serious play with a happy ending. The Renaissance use of the word "comedy" was broad enough to include "drama." In a "drama," characters undergo great stress, hardship, and privation, only to be rescued by the most fortuitous of endings. In order to bring about such a conclusion, a playwright will use every device of coincidence and improbable character reaction at his command. He will spend three-quarters of his play building up a situation which should lead to a catastrophe and then, by means of the unexpected arrival of a letter or the unmotivated repentance or conversion of one of the characters, will

[22] *Ibid.,* p. 73; V, vi, 93–95.

manage to close his play with a scene of general rejoicing. Such is the material of "drama."

Through most of the history of domestic tragedy, playwrights have found it easy to slip into the use of "drama." Many of the plays from 1603 to 1642 employ such a story as subplot for a domestic tragedy or, later, use a domestic tragedy as subplot for a "drama." Stories originally tragic are altered to conform to this genre. An example of the practice is the change in the ending of the Calverley case in the Wilkins dramatization, *The Miseries of Enforced Marriage.* The subplot of *A Woman Killed with Kindness* has no known tragic version, but the action might easily have led to catastrophe rather than to reconciliation.

Sir Francis Acton, loser in a hunting match with Sir Charles Mountford, refuses to admit defeat. Words lead to blows, and two of Sir Francis's men are slain. Sir Charles is exonerated of murder, but his acquittal deprives him of his fortune. Left in penury, he is quick to embrace the offer of a loan from one Shafton. Shafton reveals himself to be a villain who made the loan to bring further disgrace on the honest Sir Charles. Arrested at the instigation of Shafton, Sir Charles languishes in prison. In the meantime, Sir Francis Acton has fallen a victim to the charms of Susan, the sister of Sir Charles Mountford. Unsuccessful in his attempts to win her, he seeks, by economic pressure, to gain her as his mistress. He pays the debts of Sir Charles, who is set free. Learning the identity of his benefactor and the reasons for the action, Sir Charles persuades Susan to submit to the desires of Sir Francis that their debts may be paid. He then plans to kill his sister and himself. Sir Francis, won over to a life of virtue by his love for Susan, ceases his persecutions and pleads for her as his bride. Thus all ends happily.

No theological emphasis carries over into the story of Sir Charles. The motivation of the subplot is sentimental; this part of the play is filled with the usual paraphernalia of sentiment—tears and the reformation of a villain at the contemplation of feminine virtue.

Heywood's *A Woman Killed with Kindness* possesses undoubted dramatic power. Its merits have long tended to blind readers to its less obvious shortcomings. Heywood's great ability as a dramatist was to make actions lively and plots engrossing, so that absurdities frequently escape detection. The most prolific of Elizabethan dramatists, he left in all his surviving dramatic works traces of haste. *A Woman Killed with*

Kindness is no exception. At several of the crucial stages in the action motivation is insufficiently presented. Sir Francis Acton's sudden infatuation with Susan, the fall from virtue of Mistress Frankford, the decision of Wendoll to betray his patron—none of these incidents is made convincing. Although each is accepted as a dramatic fact, at these points there is a break in the illusion of reality. With the exception of Nicholas, who reveals to her husband the treachery of Anne Frankford, the servants have little connection with the two plots. Either they echo the action of their masters, as with their dance in the second scene where they imitate the wedding feast, or they act as a kind of chorus to give information to the audience and to comment on the progress of the events.

When Heywood introduced the subplot, his dramatic vision was singularly obtuse. He included it to fill out the play and to offer relief from the main action. The secondary story is palpably impossible, and his great pains to bring local color into it only make the unreality the more apparent. The subplot continually interferes with and interrupts the important main action, and the motivations and the psychological processes of the characters are so incomprehensible that they detract from the play. Heywood might better have employed the "two hours traffic" of his stage in filling out the story of the Frankfords.

In spite of all these shortcomings, Heywood deserves credit for having, to a great extent, overcome his characteristic looseness of dramatic structure. In comparison with *The Fair Maid of the West*, *The English Traveller*, *The Iron Age*, or *Edward IV*, *A Woman Killed with Kindness* is a dramaturgical masterpiece.

In characterization also, the play is uneven. The virtue of Master Frankford fails to convince. His generosity to Wendoll is almost totally unmotivated and appears to be a fair sample of his munificence. His exemplary Christianlike conduct in dealing with his adulterous wife also offends credibility. Frankford is normally so devoid of any natural emotion that he seems no man but a theological prig. On the other hand, in a few places Heywood briefly invests him with flesh and blood. Frankford completely captures the sympathy of the audience as he hesitates to enter the room where he knows the lovers are together, and again as he rushes out with his last hopes dashed to the ground. His burst of anger when, with drawn sword, he pursues

Wendoll is a natural action which the spectators immediately approve. In the moralizing sentences which follow, Heywood rebukes the audience for this approval. During the remainder of the play, Frankford steadily loses the common attributes of humanity as he grows more and more to exemplify the ideal Christian conduct.

Mistress Anne Frankford is, at no point, completely convincing. Neither her acceptance of Wendoll as her lover nor her subsequent return to virtue is adequately motivated. She is primarily employed to teach a moral lesson by her conduct. Wendoll is, perhaps, the most completely characterized figure in the play. Heywood made an effort to show the conflict within Wendoll as he struggles against the passion which impels him to betray his patron and his friend. After he is discovered, he displays sincere concern over Anne's fate. Although Wendoll is the villain of the play, Heywood endeavored to make him as little as possible the malignant stage villain. The presentation is as sympathetic as can be made commensurate with the role he plays.

Sir Charles Mountford is the only character in the subplot who is depicted with any feeling for psychological realities. He arouses considerable sympathy and interest. Before the end of the play, however, his mental processes and his conduct degenerate into absurdity. His sister, Susan, is not as well realized as her brother, but far better than are Shafton and Sir Francis Acton, who are stage puppets.

The play abounds with some of Heywood's happiest dialogue. In both plots and in the rustic scenes, the lines are expressive, eloquent, and, at times, powerful. The prologue apologizes for the meanness of the scene and subject, and for Heywood's realistic treatment.

> I come but like a harbinger, being sent
> To tell you what these preparations mean:
> Look for no glorious state; our Muse is bent
> Upon a barren subject, a bare scene.
> We could afford this twig a timber tree,
> Whose strength might boldly on your favours build;
> Our russet, tissue; drone, a honey-bee;
> Our barren plot, a large and spacious field;
> Our coarse fare, banquets; our thin water, wine;
> Our brook, a sea; our bat's eyes, eagle's sight;
> Our poet's dull and earthy Muse, divine;
> Our ravens, doves; our crow's black feathers, white;

> But gentle thoughts, when they may give the foil,
> Save them that yield, and spare where they may spoil.[23]

The play gives as realistic an impression of early seventeenth-century England as do the comedies of Jonson. The opening wedding feast and the hawking scenes are drawn from life. Business affairs occupy most of the characters; money is seldom used carelessly as in the court tragedies, but is something to be earned and conserved.

Heywood, nevertheless, makes a concession to the rule that a tragedy may not depict the lowest elements in society. The chief actors are all of the class known as "gentlemen." However, characters from the kitchen and the barnyard appear in scenes of country reveling, dancing, and merrymaking, episodes having no real connection with the course of either plot. There is nothing new or daring in the use of low-comedy characters for such a purpose or in depicting them more realistically than the gentry. The introduction of rustic personages is a frequent practice in Heywood's plays. While these scenes serve the purpose of comic relief, they also provide social contrast to maintain the proper position and dignity of the tragic characters.

The virtues of the citizenry of England appear as emphatically here as they do in *Edward IV*. Most of the characters seem contented with their social stations. Frankford puts his case thus:

> How happy am I amongst other men,
> That in my mean estate embrace content!
> I am a gentleman, and by my birth
> Companion with a king; a king's no more.
> I am possessed of many fair revenues,
> Sufficient to maintain a gentleman.[24]

The knowledge of the servants that they are necessary and integral parts of society gives them a large measure of self-respect. They show this pride in their position as Jack Slime says:

> Truly Nick, though we were never brought up like serving courtiers, yet we have been brought up with serving creatures, ay, and God's creatures too . . .[25]

While Heywood is careful to maintain social distinctions, he displays sympathy with people of all conditions, accepting everyone as a necessary part of the social structure.

---

[23] *Ibid.*, p. 3, Prologue.   [24] *Ibid.*, p. 16; II, i, 1–6.
[25] *Ibid.*, p. 10; I, ii, 9–11.

A Woman Killed with Kindness leaves the reader with a feeling that the play falls short of its dramatic possibilities. The subordination of the action of the main plot to the demonstration of religious teaching spoils any effect of tragedy which might arise from the situation. Because Heywood is eager to present his thesis, he makes the characters act in a way which will best serve his ends, not in a manner best calculated to create the illusion of reality. *Arden of Feversham* and *A Yorkshire Tragedy* far surpass *A Woman Killed with Kindness* in dramatic power and intensity. Heywood was attempting to appeal to the shopkeepers and artisans of his audience by giving them instructive and wholesome entertainment, and he knew his trade. The morality, the sentiment, the pathos, the comedy, and the tragedy in this work are all directed to the edification and amusement of this audience. Only as the play is examined critically in relation to the conventions of the genre of domestic tragedy or compared with the really great plays of the period do its deficiencies become apparent. The tragedy rewards the reader, but leaves him with a slight feeling of disappointment that Heywood lacked that extra power necessary to make a great play of *A Woman Killed with Kindness.*

Chapter Nine

THE DECLINE OF DOMESTIC TRAGEDIES

In ADDITION to the murder plays and those based on history and legend, several other domestic tragedies are important enough to receive consideration. Miscellaneous in subject matter, treating such themes as seduction, betrayal, and the erring of a prodigal son, they illustrate the debility of the genre and the causes leading to its imminent disappearance from the stage. Some of the later plays appeal to a decadent interest in such subjects as witchcraft and incest. The devices intended for teaching religious morality continued to be employed by writers of domestic tragedy throughout the reigns of James I and Charles I. Frequently, however, these playwrights give the impression that they are following a convention.

A part of Chapter Seven contains an analysis of *A Yorkshire Tragedy*, the first of the two plays on the subject of the notorious Calverley murders. George Wilkins, in *The Miseries of Enforced Marriage*, the second dramatization of the story, mutilates it almost beyond recognition. He concentrates on the early events of the history, entirely omitting the murders which were the main interest in *A Yorkshire Tragedy*. Tragedy occurs in the play, but early enough not to interfere with the happy conclusion. The story of the drama is this: Young Scarborow (William Calverley) has plighted his troth to Clare, daughter of Sir John Harcop. When he returns home, he is constrained by a friend of his father's to marry Katherine. Clare, on hearing of the marriage, commits suicide. Scarborow's reaction is dreadful to behold. He deserts his wife and children and goes to London with the express purpose of squandering the family fortunes. His brothers and sister are forced to steal for a living. Butler, the faithful servant, tricks Sir Francis Ilford, a wastrel, into marrying the sister. After the marriage has been consummated, Ilford, learning that she is penniless, deserts her. In spite of these fearful complications, all ends happily; Ilford is persuaded to accept the sister as his wife, Katherine is restored to her husband, and Old Falconbridge, the friend of Scarborow's father, dies, leaving them a fortune.

Of this drama, only the first two acts are at all tragic. The remainder of the play is devoted to an exposition of the theme expressed in the title.

In the death scene of Clare, pathos and sentiment mingle with theology. The crudest possible use is made of dramatic irony, as Clare, attempting to protract her joy in the missive, trifles with a letter she has just received from her beloved Scarborow. Its contents are already known to the audience. It says curtly, "Forgive me, Clare, for I am married." After she reads the letter, her lamentations fill two pages of the play. Since she is trothplight to Scarborow, she would commit a sin to accept the attentions of another, and her desire to avoid sin far surpasses any other emotion. She moans:

> Whoever fues to me commits a fin,
> Befiegeth me, and who fhall marry me
> Is like myfelf, lives in adultery . . .[1]

Having mused thus for some time, Clare decides on her course of action. She forgives her faithless lover, and writes him a note, "Forgive me, I am dead." She addresses the audience in justification of her conduct and then kills herself to save the soul of her betrothed from sin, saying:

> . . . be judge you maids,
> Have trufted the falfe promifes of men.
> Be judge you wives, the which have been inforc'd
> From the white fheets you lov'd to them ye loathed:
> Whether this axiom may not be affured,
> —*Better one fin, than many be endured.*
> My arms imbracings, kiffes, chaftity,
> Were his poffeffions: and whilft I live
> He doth but fteal thofe pleafures he enjoys,
> Is an adulterer in his married arms,
> And never goes to his defiled bed,
> But God writes fin upon the fefter's head.
> I'll be a wife now, help to fave his foul

---

[1] George Wilkins, *The Miferies of Inforft Marriage,* in Robert Dodsley, *A Select Collection of Old Plays,* 2d ed., V, 35.

> Though I have loſt his body, give a ſlake
> To his iniquities, and with one ſin,
> Done by this hand, end many done by him.
>
> . . . .
>
> Yet record world, though by an act too foul,
> A wife thus died, to cleanſe her huſband's ſoul.[2]

The remainder of this scene is laden with sentiment. Sir John Harcop, mourning his daughter, invokes destruction on the man who has brought her to an untimely end.

> Curſe on his traiterous tongue, his youth, his blood,
> His pleaſures, children, and poſſeſſions!
> Be all his days like winter, comfortleſs!
> Reſtleſs his nights, his wants remorſeleſs!
> And may his corpſe be the phyſician's ſtage,
> Which, plaid upon, ſtands not to honoured age!
> Or with diſeaſes may he lie and pine,
> Till grief wax blind his eyes, as grief doth mine! [3]

All these things come to pass, except Scarborow's death or life of disease. He escapes these extremities because he was not guilty of voluntarily breaking the vow of trothplight. Since he was weak enough to accept the marriage to Katherine which had been forced upon him, he had to suffer, but because compulsion had been used, and since by her suicide Clare had kept him from a sin equivalent to adultery, he was spared the punishment of death. The final scene of the play indicates this clearly. Scarborow has just learned of the death of the man who had compelled him to marry Katherine.

> *Butler.*
> And that he knew,
> Your ſin was his, the puniſhment his due.
> *Scarborow.*
> All this is here:
> Is heaven ſo gracious to ſinners then?
> *Butler.*
> Heaven is, and has his gracious eyes,
> To give men life not like intrapping ſpies.
> *Scarborow.*
> Your hand, yours, yours, to my ſoul; to you a kiſs;

---

[2] *Ibid.*, p. 36.   [3] *Ibid.*, p. 38.

Introth I am ſorry I have ſtray'd amiſs;
To whom ſhall I be thankful? all ſilent?
None ſpeak? whiſt: why then to God,
That gives men comfort as he gives his rod . . .[4]

This play embodies the usual popular theology of the period, but it varies from the customary pattern because the sinner repents his relatively trifling sins and is allowed to enjoy earthly prosperity. He is not required to pay the penalty to the law or to human justice. Forgiven on earth, he has a chance to become an upright Christian, leading a godly life. The apparent softening of the consequences of libertinism admits of ready explanation. The root of the trouble was the marriage forced on Scarborow. In reaction, he took to the life of the tavern. Thus the play is something of a *pièce à thèse,* whose main argument teaches that a great wrong is committed when dependents are forced to marry against their wills. The action of the play is a clear exposition of this thesis. The death of Clare is only an episode illustrating one of the many errors to be charged to the instigator of the marriage. Theological justice is satisfied by the punishment of Old Falconbridge at the critical time in the action. His death is an example of the intervention of Divine Providence. The sins of the others have been slight errors which deserve punishment but not death. The suicide of Clare keeps both her and Scarborow from a sin greater than that of self-destruction. The assumption is that she will find her reward in heaven.

II

As in the case of *The Miseries of Enforced Marriage,* fortuitous circumstances bring about a happy conclusion to Heywood and Rowley's *Fortune by Land and Sea* (c. 1607). The collaborators called their play a tragicomedy. By this they meant that the play began with a tragic episode and then, technically, at least, became a comedy. Of the two stories, one has tragic moments. Both plots reveal the same attention to didacticism observed in the plays already discussed.

Frank Forest disobeys his father, falls into evil company, and is killed in a tavern quarrel. His brother slays the murderer in a duel, but because the latter has powerful friends at court, Young Forest is compelled to flee the country. Eventually, after he has captured a crew

[4] *Ibid.,* pp. 112–13.

of pirates, he receives royal pardon for the duel and, prosperous, returns to England.

In the early parts, strong didactic elements overload the play. The prodigal-son theme appears in the opening scenes. Old Forest voices his opinion of the life Frank has been leading. He tells the boon companions of his son:

> I love my ſon but do not doat on him;
> Nor is he ſuch a darling in mine eye,
> That I am lought to haue him from my ſight;
> Yet let me tell you, had you gentlemen
> Called him to any fairer exercise,
>
> . . . .
>
> I could have ſpared him to you half his age:
> But call him out to drinking, of all ſkill
> I hold that much us'd practice, the moſt ill.
>
> . . . .
>
> Oh ſonne that thou wilt follow rioting,
> Surfeit by drinking and unſeaſoned hours;
> Theſe Gentlemen perhaps may do't they're rich,
>
> . . . .
>
> Where I heauen knowes the world ſtill frowning on me,
> Am forc'd to ſell and Margage to keep you.[5]

In spite of his love of gambling and drink, Frank displays proper filial affection. It is in defense of his father's honor that he is killed. After lamenting for his brother, Young Forest admits that Frank's death came as a just punishment for a wayward life.

> Come Father and dear Siſter, joyn with me,
> Let us all learn our ſorrows to forget,
> He owed a death, and he hath payd that debt.[6]

Again, the wages of prodigal living are death. This idea is stated once more as Young Forest, about to fight a duel with Rainsforth, the murderer of his brother, remarks:

> I would my brother liv'd that this our difference
> Might end in an embrace of folded love;

---

[5] Thomas Heywood and William Rowley, *Fortune by Land and Sea, a Tragi-Comedy*, in *The Dramatic Works of Thomas Heywood*, 1874 ed., VI, 364; I, i, 22–46.
[6] *Ibid.*, p. 371; I, i, 254–56.

> But 'twas heaven's will that for fome guilt of his
> He fhould be fcourged by thee, and for that guilt
> In fcourging him thou by my vengeance punifht . . .[7]

Rainsforth had acted as the "scourge of God" in killing Frank Forest in punishment of his licentious living, but Rainsforth himself was not spared the consequences of murder.[8] The significance of the episode is obvious.

Rainsforth appears to be unconscious of his role as the "scourge of God." His own sins of gaming and of murder prey upon his mind. He refers to the "chain of vice" idea when he realizes that he may have to add the death of Young Forest to his list of crimes. He soliloquizes:

> He feekes his fate, and murderers once being in
> Wade further till they drown: fin pulls on fin.[9]

After the duel in which Young Forest kills Rainsforth, the didactic motif disappears from this portion of the play.

Although the action of the second plot is not tragic, it, too, contains much religious emphasis. This story is bound to the first by the fact that Susan, the sister of Young Forest, marries Philip, the eldest son of Old Harding. The old man disinherits his son for the marriage which he thinks is beneath the dignity of the family. Philip and his bride become servants on the Harding estate, bullied by the two younger brothers who rejoice in the unhoped-for prospect of inheriting their father's money. When things are at their worst, Old Harding dies intestate, and, by the laws of primogeniture, the property comes to Philip. He forgives his brothers the slights they have put upon him. The two parts of the play are further tied together by the marriage of Anne, the young wife of Old Harding, to Young Forest.

This plot also seems contrived to illustrate the operations of Divine Providence. By all laws, human and divine, Philip, the first born, should inherit his father's property. In opposing this custom, Old Harding was attempting to thwart the Divine Will, which punished him through the intervention of Divine Providence. The news that his goods have been lost at sea strikes Old Harding down. He tells his younger sons, "if I furvive this night, you two fhal be my heirs." He soon recognizes this is not to be, for he continues:

---

[7] *Ibid.*, p. 386; II, i, 27–31.   [8] See above, Chapter III.

[9] Heywood and Rowley, *Fortune by Land and Sea,* in *The Dramatic Works of Thomas Heywood,* VI, 378; I, iii, 88–89.

> Support me to my bed, and my kind neighbors,
> Aſſiſt me with your prayers, for I divine
> My ſoul this night ſhall amongſt Angels ſhine.[10]

His death before he could sign the will was clearly an indication of the intent of heaven. Anne, Harding's wife, notes this when she says:

> Heaven being juſt could not deal longer roughly
> With one ſo virtuous and compleatly honeſt,
> He merits all he hath, but to my ſtate.
> I am at once doubly unfortunate,
> I have loſt a huſband and a brother too.[11]

It so happens that she has not lost a brother. The agency of Providence continues its lavishness. The merchant who has befriended Young Forest enters with the news that all the goods were saved and that Young Forest has been pardoned.

Meanwhile, in spite of good advice, the two younger brothers of Philip Harding have, through waywardness, come to grief. Their way of spending their money has wrought a great change in them.

> . . . no change of paſtors, which they ſay make fat calves, but change of drink, change of women, change of ordinaries, change of gaming, and one wench in the change, all theſe helpt to make this change in us.[12]

After several jests at the expense of the prodigals, Philip closes the play with a conventional moral.

> Leave trifling, for more ſerious is the object.
> Offered before our eyes: In theſe heavens juſtice,
> In theſe a moſt remarkable preſident
> To teach within our height to know our ſelves;
> Of which I make this uſe; you are my brothers
> (A name you once diſdained to call me by)
> Your wants ſhal be relieved: you that diſtruſted
> Heavens providence, and made a mock of want
> And others miſery, no more deride;
> Part of your loſſe ſhall be by me ſupplyed
> According to my power.[13]

---

[10] *Ibid.*, p. 422; IV, vi, 58–59, 70–72.   [11] *Ibid.*, p. 426; IV, vi, 185–89.
[12] *Ibid.*, p. 434; V, ii, 125–29.
[13] *Ibid.*, p. 435; V, ii, 160–70. The period in the first line of this quotation appears thus in the original.

The implication is clear. Those who have trusted in Divine Providence, as did Philip and Susan, are saved and prosper. Those who repudiated it come to grief. As a Christian and one who believes in the power of heaven, Philip will avoid the mistakes his brothers have made. He welcomes them with open arms, and the play ends happily.

Another aspect of this play is worth noting. The theme of social injustice receives considerable development. Its appearance in some of the morality plays and in *The Witch of Edmonton* has already been mentioned.[14] Heywood deplores the privilege of the upper classes and their power over the lives of the common people. After the murder of Frank Forest, his father desires to appeal to justice, but is deterred when Young Forest reminds him:

> Have you but patience, fhould we urge the Law
> He hath fuch honourable friends to guard him,
> We fhould in that but bark againft the Moon;
>
> .   .   .   .
>
> We are poor, and the world frowns on all our fortune,
> With patience then bear this amongft the reft:
> The heavens when they are pleafed may turn the wheel
> Of Fortune round, when we that are dejected,
> May be again raifed to our former height.[15]

The wheel of fortune used by the medieval homilist to express mutability is here joined to Divine Providence. When Young Forest is compelled to flee England after the duel with Rainsforth, the theme of injustice to the poor in the courts of England reappears. Its terms are the same as indicated above. The motif, however, is not a principal one of the play.

Fortune by Land and Sea is as much a *pièce à thèse* as *The Miseries of Enforced Marriage*. Its thesis is that Divine Providence will intervene to punish prodigality and to reward virtue. The examples are manifold. The father who attempts to cast off his eldest son, defying the laws of heaven and man, and three instances of the prodigal-son theme reveal the punishments meted out to those who act in opposition to God's will. The rewards of obedience are shown by the good fortune of Philip, Susan, Young Forest, Anne Harding, and The Mariner, her brother. The theme of injustice to the poor in the courts

---

[14] See above, Chapters IV and VII.   [15] *Ibid.*, p. 370; I, i, 240–50.

of England could not be stressed. Where the officers of the courts were agents of God, no injustice could be done. The presence of such a theme in the play shows an inconsistency easily accounted for in dramas written by professional playwrights who were not theologians.

III

A much more famous play than *Fortune by Land and Sea*, *Women Beware Women* (c. 1621), by Thomas Middleton, recounts the story of the notorious Bianca Capello, a commoner's wife, who became first the mistress and then the wife of the Duke Francesco de' Medici. The story of this virtuous wife forced to become the mistress of the ruler of the state bears a superficial resemblance to that of Jane Shore. The similarity, however, is only superficial. The comparatively healthy atmosphere of the English court of Edward IV gleams with a white light of purity when compared with the lust, intrigue, and lasciviousness of the Medicean house as presented by Middleton. Infidelity, incest, and murder are shown to be common in court life. Into this atmosphere are brought Bianca, her husband, and her mother-in-law. They fall into the net of court intrigue, accept the favors offered them, and eventually pay dearly for their advancement.

The opening scenes of the play present, as a contrast to the fetid air of the court, the household of Leantio, a factor or merchant's clerk. He has recently married Bianca, the daughter of wealthy Venetians.[16] Leantio's mother at first questions the wisdom of her son's having chosen a wife from a station above him, but soon accepts the situation. All is happiness until business calls Leantio from home. Then the duke sees Bianca and sends for her. Having enjoyed court life, she becomes querulously discontented with her lot in the home of Leantio and obeys a summons to the palace on the day of her husband's homecoming. In response to a further order of the duke's, Leantio follows her and is given a captaincy of the Rouen citadel. Instead of emulating Matthew Shore, he accepts the preferment won by his wife's position, soliloquizing:

> This is some good yet,
> And more than e'er I looked for; a fine bit
> To stay a cuckold's stomach: all preferment

---

[16] *Women Beware Women*, in *Thomas Middleton*, ed. Algernon Charles Swinburne, Mermaid edition, I, 265; I, i, 54.

That springs from sin and lust it shoots up quickly,
As gardeners' crops do in the rotten'st grounds;
So is all means raised from base prostitution
Even like a salad growing upon a dunghill.
I'm like a thing that never was yet heard of,
Half merry and half mad; much like a fellow
That eats his meat with a good appetite,
And wears a plague-sore that would fright a country;
Or rather like the barren, hardened ass,
That feeds on thistles till he bleeds again;
And such is the condition of my misery.[17]

Acquiescing to the position of his wife, he willingly seizes the opportunity to become the lover of Livia, a lady of the court. Hippolito, the brother of Livia, hears of their affair and kills Leantio, who dies without repentance. Bianca is now free, and the duke, in spite of the portests of his brother, the cardinal, marries her. Bianca, in a fruitless attempt to murder the cardinal, accidentally poisons the duke and then kills herself.

Middleton pays slight attention to religious morality in *Women Beware Women*. Some of the familiar language is employed in connection with the lust of the duke for Bianca Capello. The cardinal exacts from his brother a promise that he will consort with strumpets no longer.[18] This causes the duke to plan to murder Leantio so that he can legalize his relationship to Bianca. The moralizing which customarily concludes the domestic tragedies is entirely omitted. Middleton's primary interest was in depicting the atmosphere of the Medicean court. Although the work begins with elements of domestic tragedy, it soon throws aside all the trappings of the genre and becomes pure court tragedy.

IV

One of the later well-known domestic tragedies is Thomas Heywood's *The English Traveller* (1625). In this play, as in *A Woman Killed with Kindness*, Heywood for his main plot used the story of a faithless woman. The secondary plot he borrowed from Plautus's *Mostellaria*, but in the adaptation cut out the comic elements and substituted his usual moralizing. In the prologue, the author apologizes

[17] *Ibid.*, pp. 319–20; III, ii, 48–61.   [18] *Ibid.*, pp. 343–45; IV, i.

for the simplicity of his subject and ends on a note of forced self-depreciation.

> A Strange play you are like to have, for know,
> We use no drum, nor trumpet, nor dumb show;
> No combat, marriage not so much to-day
> As song, dance, masque, to bombast out a play;
> Yet these all good, and still in frequent use
> With our best poets; nor is this excuse
> Made by our author, as if want of skill
> Caused this defect; it's rather his self will.
> Will you the reason know? There have so many
> Been in that kind, that he desires not any
> At this time in his scene, no help, no strain,
> Or flash that's borrowed from another's brain;
> Nor speaks he this that he would have you fear it,
> He only tries if once bare lines will bear it:
> Yet may't afford, so please you silent sit,
> Some mirth, some matter, and perhaps some wit.[19]

The prologue is inaccurate in describing the play as wholly new, for the subplot is almost eighteen centuries old. Also, in *A Woman Killed with Kindness*, Heywood had already employed unadorned realism and the story of an adulterous wife.

In *The English Traveller*, Geraldine, a young gentleman returning from his travels, plans to wed the woman he has loved for many years. He finds, however, that she has become the wife of his friend, a worthy old man named Wincott. She promises to marry him when old Wincott dies, and Geraldine agrees to remain single till then. Indeed, they both take a solemn oath to this effect. Wincott's wife, however, is unable to resist the importunities of Delavil, Geraldine's best friend, and is unfaithful not only to her husband, but to Geraldine. The latter accidentally learns of the adultery and, heartbroken, plans to leave the country. Old Wincott insists that before Geraldine departs he come to a feast. Unable to endure the hypocrisy of Wincott's wife, who accuses him of faithlessness in deserting her, Geraldine reveals her as an adulteress. She, in despair, confesses her guilt, repents, and dies.

The plot soon reveals its background of religious doctrine. Young Geraldine says:

[19] *The Engliſh Traveller*, in *Thomas Heywood*, ed. John Addington Symonds, Mermaid edition, p. 155; Prologue, ll. 1–16.

Geraldine. However, let us love still, I entreat:
That, neighbourhood and breeding will allow:
So much the laws divine and human both
'Twixt brother and a sister will approve;
Heaven then forbid that they should limit us
Wish well to one another!
Wife. If they should not,
We might proclaim they were not charitable,
Which were a deadly sin but to conceive.[20]

When the wife promises to marry Geraldine after her husband will have died, he asks her to seal her promise with a vow, and she replies, "As I hope mercy." In return, he swears "by Heaven." [21] Thus neither of them can break his oath sworn in God's name without peril to his soul.

When Geraldine discovers the adultery of Delavil and the wife of Wincott, he bursts out with a theological tirade:

Unchaste, impious woman,
False to all faith and true conjugal love;
There's met a serpent and a crocodile,
A Sinon and a Circe. Oh, to what
May I compare you? —Out, my sword!
I'll act a noble execution
On two unmatched for sordid villany—
I left it in my chamber, and thank Heaven
That I did so! it hath prevented me
From playing a base hangman. Sin securely,
Whilst I, although for many yet less faults,
Strive hourly to repent me! I once loved her,
And was to him entire. Although I pardon,
Heaven will find time to punish: I'll not stretch
My just revenge so far as once by blabbing
To make your brazen impudence to blush—
Damn on—revenge too great; and, to suppress
Your souls yet lower, without hope to rise,
Heap Ossa upon Pelion. You have made me
To hate my very country, because here bred
Near two such monsters.[22]

---

[20] *Ibid.*, p. 182; II, i, 267–75. [21] *Ibid.*, p. 183; II, i, 292, 301.
[22] *Ibid.*, p. 223; IV, iii, 143–63.

This speech contains such a full measure of moral and religious matter that it expresses almost no personal emotion. Geraldine's first sentence contains the words "impious" and "false to all faith." Although "faith" might refer to a human understanding, "impious" can have only a theological significance. He thanks Providence for causing him to leave his sword in his room, thus preventing him from becoming an executioner. Though he pardons her sin, he expects heaven to punish it. Later Geraldine tells Wincott's wife that Divine Providence had revealed her lewdness to him.

> Only He
> That, pitying such an innocency as mine
> Should by two such delinquents be betrayed,—
> He brought me to that place by miracle,
> And made me an ear-witness of all this.[23]

He continues:

> Tush! bow to Heaven,
> Which thou hast most offended; I, alas!
> Save in such scarce unheard-of treachery,
> Most sinful, like thyself. Wherein, oh, wherein
> Hath my unspotted and unbounded love
> Deserved the least of these? Sworn to be made a stale
> For the term of life, and all this for my goodness!
> Die, and die soon; acquit me of my oath,
> But prithee die repentant.[24]

With this pious exhortation, he leaves the woman he is supposed to love. She is overcome with remorse and, what is more important, with a realization of her sin. Beginning with a bad pun on the villain's name, she harangues Delavil as follows:

> Thou'rt then a devil, that presents before me
> My horrid sins, persuades me to despair,
> When he, like a good angel sent from Heaven,
> Besought me of repentance. Swell, sick heart,
> Even till thou burst the ribs that bound thee in! [25]

Following this display of contrition, she is led off weeping. After writing a final letter to Geraldine, in which she makes confession, asks for forgiveness, and hopes for grace and mercy from heaven, she dies.

---

[23] *Ibid.*, p. 244; V, ii, 112–16. [24] *Ibid.*, p. 245; V, ii, 124–32.
[25] *Ibid.*, p. 245; V, ii, 144–48.

> My fear [sin?] is beyond pardon. Delavil
> Hath played the villain; but for Geraldine,
> He hath been each way noble; love him still.
> My peace already I have made with Heaven;
> Oh, be not you at war with me! my honour
> Is in your hands to punish or preserve;
> I am now confessed, and only Geraldine
> Hath wrought on me this unexpected good.
> The ink I write with, I wish had been my blood,
> To witness my repentance.[26]

Wincott believes that Heaven has pardoned her, for he says, "Where Heaven forgives, I pardon." [27]

Thus the play closes, and once more the familiar pattern of redemption of the guilty through sincere repentance has been followed. Geraldine recognizes the agency of Providence when he says it was by a "miracle" that he discovered the sin. Delavil lacks human characteristics—he is, in fact, little more than a personified vice. As in *A Woman Killed with Kindness*, the seducer escapes immediate punishment. At the conclusion of *The English Traveller*, repentance and the penance of death lead to the hope of salvation for the soul of the principal sinner, Wincott's wife.[28]

The English Traveller is a far weaker play than *A Woman Killed with Kindness*. Heywood had begun to repeat himself. The play fails to hang together; the subplot vies for attention with the main story. In general, the characters are lightly sketched, and the dialogue lacks color and brilliancy. Nevertheless, Heywood's ability to make his story capture the interest of the reader comes to the rescue of this play, so that the drama must have been to the tastes of Heywood's audiences.

V

The year that *The English Traveller* was produced, William Sampson brought out a play called *The Vow Breaker; or, The Fair Maid of Clifton*. His play was based on a ballad entitled "A Godly Warning for all Maidens by the Example of Gods Judgement shewed upon one Jermans Wife of Clifton, in the County of Nottingham, who lying in

---

[26] *Ibid.*, p. 247; v, ii, 189–98.   [27] *Ibid.*, p. 248; v, ii, 203.

[28] The subplot, taken from the *Mostellaria* of Plautus, bears affinities to the prodigal-son story, but with its happy ending and its triumph of sentimentalism, it offers little of interest to the present investigation.

childbed, was born away and never heard of after . . ." [29] The ballad contains all the theological emphasis promised in the title. The girl, Anne Boote, has plighted her troth to Young Bateman, but in his absence weds German. On hearing the news, the grief-stricken Young Bateman hangs himself. His ghost haunts her, and carries her away to hell after she is delivered of the child who is innocent of her infidelity. The ballad opens with the moral stated not in religious but in social terms.

> You dainty dames, so finely fram'd
>   Of beauty's chiefest mold,
> And you that trip it up and down,
>   Like Lambs in Cupids fold,
> Here is a lesson to be learn'd;
>   A lesson, in my mind,
> For such as will prove false in love,
>   And bear a faithless mind. [30]

The reader is again addressed directly in the concluding stanza of the poem, which sounds a familiar note of religious warning:

> You maidens that desire to love,
>   And would your husbands choose,
> To him that you do vow to love
>   By no means do refuse:
> For god, that hears all secret oaths,
>   Will dreadful vengeance take
> On such that of a wilful vow
>   Do slender reckoning make. [31]

In the play, Sampson closely followed the ballad, stressing heavily the religious lesson. *The Vow Breaker* was intended to illustrate the punishments meted out to those who break oaths sworn in God's name. When Anne and Young Bateman plight their troth, she offers to swear to him eternal faith. He cautions her of the seriousness of such an oath and attempts to dissuade her from giving sanctity to obligations which she may later wish to escape.

> Sweare not, sweete *Nan!*
> The booke of fate, as now may be unclasp'd
> And record what thou speak'st.

---

[29] Hans Wallrath, *William Sampson's "Vow-Breaker," ein Beitrag zur Kunde des Nach-Shakespeareschen Dramas,* p. 13.

[30] *Ibid.,* p. 13.   [31] *Ibid.,* p. 16.

Anne, however, persists in her purpose.

> Be it writ in brasse,
> My love shall be as durable as that!
> Now by this kisse, nay I will second that,
> When I this hand bequeath to any one
> But my sweete *Bateman,* then may I ever
> From heaven, and goodness rest a cast-away,
> If e're I give this hand to anyone
> But my sweete *Bateman.*[32]

As Young Bateman and Anne are about to part, he again emphasizes the sanctity of the oath they have sworn.

> *Y*[*oung*] *Ba*[*teman*]. When eyther of us breaks this sacred bond
> Let us be made strange spectacles to the world,
> To heaven, and earth.
> *An*[*ne*]. Amen, say I.
> And let heaven loth me when I falsifie.[33]

Old German's offer to release Anne from her promise to marry him if she has previously sworn faith to Young Bateman illustrates the orthodox Christian view of the sanctity of oaths. Old German says:

> I wood not have the curse
> Of contract breaking fall upon my head.[34]

Anne, however, has fallen so far from grace that she unhesitatingly perjures herself. She stoutly maintains that her relationship with Young Bateman had been only childhood affection. Thus reassured, German proceeds with his plans for the wedding.

On his return, Young Bateman, overcome at her defection, hangs himself. Old Bateman tells Anne:

> I will not curse thee, T'was [*sic*] my boyes request.
> Such deedes as these sinke not in oblivion,
> The justnes of my cause *I* leave to Heaven.[35]

Heaven justifies this faith by allowing the ghost of Young Bateman to return. This ghost revisits the world of mortals, not to incite personal

[32] William Sampson, *The Vow Breaker; or, The Faire Maide of Clifton,* in *Materialen zur Kunde des älteren englischen Dramas,* ed. Hans Wallrath, XLII, 10; I, i, 39–48.

[33] *Ibid.,* p. 15; I, ii, 69–72.　　　　[34] *Ibid.,* p. 22; I, iv, 83–84.

[35] *Ibid.,* p. 38; II, iv, 127–29.

revenge, but to serve as an instrument of God's retributive justice. It has the power personally to accomplish its mission rather than to drive others to action. In a series of appearances which seem to be modeled on the ghost scenes in *Hamlet,* the apparition warns Anne that it will bear her soul to hell as soon as she has given birth to the infant she is carrying. The child, innocent of her sin, escapes her damnation. After the birth of the baby, the spectre of Young Bateman appears to Anne and tells her:

> The Ferry-man attends thee at the verge
> of *Cocitus,* and sooty *Acheron,*
> And he shall waft thee into *Tartary,*
> Where perjury, and false-hood finds reward;
> There shalt thou reade thy history of faults,
> And mong'st the furies find just recompence;
> I'le bring thee over Turrets, Towres, and Steeples,
> O're shady Groves, brineish Mears, and Brookes,
> The flattering Sea to me is navigable,
> O're steepy Mountaines, and the craggy Rocks,
> Whose heights Kisse Stares, and stop in flying Clouds,
> Wee'le through as swift as *Swallowes* in recourse.
> The Chauntecleer summons my retreat,
> Singing [signing?] a period to my pilgrimage;
> From nipping frosts, and penetrating blastes,
> Could snowes, blacke thawes, and misty killing deawes,
> I'le lead thee to the ever-flaming Furnace,
> That like a Feaver fed by opposite meates,
> Engenders, and consumes it selfe with heate.
> I'le peirce the Aire as with a Thunder bolt,
> And make thy passage free; make speede, away!
> Thy broken contract now thou goest to pay.[36]

This horrible fate is in store for Anne, not because she has broken her vow, but because she would not repent of her faithlessness. Each visitation of the ghost afforded her an opportunity for repentance. The pagan references in this speech might seem to indicate some confusion of intention on the part of the author. However, the mixture of classical and Christian allusions and the use of pagan examples to point a Christian moral were frequent practices in the Renaissance. When all

[36] *Ibid.,* p. 60; IV, ii, 187–208,

the evidence is considered, the intention of the author is clear. His chief concern was to demonstrate the consequences of the sin of perjury. Divine Providence acts in a familiar way to punish a sinner who had broken no laws of men and so could not be punished by earthly agencies. The warnings given Anne show the mercy of God in allowing her time for repentance, but when she ignored them, she was ruthlessly dragged to the eternal fire.[37]

VI

In *'Tis Pity She's a Whore* (c. 1627), John Ford combined the intrigue of an Italian court with domestic tragedy. The principal characters of the play are citizens of Parma, well to do, but not of noble stock. One of the manifold plots presents the tragedy of a nobleman, but the tale which gives the title to the work is a domestic tragedy showing all the characteristics of the genre.

Giovanni has an incestuous passion for his sister, Annabella, who returns his love. In order to escape the disgrace of bearing her brother's child, she marries Soranzo, a nobleman. When Soranzo discovers her condition, she refuses to reveal the name of her lover, but Vasques, the servant of Soranzo, discovers who he is. Soranzo then plans to wreak his vengeance on her at a feast in the presence of Annabella's father and Giovanni. Learning Soranzo's intention, Giovanni himself kills Annabella. He vanquishes Soranzo in a fight, but is slain by Vasques.

The presence of the highly born Soranzo in the play may be taken as evidence of the "orthodoxy" of this tragedy, although the two real tragic protagonists are Giovanni and Annabella, son and daughter of Florio, a citizen of Parma. In addition to presenting citizen-heroes, *'Tis Pity She's a Whore* is as lavish with religious and didactic platitudes as any of the other domestic tragedies.

Ford's dedication contains an important sentence. He says: "The gravity of the subject may easily excuse the lightness of the title, otherwise I had been a severe judge against mine own guilt." [38] This is precisely the sort of language used in dedications of didactic works. Taken

---

[37] The subplot is of no interest here, for it deals with the war of Queen Elizabeth against the Scotch and the French. Its only connection with the main plot is to motivate the departure of Young Bateman. For the relationship of this play to the lost *Black Bateman of the North*, see Appendix A.

[38] *'Tis Pity She's a Whore*, in *The Works of John Ford*, ed. William Gifford and Alexander Dyce, I, 110.

alone, this statement might mean nothing, but in connection with the pattern of the play, it suggests that Ford put considerable emphasis on moral teaching.

The theological note is sounded early. The first act opens with a conversation between Giovanni and a friar, in which the latter warns the young man against the perils of atheism. Then Giovanni confesses his passion for his sister. At once, the friar voices the position of the Church. To Giovanni's protestations, the friar replies: "Have done, unhappy youth! for thou art lost." Asked what will cure the lust, he answers:

> Repentance, son, and sorrow for this sin:
> For thou hast mov'd a Majesty above
> With thy unrangèd almost blasphemy.
>
> . . . .
>
> O, Giovanni! hast thou left the schools
> Of knowledge to converse with lust and death?
> For death waits on thy lust.[39]

In spite of this warning, Giovanni finds his yearning for his sister too strong to be denied, so the friar again counsels repentance.

> *Friar.* Then I have done, and in thy wilful flames
> Already see thy ruin; Heaven is just.
> Yet hear my counsel.
>
> . . . .
>
> Hie to thy father's house; there lock thee fast
> Alone within thy chamber; then fall down
> On both thy knees, and grovel on the ground;
> Cry to thy heart; wash every word thou utter'st
> In tears—and if't be possible—of blood:
> Beg Heaven to cleanse the leprosy of lust
> That rots thy soul; acknowledge what thou art,
> A wretch, a worm, a nothing; weep, sigh, pray
> Three times a-day and three times every night:
> For seven days' space do this; then, if thou find'st
> No change in thy desires, return to me:
> I'll think on remedy. Pray for thyself
> At home, whilst I pray for thee here.—Away!
> My blessing with thee! we have need to pray.

---

[39] *Ibid.*, pp. 114–15; I, i, 35–59.

Gio[vanni]. All this I'll do, to free me from the rod
Of vengeance; else I'll swear my fate's my God.[40]

Notwithstanding this good advice, Giovanni remains completely at
the mercy of his lust. His attempts to pray proving fruitless, he in-
veighs against fate.

Lost! I am lost! my fates have doomed my death:
The more I strive, I love; the more I love,
The less I hope: I see my ruin certain.
What judgment or endeavours could apply
To my incurable and restless wounds,
I throughly have examin'd, but in vain.
O, that it were not in religion sin
To make our love a god, and worship it!
I have even wearied heaven with prayers, dried up
The spring of my continual tears, even starv'd
My veins with daily fasts: what wit or art
Could counsel, I have practis'd; but, alas,
I find all these but dreams, and old men's tales,
To fright unsteady youth; I'm still the same:
Or I must speak, or burst. 'Tis not, I know,
My lust, but 'tis my fate that leads me on.[41]

Having thus rationalized his yielding to temptation, he tells his sister
of his love, which she returns. Some time after the incest, he repairs
again to the friar for further advice and consolation. But the friar now
has no comfort for him, saying:

Peace! thou hast told a tale whose every word
—Threatens eternal slaughter to the soul;
I'm sorry I have heard it: would mine ears
Had been one minute deaf, before the hour
That thou cam'st to me! O young man, castaway,
By the religious number of mine order,
I day and night have wak'd my agèd eyes
Above my strength, to weep on thy behalf;
But Heaven is angry, and be thou resolv'd
Thou art a man remarked to taste a mischief.
Look for't; though it comes late, it will come sure.[42]

---

[40] *Ibid.*, pp. 115–16; I, i, 66–84.   [41] *Ibid.*, pp. 122–23; I, iii, 1–16.
[42] *Ibid.*, pp. 145–46; II, v, 1–11.

The next speech of the friar puts the whole play firmly on a theological basis.

> Indeed, if we were sure there were no Deity,
> Nor Heaven nor Hell, then to be led alone
> By Nature's light—as were philosophers
> Of elder times—might instance some defence.
> But 'tis not so: then, madman, thou wilt find
> That Nature is in Heaven's positions blind.[43]

Throughout this scene the friar emphasizes the damnation which will come to them both. He firmly believes that Giovanni has committed mortal sin, for he says:

> Nay, then I see thou'rt too far sold to hell:
> It lies not in the compass of my prayers
> To call thee back . . .[44]

The friar hopes that Annabella's sin may yet prove to be venial and attempts to ensure her pardon. When he has received her contrite confession of her relations with Giovanni, the friar replies:

> I'm glad to see this penance; for, believe me,
> You have unripp'd a soul so foul and guilty,
> As, I must tell you true, I marvel how
> The earth hath borne you up; but weep, weep on,
> These tears may do you good; weep faster yet,
> Whiles I do read a lecture.[45]

His lecture proves to be a dreadful picture of hell-fire, a description so awful that it forces her to cry: "Is there no way left to redeem my miseries?" To which he answers:

> There is, despair not; Heaven is merciful,
> And offers grace even now. 'Tis thus agreed:
> First, for your honour's safety, that you marry
> My Lord Soranzo; next, to save your soul,
> Leave off this life, and henceforth live to him.[46]

The spiritual counsel is good, but the friar is mistaken in thinking that Annabella may escape all the consequences of her sin. The subterfuge of marriage to Soranzo is not successful, for Soranzo discovers her pregnancy, and she knows that she must die. The penance of death and

[43] *Ibid.*, p. 146; II, v, 24–29. [44] *Ibid.*, p. 146; II, v, 39–41.
[45] *Ibid.*, p. 164; III, vi, 1–6. [46] *Ibid.*, p. 165; III, ii, 33–38.

her repentance save her soul in the next world. With the help of the friar, who passes by the room in which she is imprisoned, she makes her peace with heaven.

> My conscience now stands up against my lust
> With depositions character'd in guilt,
> > *Enter* Friar *below.*
> And tells me I am lost: now I confess
> Beauty that clothes the outside of the face
> Is cursèd if it be not cloth'd with grace.
>
> . . . .
>
> > That man, that blessèd friar,
> Who join'd in ceremonial knot my hand
> To him whose wife I now am, told me oft
> I trod the path to death, and showed me how.
> But they who sleep in lethargies of lust
> Hug their confusion, making Heaven unjust;
> And so did I.[47]

The friar promises to deliver a letter to her brother exhorting him to repent. Then she sighs:

> Thanks to the heavens, who have prolong'd my breath
> To this good use! now I can welcome death.[48]

The death she awaits come soon. Either by accident or by Divine Providence, Soranzo discovers the lover of his wife and plans his vengeance. Annabella, realizing that Soranzo intends to kill her at the banquet to which he has bidden her, seeks to prepare both her brother and herself for death. However, her attempts to turn him to repentance fall upon deaf ears. They do extract from him a kind of agonized tribute to her:

> Go thou, white in thy soul, to fill a throne
> Of innocence and sanctity in heaven.[49]

To save her from the ignominy of public disgrace, he stabs her. As she dies, she hopes for mercy. Firm in her conversion to faith, she forgives her slayer and asks pardon for him:

> Forgive him, Heaven—and me, my sins! Farewell,
> Brother unkind, unkind,—Mercy, great Heaven![50]

Since she has repented and has died with her soul at peace, she is presumably saved. Giovanni, whose reason has been perverted by sin, has

[47] *Ibid.,* pp. 188–89; V, i, 9–30.
[48] *Ibid.,* p. 190; V, i, 58–59.
[49] *Ibid.,* p. 200; V, v, 63–64.
[50] *Ibid.,* p. 201; V, v, 91–92.

allowed his carnal desires to overcome his will; he has no hope of divine mercy, desiring only:

> Where'er I go, let me enjoy this grace,
> Freely to view Annabella's face.[51]

'Tis Pity She's a Whore shows that domestic tragedy as a distinctive genre had almost disappeared. None of the realism, the intimacy, and the immediacy which had justified the use of the citizen for hero or tragic protagonist remains in this play. Part of the action occurs in court circles. Indeed, all the characters are at home in the palace, and there is no distinction between the language or the interests of the courtier and those of the commoner. Ford makes nothing of the lowly position of Giovanni and Annabella; it is not even a bar to the marriage of Annabella and Soranzo. In fact, if Ford did not specifically state that the brother and sister were the children of a citizen, this play would be an ordinary romantic tragedy.

When Ford wrote the domestic tragedy of Annabella and Giovanni, he employed the theological framework used by his predecessors in the field. He pretended to be a complete moralist and at every stage in the action used religious language. Nevertheless, his play creates the impression that he was much more interested in the decadent atmosphere than in religious morality. The friar is the only virtuous character in the entire play, but his judgment as applied to practical affairs has been tainted with worldliness. His worthless advice to Annabella that she marry Soranzo to conceal her condition shows this ineptitude of worldly counsel. The friar's spiritual counsel, however, is uniformly good.

The construction of the plot is so complicated that it is difficult to retain many of the details, yet the play grips the attention. Although the audience cannot sympathize with many of the motives in the action, it believes in their reality, for Ford makes them credible. A real tragic feeling is engendered for the unfortunate brother and sister, and, in the case of Giovanni, at least, no final repentance spoils the catharsis.

In all parts of the play, the language is a worthy vehicle for the action. Some of the most effective passages appear in the speeches of the friar and in the final scene between Giovanni and Annabella, as in the following:

---

[51] *Ibid.*, p. 205; V, vi, 104–5.

Gio[*vanni*]. I do indeed: these are funeral tears
Shed on your grave; these furrow'd-up my cheeks
When first I lov'd and knew not how to woo,
Fair Annabella, should I here repeat
The story of my life, we might lose time.
Be record all the spirits of the air,
And all things else that are, that day and night,
Early and late, the tribute which my heart
Hath paid to Annabella's sacred love
Hath been these tears, which are her mourners now!
Never till now did Nature do her best
To show a matchless beauty to the world,
Which in an instant, ere it scarce was seen,
The jealous Destinies requir'd again.[52]

'*Tis Pity She's a Whore* and *Women Beware Women* illustrate strikingly the tendency of domestic tragedy to merge with orthodox romantic tragedy. These two plays begin in situations familiar to domestic tragedy, but the action, set in the court and .permeated with an atmosphere of decadent high society, contains almost no trace of the realism of citizen life or of the domestic milieu. The sensationalism is decadent, not, as in *Arden of Feversham* and *A Woman Killed with Kindness*, naïve. Shortly after the accession of James I in 1603, domestic tragedy began to lose its importance. Gradually playwrights found other forms to take its place; as they lost the unsophisticated audiences of the earlier generations, they turned more and more to violence and sensationalism—to "drama" and to tragicomedy. Domestic tragedies began to be relegated to subplots or to a limited portion of a complicated action. The authors of domestic tragedies more frequently than in the past laid the scene of their actions in foreign lands, where they brought their characters into close association with the court. New playwrights found little to attract them in the form, and older ones employed it less frequently than in the past. All these tendencies to subordinate domestic tragedies to other forms of drama caused the extinction of the genre long before legal restrictions in 1642 closed the public theatres.[53]

[52] *Ibid.*, pp. 199–200; V, v, 49–62.
[53] A play by Heywood and Brome entitled *The Late Lancashire Witches* (1634) exhibits many characteristics of domestic tragedy, without actually carrying out the tragic consequences of the action. A description of it will be found in Appendix B.

Chapter Ten

CONCLUSION

ENGLISH domestic tragedies of the sixteenth and seventeenth centuries differed in many important respects from most of the plays presented during the same period at the Rose, the Curtain, the Globe, Blackfriars, and other London theatres. Indeed, they may be said to form a distinct dramatic genre, marked by a few clearly defined characteristics. All domestic tragedies, of course, present commoners as their heroes instead of men of royal or high estate. But they are alike in a still more important feature. They are all homiletic plays, expressing in their own popular melodramatic fashion the official theology of the day.

With the single exception of Middleton's *Women Beware Women*, which is only partly a domestic tragedy, all the plays belonging to this genre, from its earliest appearance until the closing of the theatres in 1642, contain too much moralizing, too much religious didacticism, for the phenomenon to be dismissed as accidental. Furthermore, the moralizing was of a sort widely different from that which appeared in the contemporary orthodox tragedies. The authors of domestic tragedy had been taught clear and obvious solutions to the problems of man's relation to God and wrote their plays to teach the doctrines which they knew were altogether true and righteous. The writers of orthodox tragedies, on the other hand, found many of these problems a mystery, a fact which gave a larger reach to their speculations and to the meaning of their plots. These authors sought to exhibit the nobility of man even in the midst of his afflictions, while the authors of domestic tragedy, limited in their view of human nature by the religious doctrines they taught, were compelled to exhibit man as a vile and wicked sinner. In their plays, they presented a God far more interested in administering laws of heavenly justice than in the fate of an individual, while writers of conventional tragedy made their chief interest the revelation of the greatness of human character.

Domestic tragedy was thus the dramatic equivalent of the homiletic tract and the broadside ballad. In all these works of literature, the author's primary purpose was to teach the people by means of examples couched in terms of their own experiences. The instruction imparted principles deprived from the religious beliefs of the man in the street. The essential tenets were these:

Sin they conceived to be any action against the word of God, a violation of any of the Ten Commandments, a yielding to any of the Seven Deadly Sins. No matter how completely a sin might be concealed from man, God always knew of it and was sure to punish it. By means of His Providence, God punished sin through the agency of direct intervention in the form of miracles or other supernatural manifestations, or He might employ His lawfully constituted agents, the king and the magistrates, to execute justice. Once the sin had been revealed and the sinner had shown sorrow for his past errors, he might still hope, no matter how great his sin, to escape the everlasting damnation he had earned and to attain divine mercy if only he expressed heartfelt and sincere repentance and paid a penance. Repentance required a complete confession of his past errors, earnest contrition for them, a recognition of their gravity, and an ardent plea for the salvation of his soul. The penance in these domestic tragedies usually took the form of death, the total negation of worldliness. Only as a man cut his mind off from earthly things and turned it to the life to come could he hope for grace. The "scaffold speech," a confession, a declaration of faith made by the protagonist of any of these plays just before his death, was accepted by others in the play and by the audience to indicate that the soul of the victim would receive the mercy of God. It was not a goodness suddenly developed in the man, it was the infinite benevolence of God and His Son, Jesus Christ, which provided for the salvation of the sinner.

Theologians made a distinction between mortal and venial sin. A venial sin could be pardoned following sincere repentance, while a mortal sin, in which the mind had been perverted to evil courses, was unforgivable. The playwrights tried to follow these distinctions, but, not being professional theologians, they had only a partial understanding of the meanings and limitations of the terms.

The interpretation of domestic tragedies in terms of popular religious beliefs offers a solution to many problems hitherto unsolved in the consideration of this genre. Previous investigators have made no effort to relate this group of plays to the thought of the time. Their favorite descriptive terms are "moral," "sentimental," and "realistic." Their use of the first term is justified, but they have made no effort to discover the basis of this morality. In calling these dramas "sentimental," the critics appear to forget that sentimentalism is based on a belief in the innate goodness of man, while these plays illustrate the innate viciousness of man—his certainty of turning to evil courses when he follows his nature rather than his faith. Care must be taken lest speeches really indicative of Christian repentance be interpreted as sentimental. Sentimentalism implies a compromise with strict moral justice to bring about the forgiveness and reconciliation of a penitent with his family and his friends. The repentant sinners in these domestic tragedies seek not earthly but divine forgiveness; they are willing to accept any penance, even death, as a means of gaining divine mercy. Thus it is clear that these "scaffold speeches," though gaining some sympathy for the sinner, are designed to have a religious rather than a sentimental significance.

The term "realistic," however, is more justly applied to these dramas. When setting the action of their plays in a domestic milieu, the authors naturally desired to appeal to a sense of self-recognition in the members of their audience. Therefore they made a great effort to catch the speech of the people, even making some of their characters talk in familiar dialects. In the interest of verisimilitude, they also wrote a larger part of their plays in prose than was the custom in the conventional tragedies. And in the verse itself, the playwrights avoid, for the most part, poetic fancy and "purple patches." Their object in writing in a deliberately realistic manner was to increase the cogency of the moral lesson by making the action seem like a page torn from the lives of the auditors.

Frequently the moralizing appears to be sincere; at other times it is obvious that the dramatist is only complying with a convention. As so often happens, the authors with the greatest desire to employ domestic tragedy as a vehicle for a "message" wrote with so heavy a didactic hand that they did a disservice both to their message and to domestic tragedy. Robert Yarington's *Two Lamentable Tragedies* illustrates the aesthetic depths to which moral overemphasis could sink a domestic tragedy. On the other hand, in Ford's *'Tis Pity She's a Whore* the religious morality is effectively woven into the texture of the play by a man who was, first of all, an accomplished playwright.

Thus the few domestic tragedies still extant from the large number written during the Elizabethan, Jacobean, and Caroline periods vary in quality from near-greatness to almost incredible feebleness. None of the domestic tragedies equals the work of the mature Shakespeare either in poetic level or in characterization, although it is possible to find passages in the domestic tragedies better than some of the poorer Shakespearean lines. Shakespeare apart, some domestic tragedies are almost as good as the best and others are fully as bad as the worst of Tudor and Stuart tragedies.

As long as *Arden of Feversham*, *A Yorkshire Tragedy*, and *A Woman Killed with Kindness* are read, critics will continue to find manifold excellences in them. It is quite true that these plays have many virtues and, together with *'Tis Pity She's a Whore*, stand like colossi while most of the remaining domestic tragedies have found dishonorable graves in dusty, forgotten books. Three of these four plays, *Arden of Feversham*, *A Yorkshire Tragedy*, and *'Tis Pity She's a Whore*, hold the reader in the grip of powerful emotions. They present to him people who, for a time, transcend their petty existences through the terrifying power of their ruling passions. The fourth, *A Woman Killed with Kindness*, makes as strong an appeal to pity as do these others to terror. In all except *'Tis Pity She's a Whore*, the effective realism of the author's method gives his fiction an immediacy that adds to the weight of the moral lesson. In addition to these four, other domestic tragedies exhibit flashes of power, although none of them so well maintains a high level of excellence.

In spite of the many virtues of these, the best of the early English domestic tragedies, the common characteristic of the genre—egregious moralizing—interferes to rob these four tragedies of the excellences they might otherwise have attained. The awe-inspiring figures of Mosbie and Alice in *Arden of Feversham* and the husband in *A Yorkshire Tragedy* dwindle into the stock repentant sinners of moral literature. They lose the attributes of humanity as they become characters in dramatic exempla. The other plays of the kind suffer from the same fault and have none of the greatness of characterization or dramatic effectiveness which characterizes the four above-mentioned plays.

While the selection of a middle-class hero increased the moral effectiveness of the plays, it also prevented the excitation of the emotions ordinarily connected with tragedy. Although rivalry, ambition, love, and hatred when viewed through the rose-tinted glasses of time and distance may seem great in the palace of a king, they become jealousy, cupidity, lust, and malevolence in the cold light of realistic treatment. Persons dominated by these lesser emotions seem to be petty men, incapable of arousing sufficient pity and terror for any tragedy, persons whose deaths offer nothing but a lesson in conduct. However, playwrights did little to make even the petty emotions credible, for, in their eagerness to moralize, they consciously avoided making sin attractive, sacrificing psychological truth in order to show the readiness of a person to fall into sin. A character would have some unexplained weakness of the flesh which would drive him even against his will to commit what he knew full well to be a sin. Dramatists seemed to fear that if they made the fall of the hero plausible they would vitiate their moral lessons. Domestic tragedy had not as yet learned how to reveal the greatness of simple people. Only in this way can it ever aspire to the eminence of orthodox tragedy. Perhaps audiences may not be prepared to recognize among people like themselves greatness in sufficient quantity ever to make domestic tragedy anything but a contradiction in terms.

Before 1642, these plays rely for their appeal on the pathetic situation involving a young man or woman who is prevented from having a prosperous and happy life; or they offer, in place of catharsis of pity and terror, spiritual satisfaction that a soul has been saved from perdition. None of the protagonists in these tragedies arouses the feeling of potential ability so necessary for creating an appreciation of tragic waste. These people are, at best, poor creatures in comparison with Tamburlaine, Hamlet, Lear, Macbeth, Oedipus, and Orestes, but they were, perhaps, more useful in teaching the members of the audience homely lessons and in moving them to easy tears.

The appeal of tears is, of course, as old as drama itself. When the audience is moved to tears by being asked to contemplate the moral goodness of man, it is called sentimentalism. When a work of art evokes a feeling of the grandeur of man by the contemplation of a great man's magnificent struggle against overwhelming forces and when there is the potentiality of victory for the hero, it is called tragedy. In none of the Elizabethan domestic tragedies is real tragedy achieved.

The idea that the hero is a miserable sinner is incompatible with the appreciation of tragic grandeur. The concept of divine mercy, which had been either denied or completely realized in the great tragedies, was too much used as a convenient exit by the dramatist. In the greatest tragedies, divine mercy comes only to those who, like Lear or Orestes, have, by deep suffering, shown themselves worthy of it. The negation of mercy may intensify the magnitude of the hero's loss. The reliance on the principle of easily achieved divine mercy in the domestic tragedies is the result of their subordination to popular theology.

Heywood, in *A Woman Killed with Kindness*, particularly relied on the appeal of tears to carry him through the early scenes, and then he changed his emphasis to religious moralizing. The audience pities Master Frankford when he finds that he has been betrayed, and then glows with self-conscious rectitude as, by his treatment of his wife, Frankford acts the beau ideal of Christianity.

Domestic tragedy as it was written between 1576 and 1642 was more than a haphazard form which chanced to employ a hero taken from the lower classes of society. It was a vehicle for reiterating commonplace moral lessons to naïve audiences. It chose its heroes from common ranks of society because these persons afforded the best lessons to the men and women of similar ranks who made up the audiences. Its methods were those of the broadside ballad, the homiletic tract, and other didactic literature. Its tenets were founded on orthodox theology. It sacrificed dramatic, psychological, and human values to make its obvious lessons yet more obvious.

As the four best of the domestic tragedies suffer from pious moralizing, those that are devoid of dramatic excellence are in no way improved by that same didactic method. Yarington's *Two Lamentable Tragedies*, unquestionably the worst of these plays, at times omits important parts of the action the better to preach. In the weaker plays, the moments of comparative excellence most frequently appear in passages in which the moralizing is briefly forgotten, as in Mother Sawyer's vituperation of the court in *The Witch of Edmonton*. Thus it happens that in these domestic tragedies the excellences are those they win in spite of the powerful influence of background and custom to turn them to moralizing. As long as domestic tragedy concerned itself with the things of the next world rather than with the things of this, it remained a subordinate genre, one really apart from the actual lives of the people, one whose products were largely ephemeral literature. All Renaissance dramatists had to pay lip service to the moral aim of drama. The greater ones made their art absorb their didacticism. The lesser ones either reversed the process or allowed the art and the moral teaching to exist separately, alternating action and sermonizing in the course of their plays. Elizabethan domestic tragedy failed both in developing a real tragedy expressive of the actual problems of the citizen of England and in developing a drama able to deal significantly with moral problems which were subtler than the obvious equating of providential operations and the popular conception of right and wrong.

In spite of the readiness of the authors of domestic tragedies to indulge in egregious moralizing, the plays themselves present no real moral problems. Sinners and virtuous characters alike are in complete agreement on their definitions of good and evil. A character never undergoes an inner conflict as to which of two courses is morally right. He knows the path of virtue and the path of vice and easily sees a clear line dividing the one from the other. When he submits to sin, it is because he sees he is a weak mortal, whose nature lacks the strength to keep him in the paths of righteousness. His occasional hesitation is a result of fear of the consequences or reluctance to commit sin. He is never asked to select one of two alternatives neither of which seems to be entirely good or entirely bad. Hamlet is commanded by the ghost and by custom to revenge the death of his father. To do this, however, is to commit a murder. The hero of a domestic tragedy, on the other hand, is faced with the choice between a life of virtue and one of sin, the latter requiring murder and adultery in the satisfaction of his sensual desires. When he accedes to vice, he knows it to be against the commands of God, but he submits to the demands of his flesh, acting in opposition to his reason.

The persons at whom the moralizing was aimed had clearly accepted it, for they continued to receive the same kinds of literature from the pens of playwrights and pamphleteers and, above all, from the preachers. As these artisans, shopkeepers, and other humble, God-fearing people began to stay away from the theatres, forced out by the removal of the best playhouses to fashionable locations in London and by the increased costs of admission to the plays, as the wealthy, gay, and well-educated Cavaliers became the chief patrons of the dramatic companies, domestic tragedy passed from the repertories. The taste for extravagance and bloodshed made domestic tragedies tame, and the growing love for tragicomedy and "drama" caused the slackening of appreciation for the tragic conclusions to the plays. Realistic tragedy was giving way to epic types, to extravagant sensationalism; the stories of national history were being supplanted by tales of Italian, French, and Spanish heroes; questions of moral conduct were being replaced by decadent passions. When the theatres were closed in 1642, domestic tragedy had quite probably disappeared from the repertories. It had settled down in England for a sleep of nearly a hundred years. There were signs, as early as 1694, that the sleeper was stirring, but with the chill storm of imported French classicism and the heated blasts of heroic bombast raging in English tragedy after 1660, there is small wonder that domestic tragedy continued its hibernation until 1731, when George Lillo produced *The London Merchant*.

But I will make an end, for I am too tedious.

Appendix A

LOST DOMESTIC TRAGEDIES

RECORDS SURVIVE of a number of lost plays which may have been domestic tragedies. The available evidence concerning the subject of many of these dramas warrants their inclusion in this book. Some plays, as their titles clearly reveal, belong to the genre. Of others, it is possible to say only that they may have been domestic tragedies.

Anonymous, *The Cruelty of a Stepmother*, Sussex's Company, 1578.

The Cruelty of a Stepmother was produced at court on December 28, 1578, and is thought to have been a murder play.[1] The Earl of Sussex's Men received the customary ten pounds for the performance.

Anonymous, *Murderous Michael*, Sussex's Company, 1578/9.

Sussex's Men produced *Murderous Michael* at court on March 3, 1578/9. Possibly this tragedy was a dramatization of the events which formed the basis for the play *Arden of Feversham*.[2]

Anonymous, *The History of Friar Francis*, Sussex's Company, before 1590.

The History of Friar Francis was produced as an old play on January 7, 14, and 20 (21), 1593/4.[3] Heywood, in his *An Apology for Actors* (1612), gives a brief summary of the plot.

It followes that we prove these exercises to have beene the discoverers of many notorious murders, long concealed from the eyes of the world. To omit all farre-fetcht instances, we will prove it by a domestike and home-borne

---

[1] Edmund K. Chambers, *The Elizabethan Stage*, II, 93; IV, 95, 154.
[2] *Ibid.*, II, 93; IV, 4, 96, 155. See above, Chapter VI.
[3] *Henslowe's Diary*, ed. Walter W. Greg, I, 16. The correction of the date of the third production was made by Greg.

truth, which within these few years happened. At Lin, in Norfolke, the then Earl of Sussex players acting the old History of Feyer Francis, and presenting a woman who, insatiately doting on a yong gentleman, (the more securely to enjoy his affection) mischievously and secreetly murdered her husband, whose ghost haunted her; and, at divers times, in her most solitary and private contemplations, in most horrid and feareful shapes, appeared and stood before her. As this was acted, a towne's-woman (till then of good estimation and report) finding her conscience (at this presentment) extremely troubled, suddenly skritched and cryd out, Oh! my husband, my husband! I see the ghost of my husband fiercely threatening and menacing me! At which shrill and unexpected outcry, the people about her, moov'd to a strange amazement, inquired the reason of her clamour, when presently, un-urged, she told them that seven yeares ago she, to be possest of such a gentleman (meaning him), had poysoned her husband, whose fearefull image personated it selfe in the shape of that ghost. Whereupon the murdresse was apprehended, before the justices further examined, and by her voluntary confession after condemned. That this is true, as well by the report of the actors as the records of the towne, there are many eyewitnesses of this accident yet living vocally to confirme it.[4]

The ghost employed is not a revenge ghost or a warning of a portent, but an instance of the power of Divine Providence used to punish the murderess by terror. Heywood carries his account of the story no further, and no additional moral methods can be observed. It is impossible to date the play, but all available evidence places it early in the history of domestic tragedy, probably before 1590.

Anonymous, *The Merchant of Emden,* Admiral's Company, 1594.

Henslowe's *Diary* mentions *The Merchant of Emden* in the following entry:

ye 30 of Julye 1594 .. ne .. Ṛ at the marchant of eamden .... iij^ll viij^s [5]

Collier suggested that the story had appeared in a Pepysian broadside ballad entitled "A most sweet song of an English Merchant born in Chichester." [6] This story is a tragicomedy of domestic incident.

---

[4] Thomas Heywood, *An Apology for Actors,* ed. J. P. Collier, II, 57–58; Book III.

[5] *Henslowe's Diary,* I, 18.   [6] *Ibid.,* II, 166.

Anonymous, *The Witch of Islington*, Admiral's Company, c. 1595.

The Admiral's Company produced *The Witch of Islington* twice in the year 1597, but there are indications that it was an older play. Henslowe's entries read:

July 1597 14 tt at the wiche of Jslyngton ... 01/07/02 – 00 – 00
July 1597 28 tt at the wiche of Jselyngton ... 01/08/00 – 13 – 00 [7]

The omission of the word "ne," which Henslowe used to indicate a new play, leads to the belief that the work had been produced before 1597. Harbage dates it between 1580 and 1597 and conjectures that it was a realistic tragedy.[8]

Henry Chettle, Michael Drayton, Thomas Dekker, and Robert Wilson, *Black Bateman of the North*, in Two Parts (Second Part by Wilson and Chettle alone), Admiral's Company, 1598.

The two parts of *Black Bateman of the North* are recorded several times by Henslowe in the *Diary*, and the following entry includes the names of all the authors.

Bowght of m^r willsones drayton & dickers & cheattell for
the companey a boocke called blacke battmane of the northe
the 22 of maye 1598 wch coste sixe pownd*e* J saye
layd owt for them .... [9] } vj^{li}

The appearance of a second part, for which Henslowe made final payment July 14, 1598, attests to the popularity of the first part. Harold Jenkins, in his book on Chettle, says that there is a chapbook in the British Museum entitled *Bateman's Tragedy* which tells of young Bateman who loves fair Isabella. "She returned his love, but subsequently yielded to the protestations of her parents and married a more wealthy suitor, called German. Thereupon Bateman hanged himself and his ghost haunted his former love, until, lying in child bed, she was mysteriously borne away." [10]

[7] *Ibid.*, I, 54.
[8] Alfred Harbage, *Annals of English Drama, 975–1700*, pp. 52–53.
[9] *Henslowe's Diary*, I, 87.
[10] Harold Jenkins, *The Life and Works of Henry Chettle*, pp. 212–13.

Jenkins also lists several ballads in the same subject, among them "A Godly Warning to all Maidens by the Example of God's Judgement showed on *German's* Wife of *Clifton*, in the County of *Nottingham*, who lying in Child-bed, was borne away, and never heard of after" and "A warning for fayre maides by thexample of Jarmans wyfe," registered June 8, 1603. Although Greg doubts that these ballads were based on the same story as *Black Bateman of the North*,[11] his reasons are not entirely convincing. The identity of the names of the hero of the ballads and the protagonist of the play affords good reason for accepting the theory that the poems and the drama had the same subject. Greg fails to mention the last-named ballad, but makes the statement that the story "can hardly be as old as the play." The ballads all emphasize the moral lesson, giving examples of God's judgment. A surviving play, *The Vow Breaker; or, The Fair Maid of Clifton* (1625), by William Sampson, deals with the story of Bateman, German, and German's wife.[12]

Henry Chettle, *A Woman's Tragedy*, Admiral's Company, 1598.

The following curious entry is the only evidence on Chettle's *A Woman's Tragedy*.

> Lent vnto Harey Cheattell the 14 of July 1598 ⎫
> vpon a boocke called the playe of a womon ⎪
> Tragedye the some of v^{ll} wch Robart shawe ⎬ v^{ll}
> willed me to delyuer hime J saye . . . . ⎭
> eather to dd the playe or els to paye the mony
> wth in one forthnyght . . . .[13]

Jenkins and Chambers conjecture that it was never completed.[14] Nothing is known of the play.

Henry Chettle (and Thomas Dekker?), *The Stepmother's Tragedy*, Admiral's Company, 1599.

Between August 23 and October 14, 1599, Henslowe paid six pounds to Dekker and Chettle for *The Stepmother's Tragedy*. There is no reason for connecting this play with *The Cruelty of a Stepmother* acted in 1578 by Sussex's Men.[15]

---

[11] *Henslowe's Diary*, II, 193.   [12] See above, Chapter IX.
[13] *Henslowe's Diary*, I, 90.
[14] Jenkins, *op. cit.*, pp. 213–14; Chambers, *op. cit.*, III, 265.
[15] *Henslowe's Diary*, I, 110–11, 113; II, 204.

William Haughton and John Day, *Cox of Collumpton,* Admiral's Company, 1599.

Henslowe paid five pounds for *Cox of Collumpton,* sometimes called *The Tragedy of John Cox,* the last payment of three pounds being made November 14, 1599. Collier and Greg surmise that the play related a murder committed at Collumpton in Devonshire.[16]

Ben Jonson and Thomas Dekker, *Page of Plymouth,* Admiral's Company, 1599.

Early in his career, Ben Jonson collaborated with Thomas Dekker in dramatizing the events of the murder of Master Page which occurred in Plymouth February 11, 1591. Master Glanfield, refusing to listen to his daughter's protests that she loved George Strangwidge, married her to Page. She, Strangwidge, Robert Priddis, and Tom Stone plotted to murder Page. An attempt with poison failed. Priddis and Stone then strangled the husband and afterward broke his neck. The perpetrators of the crime were discovered, arraigned before Sir Francis Drake, Knight, and condemned to death. Strangwidge testified that he had attempted to stop the others, but without success. However, his sentence was confirmed. The four murderers were executed February 20, 1591.[17]

For the dramatization of this story, Henslowe paid the unusually high price of eight pounds, and he even went further and spent ten pounds on the heroine's costumes. The entries read:

Lent vnto w^m Borne alles birde the 10 of
aguste 1599 to Lend vnto bengemyne Johnsone
& thomas deckers in earneste of ther boock   } xxxx^s
wch they [are] a writtenge called pagge of p [le] m^{oth} the some

Lent vnto w^m Birde Thomas dowton w^m Jube
the 2 of Septmb3 1599 to paye in fulle payment
for a Boocke called the lamentable tragedie   } vj^{ll}
of pagge of plemoth the some of . . . .

Lent vnto Jewbey & thomas towne the 12 of
Septmb3 1599 to bye wemen gownes for page   } x^{ll}
of plemoth the some of . . . .[18]

---

[16] *Ibid.,* I, 59, 113–14; II, 207.

[17] *A True Discourse of a Cruel and Inhumaine Murder, committed vpon M. Padge of Plymouth,* in *The Shakespeare Society Papers,* II, 79–85.

[18] *Henslowe's Diary,* I, 110, 111. Shaded brackets indicate additions by Greg to the

John Day and William Haughton, *The Tragedy of Merry*
[*Beech's Tragedy*], Admiral's Company, 1599. Henry
Chettle, *The Orphan's Tragedy*, Admiral's Company, 1599.
John Day, *The Italian Tragedy*, Admiral's Company, 1599/
1600.

Bullen first pointed out that "the tragedie of merie" (entered in
Revels office as "Beech's tragedie") for which Henslowe paid five
pounds to Day and Haughton in 1599 was related in subject to the
play *Two Lamentable Tragedies* by Robert Yarington, published in
1601. Fleay [19] and Greg [20] suggest that *Two Lamentable Tragedies*
combined *The Tragedy of Merry* and *The Orphan's Tragedy*. The
latter they identify with the nameless "Italian Tragedy" for which Day
was receiving advances in 1599/1600. Greg says that Day probably
submitted a subplot which was dropped when the two plays were
combined. He assigns the Merry story to Haughton and the Italian
murder to Chettle. Yarington is dismissed by Greg as a scribe. Professor Oliphant advanced the theory that Rob. Yarington was a mis-
reading for Wm. Haughton.[21]

A more recent view is that Yarington's *Two Lamentable Tragedies*
is the work of one author and that it dates from 1594, the year of the
murder of Beech by Merry. *The Tragedy of Merry* was, then, either
an independent dramatization of the same story or possibly a version
using Yarington's work as a basis. There are no grounds for believing
that *The Orphan's Tragedy* and *The Italian Tragedy* were similar
dramatizations of the second plot of Yarington's drama or even that
they were the same play. Professor Law finds echoes of *Richard III*
and the old *Leire* in *Two Lamentable Tragedies*.[22] Jenkins dissociates
Chettle from the extant play and sums up as follows what appears to
be the most satisfactory theory:

The resemblance between the two plots and the subjects suggested by the
titles *Thomas Merry* and *The Orphan's Tragedy* may be more than coincidence; but if there is any connection, then it is probably that Yarington's

text of the *Diary*. For ballads on the subject of Page of Plymouth, see above, Chapter
III.

[19] Frederick Gard Fleay, *A Biographical Chronicle of the English Drama, 1559–
1642*, II, 285–86.

[20] *Henslowe's Diary*, II, 208–9.   [21] Chambers, *op. cit.*, III, 518.

[22] Robert A. Law, "Yarington's *Two Lamentable Tragedies*," *Modern Language
Review*, V (1910), 167–77.

play, falling somehow into the hands of Henslowe and his associates in 1599, was used to supply material for two new plays, rather than that it is itself a composite version of the two plays by Chettle, Day, and Haughton.[23]

It seems unlikely that Henslowe would be purchasing a tragedy so old [24] and so poor, for even a patchwork of scenes by Chettle, Day, and Haughton could scarcely have the deficiencies of *Two Lamentable Tragedies*.

John Day and William Haughton, *Six Yeomen of the West*, Admiral's Company, 1601.

Six Yeomen of the West, by Day and Haughton, was purchased by Henslowe for five pounds in 1601.[25] It evidently contained as a part of its action the story of Thomas Cole of Reading, whose lamentable murder is described in Chapter Eleven of Thomas Deloney's *Thomas of Reading*. The story is a commonplace one of retribution, but the means employed for the execution are ingenious.

John Day, *Bristow Tragedy*, Admiral's Company, 1602.

A play known only from Henslowe's *Diary* is John Day's *Bristow Tragedy*.[26] The work has been identified with *The Fair Maid of Bristow*, but the latter work is not a tragedy and shows no resemblance to the recognized work of Day. *The Fair Maid of Bristow* belonged to the King's Men.[27] Three entries in Henslowe's *Diary* refer to *Bristow Tragedy* as a tragedy, and its setting indicates that it must have been a domestic tragedy.

William Haughton, *Cartwright*, Admiral's Company, 1602.

Henslowe's *Diary* records a play conjectured to have been a murder drama. The entry reads:

>   edward
> Lent vnto w^m Bird & Thomas towne & [w^m] Jube   ⎤ [iiij^{li}]
> the 8 of septmb3 1602 to pay vnto w^m hawghton   ⎬ 1^s
> for a playe [*of*] called w^m cartwryght some of . . . .^{28} ⎦

---

[23] Jenkins, *op. cit.*, pp. 254–55. For those interested in the further aspects of this controversy, there is an excellent summary of the theories presented in a critical fashion with full bibliographical references in the Jenkins book, pp. 253–55.

[24] There is a notice of a work in the Stationers' Register for August 29, 1594, which probably refers to the Yarington play. Quoted in Hans Wolfgang Singer, *Das bürgerliche Trauerspiel in England*, p. 29.

[25] *Henslowe's Diary*, I, 137, 138, 143, 144; II, 217.

[26] *Henslowe's Diary*, I, 165, 167; II, 221.   [27] Chambers, *op. cit.*, IV, 12–13.

[28] *Henslowe's Diary*, I, 170. The square brackets indicate the portions crossed out by Henslowe, but resupplied by Greg.

Of this play nothing more is known. It may never have been finished, for there is no further entry concerning it in the *Diary*. Greg says that Collier in his edition of the *Diary* omitted the "w^m" from the title and suggested that the work was founded on the murder of a clergyman named Stow [Storre] by one Cartwright, an account of which crime appeared in 1603.[29] Greg objects to Collier's theory on the ground that the narrative was not published until 1613 and that the murderer's name was Francis, not William, Cartwright. But William Cartwright was an actor in Henslowe's Company,[30] and when Henslowe made the entry, such a slip would be characteristic of his inaccurate recording. In the same entry he had already erred once in writing "w^m" for the first name of Edward Jube. Nothing in the pamphlet *Three Bloody Murders* states that the crime was a recent one. It seems quite probable that the play *Cartwright* dramatized the murder of the Reverend Mr. Storre by Francis Cartwright.[31]

Wentworth Smith, *Two* (or *Three*) *Brothers*, Worcester's Company, 1602.

Henslowe paid six pounds for a play which possibly was a domestic tragedy, whose title seemed to elude him, for it appears both as *Two Brothers* and *Three Brothers*. This play he consistently called a "tragedy," and his entries show that a witch and a devil were among the dramatis personae, while the properties included a coffin.[32] Harbage, on the other hand, describes it as Biblical history.[33]

Anonymous, *Baxter's Tragedy*, Chapel, 1602.

Baxter's Tragedy, for which licencing fees were five shillings in arrears in 1602,[34] may be the same as *Bristow Tragedy* [35] or *Barkstead's Tragedy*.[36]

---

[29] *Ibid.*, II, 224.
[30] Walter W. Greg, *Dramatic Documents from the Elizabethan Playhouses, Commentary*, p. 53.
[31] See above, Chapter III.
[32] *Henslowe's Diary*, I, 182, 183, 184; II, 231.
[33] Harbage, *Annals of English Drama*, pp. 72–73.
[34] *Henslowe Papers*, ed. Walter W. Greg, pp. 56–57.
[35] Chambers, *op. cit.*, II, 179.
[36] Harbage, *Annals of English Drama*, pp. 72–73.

John Day, Wentworth Smith, Richard Hathway, and "The other poyet," *Black Dog of Newgate,* in Two Parts, Worcester's Company, 1602/3.

The Black Dog of Newgate, which appeared in two parts in 1602 and 1603, was probably a work about the infamous Luke Hutton, a reputed son or cousin of the archbishop of York. Hutton was executed for his crimes in 1598. The play was written by Day, Wentworth Smith, Hathway, and another author whom Henslowe failed to name. Henslowe paid six pounds for the first part, seven pounds for the second, and two pounds for additions.[37]

Henry Chettle and John Day, *Shore's Wife,* Worcester's Company, 1603.

The story of Jane Shore was dramatized by Henry Chettle and John Day for Worcester's Men in 1603. Chettle wrote in Henslowe's *Diary* an acknowledgment of an advance received for the play.

> of m^r Philip Hinchloes
> Receiued /\ in earnest of the Booke of Shore, now newly to
> be written for the Earle of worcesters players at the Rose of
> m^r Henchoes xl^s. J. say receiued . . . .[38]

Some pages later, the title appears again in an entry for May 9, 1603.

> Lent at the apoyntment of Thomas hewode
> & John duck vnto harey Chettell & John
> daye in earneste of a playe wherein shores
> wiffe is writen the some of . . . . xxxx^s [39]

Greg speculates in an interesting fashion on the play, and there seems to be no reason to doubt his conclusions. He writes:

Fleay thinks that the payment was for extracting the Shore part out of *Edward IV* . . . and certainly the wording of the acquittance is suspicious, but £2 in earnest of this would be a very high payment, and the work would hardly need two playwrights. I fancy a new play is meant, though it is very possible and even likely that the authors availed themselves of the work of their predecessors.[40]

---

[37] C. F. Tucker Brooke, *The Tudor Drama,* p. 355; Chambers, *op. cit.,* III, 333; *Henslowe's Diary,* I, 185–87.

[38] *Henslowe's Diary,* I, 160.   [39] *Ibid.,* I, 190.   [40] *Ibid.,* II, 235.

Whether this play was an extract from *Edward IV* or whether it was completely new, it seems likely that it must have borne similarity to Heywood's work. It would, naturally, limit itself more strictly to the Shore episodes than did its predecessor, but there seems little to indicate that this compression would require any radical departure in style or moral significance.

George Chapman, *The Yorkshire Gentlewoman and Her Son*, Unknown Company, 1595–1613.

George Chapman's *The Yorkshire Gentlewoman and Her Son* was entered as a tragedy in the Stationers' Register on June 29, 1660. It also appears in the list of plays destroyed by Warburton's servant.[41] Nothing further is known of the work, but from its title it seems that it must have been a domestic tragedy.

Anonymous, *Proud Maid's Tragedy*, Lady Elizabeth's Company, 1611/12.

Proud Maid's Tragedy was performed at court February 25, 1611/12, by the Lady Elizabeth's players. Fleay conjectures that it may have been the same as Middleton's *A Chaste Maid in Cheapside*,[42] but that play has little to justify the use of the word "tragedy."

John Fletcher, Nathan Field, and Philip Massinger, *The Jeweller of Amsterdam* or *The Hague*, King's Men, c. 1617.

The Jeweller of Amsterdam, alternately entitled *The Hague*, written by Fletcher, Field, and Massinger about 1617, was based, according to Fleay, on the murder of Wely, the jeweler, an account of which was entered in the Stationers' Register June 5, 1616. The play itself was recorded there April 8, 1654.[43]

John Ford and Thomas Dekker, *The Bristol Merchant*, Palsgrave's Company, 1624.

Frequently *The Bristol Merchant* of Dekker and Ford has been identified with Day's *Bristow Tragedy* of 1602 and also with *The London Merchant*, a comedy of 1624, by Ford and Dekker.[44]

---

[41] Chambers, *op. cit.*, III, 260.   [42] *Ibid.*, III, 441; IV, 178.

[43] Fleay, *op. cit.*, II, 202–3. Cf. E. H. C. Oliphant, "The Works of Beaumont and Fletcher," *Englische Studien*, XVI (1892), 184.

[44] Fleay, *op. cit.*, III, 315.

Thomas Dekker, John Ford, William Rowley, and John Webster, *The Late Murder of the Son upon the Mother* [*The Late Murder in White Chapel; or, Keep the Widow Waking*], Prince's Company, 1624.

The Late Murder of the Son upon the Mother was listed for 1624 in Herbert's manuscript diary of plays he had seen.[45] The title also appeared as *The Late Murder in White Chapel; or, Keep the Widow Waking,* and the evidence reveals only that Dekker, Ford, Rowley, and Webster had a hand in its composition.

[45] *Ibid.,* I, 232–33; II, 273.

Appendix B

HEYWOOD AND BROME'S "THE LATE LANCASHIRE WITCHES"

THE LATE LANCASHIRE WITCHES (1634), by Thomas Heywood and Richard Brome, contains part of the characteristic pattern of domestic tragedy. Most of the play is farce-comedy, presenting crudely the mischievous pranks of the witches. It bases its action on the lives of several women who were on trial for witchcraft. As sentence had not been pronounced on the women, the authors could come to no conclusion to their play. Had Heywood and Brome known the nature of the final sentence, they could, with no alteration in the early part, have converted their play into a domestic tragedy. The drama is filled with the language of domestic tragedies and is based on the same religious doctrines.

The most pathetic character is Master Generous, who is horrified to discover that his wife is one of the witches. He tries desperately to convert her to a better way of life.

> With that word I am thunderſtrooke,
> And know not what to anſwer, yet reſolve me
> Haſt thou made contact with that Fiend
> The Enemy of Mankind?
>
> . . . .
>
> O cunning Divell, fooliſh woman know
> Where he can clayme but the leaſt little part,
> He will uſurpe the whole; th'art a loſt woman.[1]

Mistress Generous tells him she repents her sins, and he believes her as she says:

> I beg a gracious Pardon; when on you
> Me thinkes your Native goodneſſe ſhould not be

---

[1] Thomas Heywood and Richard Brome, *The Late Lancaſhire VVitches,* in *The Dramatic Works of Thomas Heywood,* 1874 ed., IV, 227.

> Leſſe pittiful than they: 'gainſt both I have err'd,
> From both I beg attonement.[2]

Later she indicates to a fellow witch that her repentance was merely feigned.

> Some paſſionate words mixt with forc't tears
> Did ſo inchant his eyes and eares
> I made my peace, with promiſe never
> To doe the like; but once and ever
> A Witch thou know'st.[3]

When his wife is finally seized, Generous abandons her to the law. His comment at the time is completely in accord with the duty of a Christian gentleman. He says:

> No ſir, my Prayers for her ſoules recovery
> Shall not be wanting to her, but mine eyes
> Muſt never ſee her more.[4]

Although the outcome is left in doubt and in the epilogue the authors disclaim any desire to pass judgment, it is clear that they and Mr. Generous have found her guilty. The fate of her soul is not disclosed, but without repentance she obviously faced damnation. Thus, even a farce-comedy of the type of *The Late Lancashire Witches* had a plot with tragic elements to teach religious morality.

[2] *Ibid.*, p. 227.   [3] *Ibid.*, p. 236.   [4] *Ibid.*, p. 259.

BIBLIOGRAPHY

FOR CONVENIENCE, this bibliography has been divided into four sections: reference works, nondramatic literature, the morality plays to which reference has been made in the course of this study, and the domestic tragedies themselves. The plays which have survived only by title are not included because they have already been listed in Appendix A.

No effort has been made to list all available editions of the domestic tragedies. Only the edition of each play which was actually used in this work has been included here. In many cases, other editions are readily available in any library. In the section covering the nondramatic literature an asterisk precedes the entry of a work which has never been published either in a modern facsimile or a modern edition.

Reference Books

Adams, Joseph Quincy, "The Authorship of 'A Warning for Fair Women,'" *Publications of the Modern Language Association*, XXVIII (1913), 594–620.

———— A Life of William Shakespeare. Boston, Houghton Mifflin Company, 1923.

Allen, Percy, Shakespeare, Jonson, and Wilkins as Borrowers, a Study in Elizabethan Dramatic Origins and Imitations. London, Cecil Palmer, 1928.

Battenhouse, Roy W., Marlowe's "Tamburlaine," a Study in Renaissance Moral Philosophy. Nashville, Vanderbilt University Press, 1941.

Bernbaum, Ernest, The Drama of Sensibility, a Sketch of the History of English Sentimental Comedy and Domestic Tragedy, 1696–1780. Boston, Ginn and Company, 1915. Harvard Studies in English.

Boas, Frederick S., An Introduction to Tudor Drama. Oxford, Clarendon Press, 1933.

———— Shakespeare and His Predecessors in the English Drama. London, J. Murray, 1896.

Bond, R. Warwick, Early Plays from the Italian. Oxford, Clarendon Press, 1911.

Bowers, Fredson Thayer, Elizabethan Revenge Tragedy, 1587–1642. Princeton, Princeton University Press, 1940.

Boyer, Clarence Valentine, The Villain as Hero in Elizabethan Tragedy. London, Routledge and Sons, 1914.

Bradford, John, A Sermon of Repentaunce. In The Writings of John Bradford, M.A., ed. Aubrey Townsend for the Parker Society, I, 24–81. Cambridge, University Press, 1848.

Brooke, C. F. Tucker, The Shakespeare Apocrypha. Oxford, Clarendon Press, 1929.

———— The Tudor Drama. Boston, Houghton Mifflin Company, 1911.

Bruggeman, Fritz, Die Anfänge des bürgerliche Trauerspiel in den fünfzigen Jahren. Leipzig, P. Reclam, 1934.

Butcher, S. H., Aristotle's Theory of Poetry and Fine Art, with a Critical Text and Translation of the Poetics. 4th edition, London, Macmillan, 1911.

———— The Poetics of Aristotle. 4th edition, London, Macmillan, 1925.

Cambridge History of English Literature, ed. A. W. Ward and A. R. Waller, Vols. V, VI, and X. Cambridge, University Press, 1918, 1919, 1921.

Campbell, Lily B., Shakespeare's Tragic Heroes, Slaves of Passion. Cambridge, University Press, 1930.

Certain Sermons, or Homilies, Appointed to Be Read in Churches in the Time of the Late Queen Elizabeth of Famous Memory. London, Printed for the Prayer-Book and Homily Society, 1852.

Chambers, Edmund K., The Elizabethan Stage. 4 vols. Oxford, Clarendon Press, 1923.

Charnock, Stephen, Discourses on Divine Providence. In The Complete Works of Stephen Charnock, ed. Rev. James M'Cosh, I, 1–120. Edinburgh, James Nichol, 1864.

Chaucer, Geoffrey, The Complete Works of Geoffrey Chaucer, ed. F. N. Robinson. Boston, Houghton Mifflin Company, 1933.

Clark, Arthur Melville, Thomas Heywood, Playwright and Miscellanist. Oxford, Basil Blackwell, 1931.

Crawford, Charles, "The Authorship of 'Arden of Feversham,'" *Shakespeare Jahrbuch*, XXXIX (1903), 74–86.

Creizenach, Wilhelm, The English Drama in the Age of Shakespeare, translated [by Cécile Hugon] from Geschichte des neueren Dramas. London, Sidgwick and Jackson, 1916.

———— Geschichte des neueren Dramas. Halle, Verlag von Max Niemeyer, 1901.

Cromwell, Otelia, Thomas Heywood, a Study in the Elizabethan Drama of Everyday Life. New Haven, Yale University Press, 1928.

Cunliffe, J. W., The Influence of Seneca on Elizabethan Tragedy. London, Macmillan, 1893.

Eloesser, Arthur, Das bürgerliche Drama. Berlin, W. Hertz, 1898.

Encyclopaedia of Religion and Ethics, ed. James Hastings. Edinburgh, T. and T. Clark, 1918.

Fansler, Dean Spruill, a Study of the English Domestic Tragedies from 1592–1600, Their Characteristics and Significance as a Type. Unpublished master's essay, Columbia University, 1907.

Fansler, Harriot Ely, The Evolution of Technique in Elizabethan Tragedy. Chicago, Row, Peterson and Company, 1914.

Farnham, Willard, The Medieval Heritage of Elizabethan Tragedy. Berkeley, University of California Press, 1936.

Fleay, Frederick Gard, a Biographical Chronicle of the English Drama, 1559–1642. London, Reeves and Turner, 1891.

Greg, Walter W., Dramatic Documents from the Elizabethan Playhouses, Commentary. Oxford, Clarendon Press, 1931.

Halliwell-Phillips, J. O., Outlines of the Life of Shakespeare. 8th edition, London, Longmans, Green, 1889.

Harbage, Alfred, Annals of English Drama, 975–1700. Philadelphia, University of Pennsylvania Press, 1940.

———— Shakespeare's Audience. New York, Columbia University Press, 1941.

Hunt, Rev. John H., Religious Thought in England from the Reformation to the End of the Last Century. London, Strahan Company, 1870.

Jenkins, Harold, The Life and Works of Henry Chettle. London, Sidgwick and Jackson, 1934.

Kruuse, Jens, Det følsomme Drama. Copenhagen, Levin and Murksgaard, 1934.

Lanson, Gustav, "L'Idée de la tragédie en France avant Jodelle," *Revue d'Histoire Littéraire de la France*, XI (1904), 541–85.

Latimer, Mary Ellen, English Domestic Tragedy in the Eighteenth Century. Unpublished dissertation, University of Wisconsin.

Law, Robert A., "Yarington's 'Two Lamentable Tragedies,'" *Modern Language Review*, V (1910), 167–77.

Mackenzie, W. Roy, The English Moralities. Boston, Ginn and Company, 1914.

McMahon, A. Philip, "Seven Questions on Aristotelian Definitions of Tragedy and Comedy," *Harvard Studies in Classical Philology*, XL (1914), 97–198.

Michel, Kurt, Das Wesen des Reformationsdramas entwickelt am Stoff des verloren Sohns. Düren, Spezial-Dissertations Buchdruckerei, 1934.

Morgan, Arthur Eustace, "English Domestic Drama," *Royal Society of Literature Transactions*, Series 2, Vol. XXXI (1912), pp. 175–207.

Mosher, J. A., The Exemplum in the Early Religious and Didactic Literature of England. New York, Columbia University Press, 1911.

Nolte, Fred Otto, The Early Middle Class Drama, 1696–1774. Lancaster, Pa., Lancaster Press, 1935.

Oliphant, E. H. C., "The Works of Beaumont and Fletcher," *Englishe Studien*, XVI (1892), 184.

Owst, G. R., Literature and Pulpit in Medieval England. Cambridge, University Press, 1933.

Peake, Charles H. Domestic Tragedy in Relation to Theology in the First Half of the Eighteenth Century. Unpublished dissertation, University of Michigan, 1941.

Pollard, Alfred William, English Miracle Plays, Moralities, and Interludes. 7th edition, Oxford, Clarendon Press, 1923.

Powell, Chilton Latham, English Domestic Relations, 1487–1653. New York, Columbia University Press, 1917.

Quinlan, M. A., Poetic Justice in the Drama. Notre Dame, Notre Dame University Press, 1912.

Schelling, Felix E., Elizabethan Drama, 1558–1642. Boston, Houghton Mifflin Company, 1908.

———— Elizabethan Playwrights. New York, Harpers, 1925.

Schweckendieck, Adolf, "Bühnengeschichte des verloren Sohnes in Deutschland," Theatergeschichtliche Forschungen, Vol. XV. Leipzig, Verlag von Leopold Voss, 1930.

Sidney, Sir Philip, The Defence of Poesie. In The Complete Works of Sir Philip Sidney, ed. Albert Feuillerat, III, 1–46. Cambridge, University Press, 1923.

Singer, Hans Wolfgang, Das bürgerliche Trauerspiel in England. Leipzig, Reudnitz, 1891.

Slowe, Lucy D., The Use of Prose in Domestic Tragedy. Unpublished master's essay, Columbia University, 1916.

Smart, Walter K., "The 'Castle of Perseverance': Place, Date, and a Source," The Manly Anniversary Studies in Language and Literature. Chicago, University of Chicago Press, 1923.

Smith, Gregory, Elizabethan Critical Essays. London, Oxford University Press, 1937.

Smith, Robert Metcalf, Types of Domestic Tragedy. New York, Prentice Hall, 1928.

Spingarn, J. E., A History of Literary Criticism in the Renaissance. 2d edition, New York, Columbia University Press, 1908.

Symonds, John Addington, Shakspere's Predecessors in the English Drama. London, John Murray, 1920.

Taylor, Edward Ayres, Elizabethan Domestic Tragedies. Unpublished dissertation, University of Chicago, 1925.

Thorpe, Willard, The Triumph of Realism in Elizabethan Drama, 1558–1612. Princeton, Princeton University Press, 1928.

Velte, Mowbray, The Bourgeois Elements in the Dramas of Thomas Heywood. Mysore City, India, Wesleyan Mission Press, 1924.

Wallrath, Hans, William Sampson's "Vow-Breaker," ein Beitrag zur Kunde des Nach-Shakespeareschen Dramas. Löwen, Druck und Verlag der Materialen zur Kunde des älteren englischen Dramas, 1914.

Walzel, O., "Das bürgerliche Drama," Vom Geistesleben alter und neuer Zeit. Leipzig, Insel-Verlag, 1922.

Ward, Adolphus William, A History of English Dramatic Literature to the Death of Queen Anne. New and revised edition, London, Macmillan, 1899.

———— Lillo's "The London Merchant" and "The Fatal Curiosity," Introduction. New York, D. C. Heath, Belles-Lettres Series, 1906.

Webbe, William, A Discourse of English Poetrie, in G. Gregory Smith, Elizabethan Critical Essays, I, 226–302. Oxford, Clarendon Press, 1904.

Nondramatic Works [1]

* Beard, Thomas, The Theatre of God's Judgements: of a Collection of Histories out of Sacred, Ecclesiasticall, and prophane Authours, concerning the admirable Judgements of God upon the transgressours of his commandements. Translated out of French, and Augmented by more than three hundred Examples, by Th. Beard, Printed by Adam Islip: London, 1597.

Bullein, William, A Dialogue Both Pleasant and Pitiful Wherein Is a Goodly Regiment against the Fever Pestilence. Reprinted by Early English Text Society, Vol. LII. London, Trübner, 1888.

Collier, John Payne, Broadside Black Letter Ballads, Printed in the Sixteenth and Seventeenth Centuries. [London] Printed for Private Circulation by Thomas Richards, 1868.

Deloney, Thomas, Thomas of Reading. New York, Taylor, 1903.

The Early English Versions of the "Gesta Romanorum," ed. Sidney J. H. Herritage. London, Trübner, 1879.

* A / Fearefull Example, / Shewed vpon a periured / Perſon. // Who on the 14. of this preſent / moneth of May being condemned for periury, / in the honourable Court of Starre Chamber: / did there deſperatly ſtabbe

---

[1] In this section, the asterisks indicate that the work has never been published in modern facsimile or a modern edition.

/ himſelfe. // *Containing a notable warning to all* / common Baylors. [Vignette] AT LONDON / Printed for Thomas / Nelſon [1591].

Henslowe, Philip, Henslowe's Diary, ed. Walter W. Greg. London, A. H. Bullen, 1904–8. Vol. I, Text, Vol. II, Commentary.

—— Henslowe Papers, ed. Walter W. Greg. London, A. H. Bullen, 1907.

Heywood, Thomas, An Apology for Actors. In three books by Thomas Heywood, from the edition of 1612 compared with that of W. Cartwright, with an introduction and notes by J. P. Collier. London, Reprinted for the Shakespeare Society, 1841.

Holinshed, Raphael, Holinshed's Chronicle of England, Scotland, and Ireland. 6 vols. London, Printed for J. Johnson et al., 1807–8.

Hopkinson, A. F. ed., Play Sources: the Original Stories on Which Were Founded the Tragedies of "Arden of Feversham" & "A Warning for Fair Women," to Which Is Added Thomas Kyd's Pamphlet, "The Murder of John Brewen." London, M. E. Sims & Company, 1913.

* *A Horrible Creuel and Bloudy Murther,* / Committed at Putney in Surrey on the 21. of / *Aprill laſt,* 1614, *being thurſday, vpon the body of* Edward Hall *a miller of the ſame pariſh.* // Done by the hands of *Iohn Selling, Peeter Pet* and *Edward Streater,* / his ſeruants to the ſaid *Hall,* each of them giuing / *him a deadly blow (as he lay ſleeping) with a Pickax.* // Publiſhed by Authority. [Picture] Imprinted at London for *Iohn Wright,* and are to be ſold without Newgate / at the ſigne of the Bible. 1614.

* THE / HORRIBLE / Murther of a young / *Boy of three yeres of age, whoſe Siſt-* / er had her tongue cut out: and how it / pleaſed God to reueale the offendors, by / giuing ſpeech to the tongueles / Childe. // Which Offendors were executed at *Hartford* the / 4. of Auguſt. 1606. // LONDON / Printed by *Ed. Allde* for *VVilliam Firebrand,* / and are to be ſolde at his Shop in the Popes-head / Alley, ouer againſt the Tauerne doore. / 1606.

[Kyd, Thomas] The trueth of the moſt wicked and ſecret / *murthering of Iohn Brewen, Goldſmith of* / London, committed by his owne wife, / through the prouocation of one Iohn Barker / *whom ſhe loued: for which fact ſhe was burned,* / and he hanged in Smithfield, on wedneſ- / day. the 28 of Iune, 1592. two yeares af- / ter the murther was committed. // [Picture] Imprinted at London for Iohn Kid, and are to be ſold / by Edward White, dwelling at the little North doore / of Paules, at the ſigne of the Gun. 1592. / ["Thõ Kyde" added by a contemporary hand.] In The Works of Thomas Kyd, ed. Frederick S. Boas, pp. 285–93. Oxford, Clarendon Press, 1901.

The Mirror for Magistrates, edited from the original texts in the Huntington Library by Lily B. Campbell. Cambridge, University Press, 1938.

More, Sir Thomas, The Hiſtory of king Ri- / chard the thirde (vnfiniſhed) writen by Maſter / Thomas More than one of the under-ſheriffis of London: a- / bout the yeare of our Lorde. 1513. In The English Works of Sir Thomas More, reproduced from William Rastell's edition of 1577, ed. W. E. Campbell and A. W. Reed. London, Eyre and Spottiswoode, 1931.

* THE / MOST CRVELL / AND BLOODY MVR- / ther committed by an Inkeepers / *Wife, called* Annis Dell, *and* / *her Sonne* George Dell, / *Foure yeeres ſince.* // On the bodie of a Childe, called / *Anthony Iames in Biſhops Hatfield in* / the Countie of Hartford, and now moſt miraculouſly / reuealed by the Siſter of the ſaid *Anthony,* who at the / time of the murther had her tongue cut out, and / *foure yeeres remayned dumme and ſpeechleſſe,* / *and now perfectly ſpeaketh, reuea-* / *ling the Murther, hauing* / *no tongue to be ſeen.* // . . . LONDON / Printed for *William Firebrand* and *Iohn Wright,* / and are to be ſold at Chriſts Church / dore. 1606.

* A moſt notable and worthy example of an vngratious Sonne, who in the pride of his / hart denied his owne Father: and how God for his offence turned his meate into loathſome Toades. *To the tune of* Lord Darley. Unique copy in the Huntington Library.

[Munday, Anthony] A VIEVV / of sundry Examples / Reporting many straunge / *murthers, sundry persons periu-* / red, Signes, and tokens of Gods anger to- / wards vs. What straunge and mon- / strous Children haue of late / been borne. // *And all memorable murthers* / since the murther of Maister *Saunders* by / *George Browne,* to this present and bloody / murther of *Abell Bourne,* Hosyer, / who dwelled in Newgate / Market. 1580. // *Also a short discourse of the late Earthquake,* / the sixt of Aprill. Gathered by A. M. / Honos alit Artes. // Imprinted at London for William Wright, and are / to be sold at the long shop, adionyng / vnto S. Mildreds Church in / the Poultrie. In John a Kent and John a Cumber. London, 1851. Shakespeare Society Publications, Vol. XLVII.

[Page of Plymouth] A true discourse of a cruel and inhumaine murder, committed vpon M. Padge of Plymouth, the 11 day of February last, 1591, by the consent of his owne wife, and sundry other. Reprinted in The Shakespeare Society Papers, II, 79–85. London, Printed for the Shakespeare Society, 1845.

* [Reynolds, John ?] THE / TRIUMPHS / OF / GODS REVENGE / Againſt the Crying and Abominable / SIN OF / ADULTERY. // EXPRESSED / In

Ten Severall Tragical HISTORIES. / Never Printed before. / Illuſtrated with New Sculptures. ["J: Reynolds" written in.] // LONDON. Printed by *J. Bennet* for *Thomas Lee*, at the *Turks head* in / *Fleet-ſtreet*, over againſt *Fetter-Lane-End*. 1679.

* Reynolds, John, THE / TRIUMPHS / OF / GODS REVENGE / Againſt the / Crying and Execrable / SIN OF / MURTHER : / Expreſſed in Thirty ſeu-eral Tragical Hiſtories. // Written by *JOHN REYNOLDS*. // *The Sixth Edition, Very Carefully Corrected*. // to Which is Added, / GODS REVENGE / AGAINST / The Abominable SIN of ADULTERY. / Containing Ten Several Hiſtories, Neuer Printed before. / Illuſtrated with New Sculptures. // *London*, Printed by *J. Bennet*, for *Thomas Lee*, at the *Turk's Head* / in *Fleet-ſtreet*, over againſt *Fetter-Lane-End*. 1679.

* [Rudierd, Edmund] THE / THUNDERBOLT / OF GODS WRATH / AGAINST HARD-HEARTED / and ſtiffe-necked ſinners, or an Abridge- / *ment of the Theater of Gods fearefull* / iudgements executed vpon no- / *torious ſinners*. . . . London, / Printed by *W. I.* by the Aſſignment of *Adam Iſlip*, for *Thomas Pauier* 1618.

Stow, John, *ANNALES*, / OR / A GENERALL / CHRONICLE / OF / ENG-LAND. // Begun by IOHN STOW: // CONTINVED AND / Augmented with matters For- / raigne and Domeſtique, Anci- / ent and Moderne, vnto the end of this preſent yeere, 1631 / By EDMVND HOWES, *Gent*. / LON-DONI, / Impenſis RICHARDI / MEIGHEN, / 1631.

* Three Bloodie Murders: // The firſt, committed by *Francis Cartwright* vpon *William Storre*, Mᴿ. of / Art, Miniſter and Preacher at *Market Raiſin* in the countie of *Lincolne*. // The Second, committed by *Eliza-beth Iames*, on the body of her Mayde, in the / Pariſh of *Egham* in *Surrie*: who was condemned for the ſame fact at Saint / Margarets hill in Southwark, the 2. of Iuly 1613. and lieth in the White Lion / till her deliuerie: diſcouered by a dombe Mayde, and a Dogge. // The Third, committed vpon a Stranger, very lately, neere High-gate foure miles / from *London*: very ſtrangely found out by a Dogge alſo, the 2. of Iuly, 1613. / [Picture] / Imprinted at London for *Iohn Trundle*, dwelling in Barbican 1613.

Turberville, George, Tragicall Tales and Other Poems. Reprinted from the edition of 1587. Edinburgh, Edinburgh Printing Company, 1837.

* Two moſt vnnaturall and bloodie / Murthers: / The one by Maister Cau-erley, a Yorkeſhire / *Gentleman, practiſed vpon his wife, and com-* / mitted vppon his two Children, the / three and twentie of Aprill / 1605. // The other, by Miſtris Browne and her ſeruant Peter, vpon her hus-band, / who were executed in Lent laſt paſt at Bury in Suffolke. / 1605.

// Printed at London by V. S. for Nathanael Butter dwelling in Paules / churchyard neere Saint Auſtens gate. 1605.

Vitry, Jacques de, The Exempla of Jacques de Vitry; or, Illustrative Stories from the Sermones Vulgares of Jacques de Vitry, ed. Thomas F. Crane. London, 1890. Folk-Lore Society Publications, Vol. XXVI.

Morality Plays and Interludes

The Castle of Perseverance. Reprinted in Tudor Facsimile Texts, 1908.

Everyman. In Joseph Quincy Adams, Chief Pre-Shakesperean Drama. Boston, Houghton Mifflin Company, 1924.

[Fulwell, Ulpian] An Enterlude Entituled / Like Wil to Like, Quod the Deuil to the Colier. Ve- / ry godly and ful of pleſant mirth. Wherin is declared not one- / ly what puniſhement followeth thoſe that will follow licentious liuing, than to eſteem & followe good / councel: and what great benefits and commedi- / ties they receiue that apply them vnto / vertuous living and good exerciſes. // In The Dramatic Writings of Ulpian Fulwell, ed. John S. Farmer. London, Privately Printed for Subscribers by the Early English Drama Society, 1906.

[Gascoigne, George] The Glaſſe of / Gouernement. // A tragicall Comedie ſo entituled, by- / cauſe therein are handled aſwell the re- / wardes for Vertues, as alſo the / puniſhment for Vices // . . . IMPRINTED / at London for C. Barker. Reprinted in Tudor Facsimile Texts, 1914.

[Ingeland, Thomas] A pretie and Mery trew Enterlude: called the Diſobedient Child. In W. C. Hazlitt, Dodsley's Old Plays, II, 265–320. London, Reeves and Turner, 1874.

Lupton, Thomas, A Moral and Pitiefvl Comedie intitled All for Money. Plainly repreſenting the maners of men and faſhion of the world noweadayes. Compiled by T. Lupton. In Huntington Library Reprints, Vol. I.

Mankind. Reprinted in John Matthews Manly, Specimens of the Pre-Shakespearean Drama, I, 315–52. Boston, Ginn and Company, 1897.

MORALITÉ / NOVVELLE TRES- / FRVCTVÉVSE, DE L'EN- / fant de perdition qui pendit / ſon pere, & tua ſa mere: & / comment il ſe deſeſpera, à ſept / perſonnages. // *Le contenu ſe voit à la page ſuyuant,* / *Imprimé nouuellement.* // *A LYON,* / PAR PIERRE RIGAVD / en ruë Merciere, au coing de ruë / Ferrandiere, à l'orloge. / 1608. Reprinted in facsimile. Paris, A. Pinard, 1833.

[Nice Wanton] A PREATY INTERLUDE / CALLED, NICE WANTON . . . In John Matthews Manly, Specimens of the Pre-Shakespearean Drama, I, 457–516. Boston, Ginn and Company, 1897.

Wager, W., A Comedy or Enter- / lude intitled, Inough is as good as a feaſt. / Very frutefull godly and ful of plea- / ſant mirth. Compiled by W. Wager. Reprinted in Henry E. Huntington Facsimile Reprints, with an introductory note by Weymore de Ricci. New York, George D. Smith, 1920.

──── The Cruell Debtter, ed. Walter W. Greg. In Malone Society Collections, 1911, 1923.

──── A very mery and / Pythie Commedie, called *The longer / thou liueſt, the more foole thou art.* / A Myrrour very neceſſarie for youth, and / ſpecially, for ſuch as are like to come to dig- / nity and promotion: As it maye / well appeare in the Matter / folowynge. // Newly compiled by W. Wager. // Imprinted at / London, by Willyam HoW / for Richarde Johnes: and / are to be ſolde at his ſhop / under the Lotterie / houſe. Reprinted in Tudor Facsimile Texts, 1910.

Wapull, George, The / Tyde taryeth no Man. / *A MOST PLEA-* / *ſant and merry commody, right / pythie and full of delight.* // Compiled by George Wapull. // *Imprinted at London, in Fleete* / ſtreate, beneath the Conduite, at the Signe of Saynt Iohn Euangeliſt, / by Hugh Iackſon. / 1576. Reprinted in Tudor Facsimile Texts, 1910.

Domestic Tragedies

Arden of Feversham, c. 1591, printed 1592, Unknown Company.

     T H E / L A M E N T A - / *BLE AND TRVE TRA-* / GEDIE OF M. AR- / *DEN DF FEVERSHAM* / IN KENT. // *Who was moſt wickedlye murdered, by* / the meanes of his diſloyall and wanton / *wyfe, who for the loue ſhe bare to one* / Moſbie, hyred two deſperat ruf- / fins Blackwill and Shakbag, / *to kill him.* // Wherein is ſhewed the great mal- / ice and diſcimulation of a wicked wom / man, the vnſatiable deſire of filthie luſt / and the ſhamefull end of all / murderers. // *Imprinted at London for Edward* / White, dwelling at the lyttle North / dore of Paules Church at / the ſigne of the / Gun 1592. / * / In C. F. Tucker Brooke, The Shakespeare Apocrypha. Oxford, Clarendon Press, 1929.

B., R., Appius and Virginia, c. 1559–67, printed 1575, Westminster's Boys (?).

     A new and Tragicall Comedie of Apius and Virginia, Wherein is liuely expressed a rare example of the vertue of Chastitie, by Virginias constancy, in wishing rather to be slaine at her owne Father's handes, than to be dishonored of the wicked Iudge Apius. [By R. B.] In W. C. Hazlitt, Dodsley's Old Plays, IV, 105–55. London, Reeves and Turner, 1874.

Brome, Richard, *see* Heywood, Thomas, and Richard Brome.

Daborne, Robert, A Christian Turned Turk, 1609–12, printed 1612, King's (?) or Queen's Revels (?).

A Christian Turn'd Turk; or, The Tragical Lives and Deaths of the Two Famous Pirates, Ward and Dansiker, ed. A. E. H. Swaen, in *Anglia*, XX (1897–98), 188–256.

Dekker, Thomas, Old Fortunatus, 1599, printed 1600, Admiral's Company.

Old Fortunatus, ed. Oliphant Smeaton. London, J. M. Dent and Company, 1904.

—————— *see also* Rowley, William, Thomas Dekker, and John Ford.

Ford, John, 'Tis Pity She's a Whore, c. 1627, printed 1633, Queen Henrietta's Company.

'Tis Pity She's a Whore. In The Works of John Ford, ed. William Gifford and Alexander Dyce, I, 107–208. London, Lawrence and Bullen, 1895.

—————— *see also* Rowley, William, Thomas Dekker, and John Ford.

Heywood, Thomas, The English Traveller, 1625, printed 1633, Queen Henrietta's Company.

THE / ENGLISH / TRAVELLER. / AS IT HATH BEENE / Publickely acted at the COCK-PIT / *in Drury-lane:* // By Her Maiefties feruants. // Written by THOMAS HEYVVOOD. *Aut prodeffe folent, aut delectare* / LONDON, Printed by *Robert Raworth*. . . . 1633. In Thomas Heywood, ed. John Addington Symonds. Mermaid edition, London, T. Fisher Unwin [1888].

—————— I and II King Edward IV, c. 1592–99, printed 1599, Derby's Company.

THE FIRST / and Second parts of King / *Edward the Fourth.* / CONTAINING, / His merie paftime with the Tanner of Tam- / worth, as alfo his loue to the faire Miftreffe / Shore, her great promotion, fall and / miferie, and laftly the lamentable / death of both her and her / hufband. // Likewife the befieging of London, by the Baftard Falconbridge, and the valiant / defence of the fame by the Lord / Maior and the *Citizens.* // As it hath diuers times beene publikely played by the Right Honourable the Earle of / *Derbie his feruants.* THE SECOND / PART OF KING EDWARD / THE FOURTH. // Containing / his iourney into *France*, for the obtaining of / his right there: // The trecherous falfhood of the Duke of *Bur-* / *gundie* and the Conftable of *France* / vfed againft him, and his / returne home / againe. // Likewife the profecution of the hiftorie of M. / *Shoare* and his faire wife. // Concluding with the lamentable death of them / both. In The

Dramatic Works of Thomas Heywood, I, 1–187. London, John Pearson, 1874.

——— A Woman Killed with Kindness, 1603, printed 1607, Worcester's Company.

A / WOMAN / KILDE / with Kindneſſe. / *Written by Tho: Heywood.* LONDON, / Printed by William Jaggard dwelling in Barbican, / and are to be ſold in Paules Church-yard, / by Iohn Hodgets. 1607. In Thomas Heywood, ed. John Addington Symonds. Mermaid edition, London, Vizetelly, 1888.

——— and Richard Brome, The Late Lancashire Witches, 1634, printed 1634, King's Men.

The late Lancaſhire / VVITCHES. / A well received Comedy, lately / Acted at the *Globe* on the *Banke-ſide*, / by the Kings Majieſties / Actors. // VVRITTEN, / By THOM. HEYVVOOD, AND / RICHARD BROOME. // *Aut prodeſſe ſolent, aut delectare.* / LONDON, / Printed by *Thomas Harper* for *Benjamin Fiſher*, / and are to be ſold at his Shop at the Signe of the / *Talbot,* without *Alderſgate,* / 1634. In The Dramatic Works of Thomas Heywood, IV, 167–262. London, John Pearson, 1874.

——— and William Rowley, Fortune by Land and Sea, c. 1607–9, printed 1655, Queen Anne's Company.

FORTUNE / BY / LAND and SEA. / A / TRAGI-COMEDY. // As it was Acted with great Applauſe / by the QUEENS Servants. // WRITTEN BY / *THO. HAYWOOD* / AND / WILLIAM ROWLEY. // LONDON, / Printed for *John Sweeting* at the *Angel* in *Popes-head* Alley, / and *Robert Pollard* at the *Ben Johnſon's* Head behind / the Exchange. 1655. In The Dramatic Works of Thomas Heywood, VI, 359–435. London, John Pearson, 1874.

Legge, Thomas, Richardus Tertius, 1579/80, MS only, St. John's College, Cambridge.

"The True Tragedy of Richard the Third," to Which Is Appended the Latin Play of "Richardus Tertius," by Dr. Thomas Legge, Both Anterior to Shakespeare's Drama, with an introduction and notes by Barron Field, pp. 73–166. London, Printed for the Shakespeare Society, 1844.

The Life and Death of Jack Straw, c. 1591, printed 1593, Unknown Company.

The Life and Death of Jack Straw. In W. C. Hazlitt, Dodsley's Old Plays, V, 375–414. London, Reeves and Turner, 1874.

Middleton, Thomas, Women Beware Women, c. 1621, printed 1657, King's Men (?).

Women Beware Women. In Thomas Middleton, ed. Algernon Charles Swinburne, I, 259–336. Mermaid edition, London, T. Fisher Unwin.

[Richard the Third] The True Tragedy of Richard the Third, c. 1588–94, printed 1594, Queen's Company.

THE / True Tragedie of Ri- / chard the third: // Wherein is fhowne the death of Edward the / fourth, with the fmothering of the two / yoong Princes in the Tower: // *With a lamentable ende of Shores wife, an example / for all wicked women.* // And laftly, the coniunction and ioyning of the two noble / Houfes *Lancafter* and *Yorke.* // As it was playd by the Queenes Maiefties / Players. In Malone Society Reprints. London, Oxford University Press, 1929.

Rowley, William, Thomas Dekker, and John Ford, The Witch of Edmonton, 1621, printed 1658, Prince's Men.

The Witch of Edmonton. In The Works of John Ford, ed. William Gifford and Alexander Dyce, III, 171–276. London, Lawrence and Bullen, 1895.

———— see also Heywood, Thomas, and William Rowley.

[Sachs, Hans, Fortunatus.

Tragedia, mit 22 Personen, der Fortunatus mit dem Wünschsackel und hat, VII Actus. In Hans Sachs, ed. Johann Gustav Büsching, II, 73–124. Nürnberg, Schrag, 1816.]

Sampson, William, The Vow Breaker, 1625, printed 1636, Prince's Men (?).

THE / VOW / BREAKER. / OR, / THE FAIRE MAIDE / of *Clifton.* / *In* Notinghamshire *as it hath bene diuers times Acted by / severall Companies with great applause. / by* WILLIAM SAMPSON. / *Virg: AEn: lib:* 2. 77. / *Obstupui, steterantque Comae, & vox fausibus haesit.* / LONDON. / Printed by IOHN NORTON and are to be sold by / ROGER BALL at the signe of the *Golden / Anchor* in the Strand, neere Temple- / Barre, 1636. In Materialen zur Kunde des älteren Englischen Dramas, ed. Hans Wallrath, Vol. XLII. Louvain, A. Uystpruyst, 1914.

A Warning for Fair Women, 1599, printed 1599, Chamberlain's Company.

A / WARNING / for Faire Women. // Containing / *The moft tragicall and lamentable mur-* / ther of Maſter George Sanders of London / Marchant, nigh Shooters hill. // Confented vnto / By his owne wife, acted by. M. Browne, Miſtris / Drewry and Truſty Roger agents therin: / with their feuerall ends. // As it hath beene lately diuerfe times acted by the right / Honorable, the Lord Chamberlaine

/ his Seruantes. // 1599. In Tudor Facsimile Texts, 1912.

Webster, John, Appius and Virginia, c. 1608, printed 1654, Queen Anne's Company.

> Appius and Virginia. in The Complete Works of John Webster, ed. F. L. Lucas, III, 149–224. New York, Oxford University Press, 1937.

Wilkins, George, The Miseries of Enforced Marriage, 1607, printed 1607, King's Men.

> The Miſeries of Inforſt Marriage. As it is now playd by his Maieſties Servants. Qui alios (ſeipſum) docet. By George Wilkins. London. Printed for George Vincent, and are to be ſold at his ſhop in Wood-ſtreet, 1607. Reprinted in Robert Dodsley, A Select Collection of Old Plays, V, 3–114. 2d edition, London, J. Nichols, 1780.

Yarington, Robert, Two Lamentable Tragedies, c. 1594, printed 1601, Admiral's Company.

> Two Lamentable / Tragedies. // The one, of the Murther of Mai- / ster Beech *A Chaundler in* / Thames-streete, and his boye, / done by *Thomas Merry.* // *The other of a Young childe mur-* / thered in a Wood by two Ruffins, / *with the consent of his Vnckle* // BY ROB. YARINGTON. // LONDON. / Printed for *Mathew Lawe. . . . at the signe of the Foxe* 1601. In A. H. Bullen, A Collection of Old English Plays, IV, 1–97. London, Wyman and Sons, 1885.

A Yorkshire Tragedy, c. 1608, printed 1608, King's Men.

> A / YORKSHIRE / Tragedy. / *Not ſo New as Lamentable* / and true. / *Acted by his Maieſties Players at* / the *Globe.* / *VVritten* by VV. Shak-ſpeare. / AT LONDON / Printed by *R. B.* for *Thomas Pauier* and are to be ſold at his / ſhop on Cornhill, neere to the exchange. / 1608. In C. F. Tucker Brooke, The Shakespeare Apocrypha. Oxford, Clarendon Press, 1929.

INDEX

Acolastus (Gnapheus), 68

Adams, Joseph Quincy, 125*n*

Adultery, sin of, 24; moral stories, 52 f.; death as penance for, 154

Aeschylus, 4, 6

All for Money (Lupton), 61*n*, 74

Amphitruo (Plautus), 76

Apology for Actors, An (Heywood), excerpt, 89, 193 f.

Appius and Virginia (R. B.), 75-78

Appius and Virginia (Webster), 78-80, 99

Aquinas, St. Thomas, quoted, 9

Arden of Feversham, Holinshed's account of, 101, 105

Arden of Feversham, 39, 41, 100-108, 125, 143, 144, 146, 159, 183, 187, 193; authorship, 101*n*, 107

Aristotle, 67, 118; quoted, 2

Articles of Religion (Thirty-nine Articles), 7, 14

Asotus (Macropedius), 68

B., R., *Appius and Virginia*, 75-78

Baldwin, William, 29

Ballads, 39-41, 173, 185, 196

Barkstead's Tragedy, 200

Bateman's Tragedy, 195

Battenhouse, Roy W., 22; quoted, 21

Baxter's Tragedy, 200

Beard, Thomas, 42, 43

Beech, Thomas, murder of, 108

Beech's Tragedy [*The Tragedy of Merry*] (Day and Haughton), 109*n*, 198

Black Bateman of the North (Chettle, Drayton, Dekker, and Wilson), 177*n*, 195 f.

Black Dog, 135, 138, 141

Black Dog of Newgate (Day, Smith, Hathway, and "The other poyet"), 201

Blackfriars, 184

"Blacksmith, The," 29, 30 f.

Boas, Frederick S., quoted, 73

Boccaccio, Giovanni, 29

Boethius, Chaucer's translation, 4

Bond, R. Warwick, 68

Book of Homilies, 7; *see Certain Sermons*

Bradford, John, 122, 123; quoted, 12-14, 20

Brief Discourse of the Late Murder of Master George Saunders, A, 34

Bristol Merchant, The (Ford and Dekker), 202

Bristow Tragedy (Day), 199, 200, 202

Broadside ballads, *see* Ballads

Brome, Richard, and Thomas Heywood, *The Late Lancashire Witches*, 183*n*, 204-5

Brooke, C. F. Tucker, 95, 101*n*, 201*n*; quoted, 63, 126*n*

Browne, George, story of, 33; text, 34 f.

Bullein, William, 59

Bullen, A. H., 198

Cade, Jack, story of, 29 f., 83 f., 98

Calverley murders, story of, 44, 127, 160

Cambridge History of English Literature, The, excerpt, 103

Campbell, Lily B., quoted, 9, 23

Cartwright, Francis, 46, 200

Cartwright, William, 200

Cartwright (Haughton), 46, 199 f.

Castellano, Castellani, 68

Castle of Perseverance, 55, 56

Certain Sermons, or Homilies, Appointed to Be Read in Churches, 7; excerpts, 8-17 *passim*, 22, 24 f.

Chain of vice, 118, 128, 148, 165

Chambers, Edmund K., 193*n*, 196

Chapman, George, 202

Charles I, king of England, 160

Charnock, Stephen, quoted, 20, 22

Chaste Maid in Cheapside, A (Middleton), 202

Chaucer, Geoffrey, 4, 76

Chettle, Henry, plays by, 29, 195, 196, 198, 199, 201

—— coauthor with Thomas Dekker? 196; with Michael Drayton and others, 195 f.

Christ, lived without sin, 8; redemption of mankind, 10, 15, 185; perjurers divorced from, 25

Christian Turn'd Turk, A (Daborne), 84

Chronicle-history plays, 82-99; the genre analyzed, 82 f.; plays based upon stories of famous criminals, 83 f., 98; upon story of Jane Shore, 84-98; five reasons for their place in history of domestic tragedies, 98 f.

Chrysostom, Saint John, 12

Churchyard, Thomas, 31

Cicero, 68

Citizen hero, *see* Common man

Classical tragedy, exalted position: influence, 2; rules, 3; treatment of evil, 6; prodigal-son story, 67, 68

Cole, Thomas, story of, 199

Collier, John Payne, 38, 194, 197, 200

Comedy, early concept of, 3; realism's natural expression in, 64; in *Old Fortunatus*, 81, 82; inclusion of drama, 154

Common man, why made hero of domestic tragedy, 1; earliest appearance of, in comedy only, 3; nondramatic literature's early references to, 29, 37, 38, 53; emergence as protagonist in morality plays, 54, 55, 73; use of, for moral purposes, 58; in plays from legend and history, 75, 81, 82, 95, 98, 99; sin of attempting to rise above own station, 75; fate of, unrelated to larger social and political world, 96, 99; gives place to characters in court life, 183; exhibited as wicked sinners in domestic, while noble characters in orthodox tragedy, 184, 186; why tragedy not achieved by, 188

Confession of sins, 17; a required part of repentance, 66; *see also* Scaffold speeches

Continental drama, early influences, 4; stifling conservatism, 5; free development prevented, 54; use of prodigal-son story, 67 f.

Courage, 66 f.

Courts, realistic scene, 124; attack on customs of, 139-41; theme of injustice in, 167

Court tragedies, 168 f., 177, 183

Coventry, 54

Covetousness, 60, 61*n*

Cox of Collumpton (Haughton and Day), 197

Creizenach, Wilhelm, quoted, 98

Critics and dramatic theorists, influence, 4, 5

Cruel Debtor, The (Wager), 61*n*

Cruelty of a Stepmother, The, 193, 196

Curtain, The, 184

Daborne, Robert, 84

Damnation, avoidance of, 6

Day, John, plays by, 197, 198, 199, 201, 202

——— coauthor with Henry Chettle, 29, 201; with William Haughton, 197, 198, 199; with Wentworth Smith and others, 201

Death, concept of, 6; importance in morality plays, 58, 77; pathetic possibilities of, first exploited, 77; as penance, 154, 185

De casibus virorum illustrium (Boccaccio), 3, 29

Defense of Poesy, The (Sidney), 4; excerpt, 5

Dekker, Thomas, *Old Fortunatus*, 80-82, 98

——— coauthor with Henry Chettle, 196; with Chettle and others, 195, 196; with John Ford, 202; with Ford and others, 203; with Ben Jonson, 197; with William Rowley and others, 132

Del figliuol prodigo (Castellano), 68

Deloney, Thomas, 199

Demonic possession, 131

Despard Murgatroyd, Sir, 11

Dialogue Both Pleasant and Pitiful, A (Bullein), 59

Discourse of English Poetry, A (Webbe), excerpt, 4

Disobedient Child, The (Ingeland), 67, 71*n*

Divine Providence, 18-24, 25, 55, 61, 71, 74 f., 77 f., 88, 100, 104-7, 110 f., 114, 116-19, 121 f., 124 f., 128, 130, 136, 138, 141 f., 150 f., 162-67, 172-75, 176 f., 181, 185, 194; distinguished from poetic justice, 18; operations attributed to, crudely illustrated in nondramatic literature, 26-53; used in interludes and prodigal-son plays, 63, 71; crude use in morality plays, 63; interventions of, in all the murder plays, 142; *see also* God

Domestic, two meanings of word, 1

Domestic-milieu protagonists, *see* Common man

Domestic tragedy, a new dramatic form: caused by change in conception of tragic hero, 1; two meanings: "common" hero a characteristic of the genre, 1; earliest known: has become greatest achievement of modern theatre, 2; origins, 3 f.; reasons for development of, 5; popular theology as basis of, 6-25 (*see entries under* Theology); pattern, 6; its sequence, 7; material for, provided by nondramatic literature (*see entries under* Nondramatic), 26-53; morality plays as ancestors of, 54-74 (*see* Morality plays); prodigal-son story aided development of, 67, 73; plays from legend and history that are, in essence, domestic tragedies, 75-98; five reasons for their place in history of development of the genre, 98 f.; specific kind of, designated by term "murder play," 100-143 (*see* Murder plays); most famous of Elizabethan, and the best, 100; *A Woman Killed with Kindness* the most outstanding, 143, 144-59; first alliance between "drama" and, 154; decline of: the later plays, 160-83; relegated to subplots: scenes laid in foreign lands, 183; causes of decline, 183, 190 f.; characteristics of, summarized, 184-91; the four greatest: most of the others forgotten: vary from near-greatness to incredible feebleness, 187; real tragedy not achieved by middle-class hero, 188; the worst play, 189; lost plays, 193-203; prices paid by Henslowe for, 196-201; bibliography, 216-20
Drama, meaning of term: first alliance with domestic tragedy, 154
Drayton, Michael, *see* Chettle, Henry, and others

Edward IV, king of England, 29, 84, 87, 88, 90, 91, 92, 95, 96, 168
Edward IV (Heywood), 29, 31, 125n, 156, 202; extended treatment of Jane Shore's story, 85, 88-98
Elckerlijk, 58
Election, doctrine of, 14
Elizabeth, queen of England, 7, 14, 15, 177n
Elizabethan theology, 6-25; *see* Theology

Encyclopaedia of Religion and Ethics, excerpt, 19
England, Church of, 14
English Traveller, The (Heywood), 24, 125n, 156, 169-73
Enough Is as Good as a Feast (Wager), 22, 59-63, 66, 74, 137
Eumenides, The (Aeschylus), 4
Euripides, 6
Everyman, 54, 58, 74
Everyman, 58 f.
Evil, a primary problem of tragedy, 6; *see also* Sin
"Example of Anne Averies," 36
Exempla, 26-28
Exempla of Jacques de Vitry, The, 26, 27

Fair Maid of Bristow, The, 199
Fair Maid of Clifton, The, see Vow Breaker, The (Sampson)
Fair Maid of the West, The (Heywood), 156
Fall of Princes, The (Lydgate), 29
Family life divorced from murder, first play to deal with, 144
Farnham, Willard, 21, 31, 32; quoted, 54, 58
Fearfefull and Terrible Example, A, 40n
Fearful Example, A, 38
Field, Nathan, *see* Fletcher, John, and others
Fleay, Frederick G., 198, 201, 202
Fletcher, John, Nathan Field and Philip Massinger, *The Jeweller of Amsterdam* or *The Hague*, 202
Folk origin, plays of, 75-99; *see under* History; Legend
Ford, John, *'Tis Pity She's a Whore*, 177-83, 186, 187
——— coauthor with Thomas Dekker, 202; with Dekker and others, 132-42, 189, 203
Forgiveness of sin, *see* Sin
Fornication, sin of, 23
Fortunatus and his sons, legend of, 80
Fortune, 29, 81 f.; fortune's wheel, 29, 167
Fortune by Land and Sea (Heywood and Rowley), 163-68
Fulwell, Ulpian, *Like Will to Like*, 63-66

Gascoigne, George, 72 f.
Gesta Romanorum, 26, 27
Gilbert, Sir William Schwenck, 11

Glass of Government, The (Gascoigne), 72 f.

Globe, The, 184

Gnapheus, *Acolastus*, 68

God, popular theological beliefs, 8 ff.; operation of mercy, 10; Divine Providence of (*q.v.*), 18-23, 25-53, 63, 71, 142; rulers as authorized agents of: responsible only to God, 21, 22; sin of revolt against agents, 83, 98; officers of courts as agents of, 168; dramatists' concept of, 185

Godly Warning for All Maidens, A, 173, 196

God's retributive justice, *see* Divine Providence

Good works, ideas about, 11

Gorboduc, 5

Greek tragedy, *see* Classical tragedy

Greg, Walter W., 196, 197, 198, 199*n*, 200; quoted, 201

Hague, The, or *The Jeweller of Amsterdam* (Fletcher, Field, and Massinger), 202

Halliwell-Phillips, J. O., 126*n*

Hamlet (Shakespeare), 1, 16, 149, 176, 190

Harbage, Alfred, 195, 200

Hathway, Richard, *see* Day, John, and others

Haughton, William, *Cartwright*, 46, 199
——— coauthor with John Day, 197, 198, 199

Henry VI (Shakespeare), 30, 83, 84

Henslowe's *Diary*, titles of lost plays preserved in, 46, 100, 193-201

Heywood, Thomas, 78*n*; *A Woman Killed with Kindness*, 24, 125*n*, 143, 144-59, 170, 173, 183, 187, 189; *Edward IV*, 29, 31, 85, 88-98, 125*n*, 156, 202; *An Apology for Actors*, 89, 193 f.; works giving proof of Heywood's interest in domestic tragedy, 125*n*; *The English Traveller*, 125*n*, 156, 169-73; play that surpasses his others, 144; makes first alliance between domestic tragedy and "drama," 154; abilities: shortcomings, 155 f.
——— coauthor with Richard Brome, 183*n*, 204 f.; with William Rowley, 163-68

History, tragedies derived from, 82-99; *see* Chronicle-history plays

History of Friar Francis, The, 193

History of King Richard the Third, The (More), excerpt, 85 f.

Holinshed's *Chronicle*, 86, 87, 97; account of Arden of Feversham, 101, 102, 103, 105, 106

"Homily of Repentance," 15; excerpts, 16 f.

Horrible Cruel and Bloody Murder, A (I.T.), 47

Horrible Murder of a Young Boy, The, 18, 19, 45

Human character, greatness of, 184

Hutton, Luke, work about, 201

Ibsen, Henrik, 2

Incontinence, sin of, 118

Ingeland, Thomas, 71*n*

Interludes, 63; Fulwell's play, 64-66; bibliography, 215 f.

Iron Age, The (Heywood), 156

Italian Tragedy, The (Day), 198

Jack Straw, 75, 83, 98

Jacob, Edward, 101*n*

James I, king of England, 160, 183

Jenkins, Harold, 195, 196; quoted, 198

Jeweller of Amsterdam, The, or *The Hague* (Fletcher, Field, and Massinger), 202

Jonson, Ben, and Thomas Dekker, *Page of Plymouth*, 197

Jube, Edward, 200

Keep the Widow Waking, 203

Kings and princes as heroes, 1, 2; *see* Rulers

Kyd, Thomas, 41, 101*n*, 108

Lambeth Articles, 14

Langveldt, George (Macropedius), 68

Late Lancashire Witches, The (Heywood and Brome), 183*n*, 204 f.

Late Murder of the Son upon the Mother, The [The Late Murder in White Chapel] (Dekker, Ford, Rowley, and Webster), 203

Law, Robert A., 198

Legend, plays from, 75-82, 98 f.; story of Appius and Virginia, 75; put in dramatic form by R.B., 75-78; by Webster, 78-80, 99; legend of Fortunatus and his sons: used by Dekker, 80-82, 98

Legge, Thomas, 87

Leire, 198

Life and Death of Jack Straw, The, 75, 83, 98

Like Will to Like (Fulwell), 63-66, 74

Lillo, George, 1, 191

Livy, story of Appius and Virginia, 75, 78

London Merchant, The (Ford and Dekker), 202

London Merchant, The (Lillo), 1, 191

Longer Thou Livest, The (Wager), 62*n*

Lost domestic tragedies, 100, 193-203

Lupton, Thomas, 61*n*

Lydgate, John, 29

Macbeth (Shakespeare), 125

Macropedius (George Langveldt), 68

Magistrates, moral lessons for, 29-32; *see also* Rulers

Man, *see* Common man

Mankind, 55 ff.

Mankind, 56-58

Marlowe, Christopher, fictitious account of death of, 42, 43

Massinger, Philip, *see* Fletcher, John, and others

Medicean court tragedy, 168 f.

Medieval drama, 3, 4

Medieval Heritage of Elizabethan Tragedy, The (Farnham), 31, 32

Merchant of Emden, The, 194

Merchant of Venice (Shakespeare), 77

Mercy, appearance in morality and later plays, 54

Middle-class hero, *see* Common man

Middleton, Thomas, 168 f., 184, 202

Mimes, 3

Miracles, disbelief in, 33

Mirror for Magistrates, The, 29-32, 83, 84, 85, 91, 98; literary descendants of, 32

Mirrour of Mutabilitie, The (Munday), 33

Miseries of Enforced Marriage, The (Wilkins) 44, 127, 155, 160-63, 167

Monk's Tale, The (Chaucer), 4

Moorman, F. W., quoted, 103

Moral emphasis of morality plays, 54 ff., 74; of later interludes, 63

Moral instruction, in *The Mirror for Magistrates,* 29-32; in *A View of Sundry Examples,* 33-37; technique of employing, adopted by authors, 32; in pamphlet literature, 38-48; continued in plays from legend and history, 98; play illustrating complete dedication of domestic tragedy to, 124; too much egregious moralizing a characteristic of the plays, 184, 187; domestic tragedy a vehicle for reiterating, 189; *see also* Theology

Moralité de l'enfant de perdition, La, 68, 69

Morality at root of domestic tragedies, 6 ff.

Morality plays, 54-74; analysis of: emergence of common man as protagonist, 54 f., 58, 73; earliest: outline of action employed, 53; *Mankind,* 56-58; *Everyman* the best known and finest, 58 f.; Wager's plays, 59-63; Fulwell's interlude, 63-66; Wapull's play, 66 f.; prodigal-son stories, 67-73; borrowings by domestic tragedy, 73; realism and moral emphasis: theology in, 74; elements preserved and improved, in plays from legends, 75, 76, 82; murder plays continuing tradition of, 114, 142; bibliography, 215 f.

Moral problems, real: none presented by plays, 190

More, Sir Thomas, story of Jane Shore in his *History,* 87, 97; text, 85 f.

Mortal sin, defined, 9, 185

Most Cruel and Bloody Murder, The, 18, 19, 45

Mostellaria (Plautus), 169, 173*n*

Most Notable and Worthy Example of an Vngratious Sonne, A, 40

Most Sweet Song of an English Merchant, A, 194

Mother Sawyer, the witch of Edmonton, 133, 134, 135, 137 ff.

Munday, Anthony, 32; theme, 33; *The Mirrour of Mutabilitie,* 33; *A View of Sundry Examples,* 33-37, 114

Murder of John Brewen, The (Kyd), 41, 101*n*

Murderous Michael, 193

Murder plays, 100-143; specific kind of domestic tragedy designated by the term: dramatic instruments used, 100; most outstanding plays, 100; *Arden of Feversham,* 100-108; *Two Lamentable Tragedies,* 108-14; *A Warning for Fair Women,* 114-25; *A Yorkshire Tragedy,* 126-32; *The Witch of Edmonton,* 132-42; reasons for waning popularity, 142; common characteristics: relationship to morality

Murder plays (*Continued*)
  plays and nondramatic literature, 142;
    writers of, 143
Murder stories later used by dramatists,
  29-52
Mystery plays, 54

Nemesis, 75
Nice Wanton, 69-71, 74, 128
Nondramatic literature, 26-53; exempla,
  26-28; moral lessons in *The Mirror
  for Magistrates*, 29-32; in Munday's
  A View of Sundry Examples, 32-37;
  tragedies in verse, 37; cases of operation of Providence in pamphlets, 38-
  48; repentance as used in Reynold's
  The Triumphs of God's Revenge, 48-
  53; bibliography, 211-15

Oaths, 24, 174
Old Fortunatus (Dekker), 81 f., 98
Oliphant, Professor, 198
O'Neill, Eugene, 2
Orphan's Tragedy, The (Chettle), 109*n*,
  198
Owst, G. R., 28

Pagan allusions, use of, 176
Page of Plymouth (Jonson and Dekker),
  38 f., 197
Painter, *Palace of Pleasure*, 76
Pamphlets related to sermons and mo-
  ralities and using their techniques, 38-
  48
Parents, admonition to, 65
Perjury, sin of, 25
Petriscus (Macropedius), 68
Physician's Tale (Chaucer), 76
Pièce à thèse plays, 163, 167
Plautus, 3, 76, 169, 173*n*
Poetic justice, 18
Poetics, The (Aristotle), 2
Prices paid by Henslowe for plays, 196-
  201
Prodigal-son plays, 67-73; use of Provi-
  dence in, 63, 71, 74; aided develop-
  ment of domestic tragedy, 67, 73;
  continental plays, 67 f.; English de-
  velopment, 69; *Nice Wanton* the ear-
  liest worthy of analysis, 69-71; a step
  backward taken in Gascoigne's play,
  72 f.
Protagonist, persons of exalted estate, 1;

2; new form called domestic tragedy,
  caused by change in conception of, 1;
  in classical tragedy, 2; *see also* Common man; Rulers
Protestantism means taken to establish,
  7; *see also* Theology
Proud Maid's Tragedy, 202
Providence, see Divine Providence; God
Punishment, mundane, 18

Realism, tradition of, established: natural expression in comedy, 64; as developed in morality plays, 74; technique developed in plays from legend
  and history, 99; employed as means
  to an end, 124; how moral lesson
  made effective by, 142; term justly
  applied to domestic tragedy, 186
Rebelles (Macropedius), 68
Rebellion as sin, 75, 78, 98
Religion, *see* Protestantism; Theology
Renaissance, classical influence, 2, 3
Repentance, reason for denial of, 10;
  theological beliefs reflected in dramas,
  10 ff.; defined, 12; best summary of,
  16; dramatic device of, in Reynolds's
  work, 48-53; in murder-play scaffold
  speeches, 142
Retributive justice, early embodiment in
  drama, 3; in theology, 10 ff.
Reynolds, John, *The Triumphs of God's
  Revenge against Murder*, 48-52; *The
  Triumphs of God's Revenge against
  Adultery*, 48*n*, 52 f.
Richard II, king of England, 83
Richard II (Shakespeare), 1
Richard III, king of England, 31, 85,
  87, 92, 95
Richard III (Shakespeare), 87, 96, 198
Richardus Tertius (Legge), 87
Roman de la Rose, 76
Rose, the, 184
Rowley, William, and others, plays by,
  132, 163-68, 203
Royal heroes, 1, 2; *see* Rulers
Ruddigore (Gilbert and Sullivan), 12
Rudierd, Edmund, 42 f.
Rulers, as protagonists, 1, 2; as au-
  thorized agents of God, 21, 22, 83,
  98, 168; why tyrants permitted to
  reign, 21; stories designed to teach
  moral lessons to, 29-32; in chronicle
  histories, 82, 96
Rymer, Thomas, 18

Sachs, Hans, 81
Salvation, attainment of, in drama, 6; popular theological beliefs, 10 ff.
Sampson, William, *The Vow Breaker*, 173-77, 196
Sanders, George, story of, 33, 37; text, 34 f.
Satiric attack on court, significance of, 141
Scaffold speeches, reason for extraordinary number, 17; nature of, 18, 185 f.; tiresomely familiar in the domestic tragedies, 66; excerpts from confessions in plays, 80, 120, 131, 136, 138; appearance in nearly all murder plays, 142
Schelling, Felix, quoted, 145
Scorners, 10, 129
Scourge of God, 105, 165
Seneca, 3, 5
Sentimentalism, 186, 188
"Sermon against Whoredom and Uncleanness," 23, 53
Sermon of Repentance, A (Bradford), excerpts, 12-14, 20
Sermons, reiterated basic ideas, 7; book of authorized sermons, or homilies, with excerpts, 7-18 *passim*, 22, 24 f.; exempla and other types of nondramatic literature descended from, 26, 38; play that is a dramatized sermon, 108, 113
Sexual sin, the subject of sermons, 23, 53; of moral tales, 52; incontinence, 118; death as penance, 154
Shakespeare, Richard, 58
Shakespeare, William, 1, 16, 30, 58, 77, 83, 84, 96, 125, 134, 149, 176; plays attributed to, 100, 101*n*, 107, 126, 143; domestic tragedies compared with work of, 187
Shakespeare Apocrypha, The (Brooke), 101*n*, 126
Shore, Jane, story of, 29, 31 f., 75, 84-88, 168; extended treatment of story in Heywood's *Edward IV*, 75, 85, 88-98
Shore's Wife (Chettle and Day), 29, 201
Sidney, Sir Philip, 4; quoted, 5
Sin, a primary problem of tragedy, 6; God's awareness of, 8; distinction between mortal and venial, 9, 185; popular beliefs about forgiveness of, 10 ff.; confession, 17; mundane pun-

ishment, 18; of attempting to rise above one's own station, 75; dramatists' concept of, 185
Singer, Hans W., 83, 199*n*
Sinners, man exhibited as wicked, 184, 189
Six Yeomen of the West (Day and Haughton), 199
Smith, Wentworth, 200, 201; *see also* Day, John, and others
Snitterfield, 59
Social protest, 60, 61, 167; satiric attack on customs of court, 139-41; disappearance of tendencies toward, 142
Sophocles, 6
Spanish Tragedy, A (Kyd), 108
Spingarn, J. E., distinctions between early tragedy and comedy, 3
Stationers' Register, 81, 126, 199*n*, 202
Stepmother's Tragedy, The (Chettle [and Dekker?]), 196
Storre, Reverend Mr., murder of, 200
Stow's *Chronicle*, 34; excerpt, 127
Straw, Jack, story of, 29, 75, 83, 98
Subplots, 155
Sullivan, Sir Arthur Seymour, 12
Swearing, 24
Swinburne, Algernon C., quoted, 107
Symonds, John Addington, quoted, 145
Sympathy, appeal to, 54, 60

T., I., *A Horrible . . . Murder*, 47, 48
Tamburlaine, 22
Tears, appeal of, 188, 189
Terence, 3; comedies of, 67
Theatre, the, 66
Theatre of God's Judgments, The (Beard), 41, 42
Theatres, in hands of the people, 54; London, 184
Theology, popular, 6-25; authorized sermons, with excerpts, 7-18 *passim*, 22, 24 f.; two constantly reiterated articles of faith, 8; distinction between mortal and venial sin, 9, 185; proneness to, and forgiveness of, sins, 10 ff.; Divine Providence (q.v.), 18-25, 26-53, 63, 71, 142; sins most often in the plays the subject of sermons, 23-25; ideas behind both dramatic and nondramatic literature based on, 53; increasingly orthodox in morality plays, 74; popular understanding of, the basis of the outstand-

Theology (*Continued*)
ing domestic tragedy, 146; expressed in melodramatic fashion in all the plays, 184 ff.; *see also entries under* Moral

Thirty-nine Articles, *see* Articles of Religion

Thomas Merry, 198

Thomas of Reading (Deloney), 199

Three Bloody Murders, 46 f., 200

Three Brothers or *Two Brothers* (Smith), 200

Thunderbolt of God's Wrath, The (Rudierd), 42 f.

Tide Tarrieth No Man, The (Wapull), 66, 137

'Tis Pity She's a Whore (Ford), 177-83, 186, 187

Tragedy, classical influence, 2 ff.; early concept of, 3; rise of historical form, 4; as art form, rather than moral treatise, 77; distinctions between domestic and orthodox, 96, 99; real, not achieved by middle-class hero, 188; *see also* Domestic tragedy

Tragedy of John Cox, The, 197

Tragedy of Merry, The [*Beech's Tragedy*] (Day and Haughton), 109n, 198

Tragical Tales and Other Poems (Turberville), 37 f.

Tragic hero, *see* Protagonist; Rulers

Tragodia (Sachs), 81n

Triumphs of God's Revenge against Adultery, The (Reynolds?), 48n, 52 f.

Triumphs of God's Revenge against Murder, The (Reynolds), 48-52

True Tragedy of Richard the Third, The, 87

Turberville, George, 37-38

Two Brothers or *Three Brothers* (Smith), 200

Two Lamentable Tragedies (Yarington), 75n, 108-14, 118, 125, 186, 189, 198, 199

Two Most Unnatural and Bloody Murders, 44-46

Velte, Mowbray, quoted, 146

Venial sin, defined, 9, 185

Vice, humanizing of the, 56; chain of, 118, 128, 148

View of Sundry Examples, A (Munday), 33-37, 114

Vitry, Jacques de, *Exampla*, 26, 27

Volksbuch, 81

Vow Breaker, The (Sampson), 24, 173-77, 196

Wager, W., *Enough Is as Good as a Feast*, 59-63, 66; *The Cruel Debtor*, 61n; *The Longer Thou Livest*, 62n

Wapull, George, 66

Ward, A. W., quoted, 145

Warning for Fair Women, A, 12, 34, 37, 114-25; an outstanding drama, 100; authorship, 125n

Warning for Fayre Maides, A, 196

Webbe, William, quoted, 4

Webster, John, *Appius and Virginia*, 78-80, 99; *see also* Dekker, Thomas, and others

Wilkins, George, *The Miseries of Enforced Marriage*, 44, 127, 155, 160-63 167

Wilson, Robert, *see* Chettle, Henry, and others

Witch of Edmonton, The (Rowley, Dekker, and Ford), 132-42, 167, 189; subplot, 133, 137 ff.; most noteworthy characteristic, 141

Witch of Islington, The, 195

Woman Killed with Kindness, A (Heywood), 24, 125n, 143, 144-59, 170, 173, 183, 187, 189; the best-known domestic tragedy, 143, 144; intellectual milieu, 144, 146; opinions of critics, 145 f.; subplot, 154 f., 156

Woman's Tragedy, A (Chettle), 196

Women Beware Women (Middleton), 168 f., 183, 184

Worldly Man, Mr., 22, 60-62

Yarington, Robert, *Two Lamentable Tragedies*, 18n, 75n, 108-14, 115, 116, 186, 189, 198, 199n; absence of name from records, 108, 114

York, 54

Yorkshire Gentlewoman and Her Son, The (Chapman), 202

Yorkshire Tragedy, A, 44, 100, 126-32, 142, 143, 144, 159, 160, 187; authorship, 100, 126; recognized as an outstanding drama, 100